Young People in 2003

The Health Related Behaviour Questionnaire
results for 15,526 young people between the ages of 10 and 15

John Balding

SHEU
2004

Published by
SHEU
Renslade House
Bonhay Road
Exeter, Devon EX4 3AY

ISBN 1-902445-22-8

NOTE

Each year we produce a report in the *Young People* series, and however careful we are to describe the populations involved in the surveys, the total picture is often referred to by the media as 'national data'.

The surveys that give rise to the data are large, numerous, and from many parts of the United Kingdom, but they do not form a deliberately-selected sample. The origin and structure of these surveys is described very carefully and fully on subsequent pages.

Despite this difference, the picture produced by our annual data set typically matches survey outcomes from other data-collection agencies using orthodox strategies such as stratified random sampling. On pages xx–xxvii we draw attention to evidence supporting this claim.

Young People in 2003 is the 18th in a series of annual reports
based on data collected using the Health Related Behaviour Questionnaire

SHEU
Renslade House
Bonhay Road
Exeter
Devon EX4 3AY

Tel: 01392 667272
Fax: 01392 667269
Email: sheu@sheu.org.uk
www.sheu.org.uk

Staff members

John Balding	**Director**
Michelle Dickinson	**Secretary**
David Regis	**Director & Research manager**
Angela Balding	**Director & Survey manager**
David McGeorge	**Marketing & Publications manager**
Di Bish	**Data Preparation manager**
Nigel Balding	**Computing consultant**
Cheryl Lewis	**Report writer**
Dan Hawkins	**Administrator**

Data processing and preparation personnel

David Armstrong	Liz Johns
Joan Armstrong	Jane Lavis
Margaret Bird	Anna McConachie
Kate Bish	Bruce McConachie
Mark Bish	Alison Salway
Val Cooper	Karen Scant
Hannah Davies	Heather Smallridge
Joanne Fennell	Barbara Stapleton
Dan Hawkins	Julie Stapleton
Marcia Hitt	Oliver Witkin
Debbie Hunt	

Technical support from Brian Fowler (Brian Fowler Computers, Exeter) is gratefully acknowledged.

SHEU provides a range of services to those involved in the planning, providing and commissioning of health and education programmes. The Schools Health Education Unit is part of SHEU and has been involved in the collection of robust baseline data about young people's health-related behaviour for over 25 years. Most of the work is through surveys in schools using the Health Related Behaviour Questionnaire (HRBQ).

The resulting baseline data identify and confirm priorities for health needs assessment, intervention programmes, and health education planning. Behaviour changes can also be monitored over time and compared with local and national trends.

Breaking the data down by locality prompts curriculum review by the schools, promotes stronger links between schools and health authorities, and stimulates health promotion in the community.

Repeated use of the HRBQ allows intervention programmes to be monitored and evaluated.

The data presented in this report were derived from surveys carried out during 2003, and includes data from primary and secondary schools.

You are very welcome to contact us if you would like to know more about our work, or carry out a survey of the young people in your locality.

Contents

The questionnaire and the survey

1 The Unit and its work

The Schools Health Education Unit is part of SHEU, which has its offices in the centre of Exeter, and supports and promotes:

(a) *Health Care planning at community level through co-operative survey and report writing with Primary Care Trusts, GP practices and other bodies.*

(b) *The design of intervention programmes in schools through curriculum review in health and social education, and the provision of stimulus material.*

(c) *Co-operation between teachers, parents, children, governors, and health-care professionals through survey work in both primary and secondary schools.*

These survey services are tailored to suit a co-operative method of working between different agencies supporting health promotion at community level. This has been achieved through numerous projects, including development of resource packages in PE, sex and alcohol education for classroom use, as well as generating materials to accompany The Extra Guest (a widely-disseminated video about responsible drinking) and Drawing the Line (a video to support HIV and AIDS education). Projects include the presentation of health-related behaviour data to support planning by Primary Care Trusts, Drug Action Teams and a set of classroom resources entitled the 'Healthy Schools' series.

The development of the Health Related Behaviour Questionnaire (HRBQ) for use in secondary schools was supplemented, in 1990, by a primary-school version. Special questionnaires have been developed for particular needs, such as monitoring young people's smoking levels. The primary and secondary versions of the HRBQ have been used in more than 5,000 separate school surveys, some schools repeating surveys of their pupils on five occasions, and more than 640,000 pupils between the ages of 9 and 16+ have taken part in the surveys from across the UK. (School and pupil numbers have been revised this year to coincide with our annual figures of schools surveyed.)

2 The Health Related Behaviour Questionnaire surveys

An increasing number of authorities have become involved in funding and in co-ordinating the surveys in schools in their localities.

The outcomes from this are numerous:

(a) *Strong links between individual schools and health personnel are created or maintained.*

(b) *Priorities for intervention/education programmes can be identified, from within schools or from without, or, co-operatively.*

(c) *Primary Care Trusts (PCTs) can receive the combined results from children on their GP practice lists, together with a report.*

(d) *Methods and stimulus materials have been developed using the specific data from the school, the district, or the region.*

A secondary school carrying out a Health Related Behaviour Questionnaire survey selects a mixed-ability sample of about a hundred pupils from each year group being studied. A primary school, being smaller, may survey the entire year group. An hour is normally enough, but the less able, whose data are just as important, may work at their own pace in special groups with extra support from the supervisor. The Unit processes the anonymous questionnaires, and the school receives a set of tables showing the percentages of pupils (divided into gender and year group) that gave particular responses to the questions. Each school also receives a selection of its own results set out in a written report. If desired, the data can be returned in graphical form, or in computer-readable form for interrogation by staff or pupils. See pages xii-xiii for the full range of options available.

The topic areas included in the current editions of the HRBQ include:

Accidents*	**Locality***
AIDS/HIV*	**Medication**
Alcohol consumption*	**Money***
Asthma*	**National Lottery**
Bicycle use*	**Paid work**
Bullying*	**Personal safety**
Dental care*	**Physical activity**
Diet*	**Problem sharing**
Doctor visits	**Puberty***
Drugs*	**Relationships**
Dyslexia	**Self-esteem*, autonomy**
Eczema	**Sexual health**
Ethnicity*	**Smoking***
Family background*	**Social activities**
Fitness & sports*	**Stranger danger****
Gambling	**Sun protection***
Homework	**Travel to school**
Hygiene*	**TV, videos, computers**
Internet access	**Worries***
Leisure pursuits*	

A single asterisk means that the topic is also covered in the primary-school version. A double asterisk means that it is found only in the primary-school version.

The Unit's questionnaire versions, 1976–2004

1976–80
Secondary HRBQ, Versions 1–6.

1980–83
Secondary HRBQ, Versions 7, 8 & 9.

1984
Secondary HRBQ, Version 10.

1987-8
Secondary HRBQ, Version 11 (with 'illegal drugs' questions).

1989
Secondary HRBQ, Version 12 (containing HIV/AIDS and mental health questions). Version 13 never used; 14 similar to 12.

1990
Secondary HRBQ, Version 15 (completely re-set, with amendments). Primary HRBQ, Versions 1–4 (trial versions).

1992
Secondary HRBQ, Version 16 (with a section on personal aspirations).

1993
Primary HRBQ, Version 5 (with AIDS and illegal drugs).

1995
Secondary HRBQ, Versions 17 & 18 (with new sections on gaming machines and personal protection). Version 18 permitted selection of topics if required.

1996
Secondary HRBQ, Version 19 (as 17, without sections on gaming machines or personal protection, but with new questions on recent accidents).

1997
Primary HRBQ, Version 6 (several new topics, including worries, 'growing up', stranger danger, bullying, accidents, sun safety and collecting stickers). Version 7 (newspapers at home and cycling) followed later.

1999
Primary HRBQ, Versions 8 (fitness question) & 9 (female puberty question).
Secondary HRBQ, Versions 20 (with extra questions about use of cannabis, and revised dietary checklist) & 21(female puberty question, other minor amendments).

2000
Primary HRBQ, Version 9.
Secondary HRBQ, Version 21.

2002
Primary HRBQ, Version 10.
Secondary HRBQ, Version 22. (Revised STI/contraception.)

3 Origins of the questionnaire content in 1976

The preparation of Version 1 of the HRBQ in 1976 involved around 50 secondary school teachers, who were invited to examine 30 suggested questions for inclusion.

These questions had been taken from an American source, and the teachers were asked to comment on the appropriateness of their structure and relevance with respect to inclusion in the questionnaire. Most of the teachers were highly critical, used their red ink freely over the document, and then produced prototypes of 'better' questions for inclusion. Around 90 questions were produced from this process, reflecting the views of important health issues for these teachers.

Refinement

The structure of the questions was refined in consultation with experienced teachers and with trials and interview work with pupils in schools. The bank of questions was also reviewed by professional groups other than teachers, including road safety officers, school nurses, and health authority personnel (health education officers and district community physicians).

It is important to note a third process that was applied at this time: circulating the refined list to a number of headteachers and deputy headteachers for their comments on any sensitive questions. The invitation was to put a red line through any questions that were considered best excluded because they might cause anxiety amongst some parents. They were not asked for any further information or explanation of any deletions they suggested. This process resulted in the exclusion of all the proposed questions on shoplifting, on vandalism, and many of the questions on sexual behaviour.

4 Evolution and development (1976–2004)

Over 25 years of evolution and development the content has been under continuous scrutiny, and much revision has taken place. Professions other than teaching have been deliberately drawn in to influence the content, and the teachers' concept of health behaviour has had to be balanced against other professional views.

It is interesting to note that, at one stage in the development of the questionnaire, it was possible to have the content reviewed by numerous teachers around the country who were involved with the Southampton-based 13–18 Health Education Project. The teachers were invited to assign each question to one of three categories:

Useful *Undecided* *Not relevant*

and they found no difficulty in the task. Most questions were 'Useful', and the one or two considered 'Not relevant' were excluded from subsequent versions.

A few questions received positive approval from some teachers and negative appraisal from others. These were retained, and do draw attention to the differing views that can be held on the relative importance of aspects of health.

Two questions producing this polarity of view were in connection with (a) the importance of the amount of sleep a child was getting and (b) whether or not he or she had eaten breakfast before coming to school.

Individual questions

Individual questions have been revised to meet particular professional needs. For example, the frequency of intake of iron-containing medicines, either prescribed or non-prescribed, is of particular concern, and questions to discover how many children may have undetected asthma were added to Version 15 in 1990.

Groups of questions have similarly been revised in consequence of the attention paid to the data derived from them. The dietary questions probably receive the most criticism and revision of all sections; each expert who has paid attention to them decides that there is room for improvement, and this results in further changes. The questions connected with watching a television screen are another example of evolution, and now distinguish between TV programmes, videos, computer games, word processing, and using the Internet. This has happened in step with (or perhaps a little behind) the changing reported practices of young people.

Levels of use

Another measure that has been applied to the content of the questionnaire is that of the level of use made by the 'consumers' on the return of the summarised data to them.

Enquiries reveal that some sections of the questionnaire are much used — for example, consumption of alcohol and tobacco, and diet — whilst others receive less attention. Some sections are receiving more and more use as they become better tailored to meet the needs of the users; the section on sports and physical activities is an example of this type of evolution, and currently enables a comparison to be made between the provision available in school and the variety of activities and the levels of involvement outside lesson time.

Recent revisions

Locality In order to attribute survey response patterns to the parts of a city where young people live, and to retain anonymity and confidentiality, the health authority may allocate its own reference numbers to different wards or boroughs.

Primary Care Trusts Many health authorities ask for a question that identifies the GP or health centre with which the child's family is registered. GP practices are linked into Primary Care Trusts (PCTs), which can then be supplied with a report and combined results from the young people on their lists.

Gambling These questions examine the frequency of playing on arcade machines, updated in the more recent versions of HRBQ to include the National Lottery and scratch cards.

Personal safety Perceptions of neighbourhood safety and fear of being bullied at school are both included.

Other recent additions include requests for information about recent use of illegal drugs; Internet use; the dyslexic condition; precautions against sunburn; collecting stickers and buying scratch cards; more about the purchase of National Lottery tickets; personal enjoyment of physical activities, and the use of bicycles and safety helmets.

Version numbers

The list on page vii indicates the progression of revisions to HRBQ.

Currently (2004) Version 22 of the Secondary HRBQ and Version 10 of the Primary HRBQ are in use.

Piloting and producing a new version is a major task, to be undertaken on average about once every 2–3 years.

However, minor changes are sometimes made during the life of a version, and these are distinguished by a decimal point.

Co-operation with authorities

This continuous review depicted above underpins the level of validity of the questions contained in the current version of the questionnaire. In addition, we have now developed a service enabling authorities to derive baseline statistics about the young people in their district, to support health-care planning. Adaptation of the questionnaire to meet these needs could lead to a further modification of the way in which different sets of professional views are incorporated.

Differences between genders and between regions

The figures presented in this document show clear differences between males and females on a nationwide scale. In the group surveys organised by local education authorities and the former health authorities, comparisons between the behaviour of children from schools grouped according to location (Balding & Shelley, 1989) provide information for health-care planning in different neighbourhoods. This is in addition to the data the authorities may already hold, which were gathered from other sources.

Taking the data back to schools

The survey method may well be unique. It is not uncommon in survey procedures for those collecting the information from the respondents to disappear with it and never deliberately reveal the results to those who have given assistance in the enquiry, publishing discoveries based on it in professional journals only read by their peers.

The Health Related Behaviour survey, however, is provided as a service to schools with the precise contract to return the results to the schools concerned.

Those who collect the raw data and who participate in the conditions under which the children completed the questionnaire examine the returned summarised results; furthermore, the results are intended for use, and are often used with classes of pupils who either participated in providing the data or are close in age to those who did, and live in the same catchment area.

Feeding back the results to the classroom situation, as a routinely-available exercise, provides ideal opportunities to check on memory and on interpretation, both significant components of validity.

The service particularly encourages a positive approach towards the data by school staff, as well as by health promotion staff from outside the school with whom they have, or may develop as a result of this initiative, a working relationship (see pages xii-xiii).

5 Researching the questionnaire content

What confidence have we in the individual data returned to schools and stored in our very large data banks?

There are two aspects to this:

- *Is the set of questions contained in the questionnaire appropriate to the needs or demands of the body of people using the survey method?*
- *Do the answers collected to the questions accurately represent the behaviours or beliefs of the respondents?*

Between pages xxii and xxviii we present evidence of *the quality of the survey data.*

We have, over the years, brought a number of lines of enquiry to bear on these important questions, as discussed below.

Interviews

As a result of this methodology there is opportunity for the schools themselves to discover problems in interpretation and memory. A standard practice throughout the evolution and development of the method has been to interview individual pupils following their completion of the questionnaire under the conditions set by a teacher supervisor working from the prescribed method. Since the beginning of the work over a hundred different interviewers have participated in this activity.

The routine practice involves a team of about eight people, experienced in working with schoolchildren, being introduced to the class near the end of the time in which they have been completing the questionnaire. Some of the team are student teachers and fairly close in age to the young people themselves.

The team leader explains something of the difficulties of question design and asks for assistance from class members. Examination in the class of one or two difficulties that all can participate in is succeeded by private and confidential interviews between individual members of the class and of the visiting team. The interviewer asks permission to examine the completed questionnaire with the pupil and to make notes on it if necessary. The interviewer is particularly looking for misinterpretations, problems of memory, and problems of unreliability arising from children presenting answers that may put themselves in too favourable a light, or are intended to shock the reader.

Exchanges between team members and supervising staff on these visits are also very valuable in highlighting supervision problems, and methods by which they have been or might be resolved can be passed on to future users.

Following the interview excursion the team members, equipped with their annotated completed questionnaires, share in a 'blow-by-blow' discussion of each question. This is an exhausting and exhaustive process by which the knowledge of the quality of each question can be built up and necessary amendments effected in the subsequent drafts.

Added to this is all the written commentary provided by the teachers involved — for every 25–30 completed questionnaires returned we also receive a supervisor's comment sheet on which attention is drawn to areas of difficulty experienced as well as to the positive aspects, such as the pupils' enthusiasm and the perceived relevance of the exercise. We received well over one thousand of these sheets in one year of surveys.

Validating the questions

The above processes shape the quality of each individual question. One observation to be made is that the longer a question has been contained in the questionnaire the more will be known about it and the more confident we will be in interpreting the responses. The level of confidence in new questions will be less than for the long-standing questions. Among recently-included questions are those to do with GCSEs, enjoyable school lessons and knowledge of sexually transmitted diseases and infections.

6 How are the data collected?

The way in which the questionnaire is used is entirely different from the style of most 'national surveys'. Typically, when planning a national survey, the smallest sample that will give reliable information about a representative cross-section of the community is chosen.

Each annual sample from the Health Related Behaviour Questionnaire, on the other hand, is an 'opportunity sample', in that the Unit exercises little or no control over which schools and which parts of the country become involved.

Since this method is at variance with the procedures in 'national' surveys, a fuller explanation drawing particular attention to its content and process is offered here, to enable the reader to give full weight to the results presented and discussed. This may open readers' eyes to the dangers of accepting statistics uncritically.

It is important to recognise, from the outset, that the results presented in this book do not arise from an organised annual survey. We are not selecting a randomised sample of schools and communities, but are responding principally to requests coming from health boards and other authorities promoting the use of the questionnaire in their schools. Naturally there will be clustering of sites.

However, as the use of the questionnaire becomes more widespread, the clusters themselves become more numerous and embrace a larger sample of the population, with the result that the 'accidental' sample becomes closer and closer to a 'random' one — as well as being far larger than the numbers in other surveys.

Confidence in the sample is raised by comparing results with those from other surveys of young people's behaviour, such as smoking prevalence studies carried out by the Office of National Statistics (ONS - formerly Office of Population Censuses and Surveys) and other research bodies (Dobbs & Marsh, 1983; Nelson et al., 1985). Consistency between annual results is further evidence of reliability.

Researchers are wisely cautious about the representative nature of the annual sample displayed in this series of publications. As mentioned above, this important topic is discussed further on pages xx–xxvii.

The school sample

Choosing a sample on paper, and deriving data from that sample, are different things. In practice, particularly where schools are concerned, any collection of results can be to some extent an 'opportunity sample', as some may decline the invitation to be included in a nationally-organised survey. For example, in one ONS study (Lader & Matheson, 1991), 15 out of the 140 English schools approached declined to be involved, and within co-operating schools data were not collected from 10% of those pupils selected for interview. Similar losses were experienced in the HEA/MORI study (HEA/MORI, 1992).

In practice, the data describe the communities represented principally by comprehensive schools, which in most places offer a coherent sample of their catchment area. If schools select the recommended sample of the year group (see below), the total effective population represented in these figures will be at least twice the number of questionnaires processed. This is also explained on the following page.

The sample needs to reflect the academic cross-section of the year group, which is straightforward if the questionnaire is completed during non-streamed time or in a mixed-ability setting.

Which year groups?

Surveys usually concentrate on the pupils in Years 8 and 10 (12-13 year olds and 14-15 year olds). Year 7 are the new intake, Year 11 are concerned with exams above all else, and Year 9 may be interpolated from the Year 8 and 10 data. If the school is involved in a 'pyamid survey', with the Year 6 children in its feeder schools completing the primary version of the HRBQ, it will be able to 'revisit' the same year groups in biennial surveys as they move up the school.

The sample size and its selection

In order to discover a reliable picture of the behaviour of the total year group in a school it is not necessary to include every individual in the sample, although in some schools the decision has been taken to do this so that no one feels excluded from the exercise.

The research method used to establish the size of the sample needed to give a reliable representation of the total school population was to carry out the survey of an entire school with very large year groups numbering around 450 individuals, fairly evenly split between the sexes.

By taking samples of different sizes and comparing the results for each of these with the results of total year groups it was established that, for this large size of year group, a sample of 50 of each sex provided a reliable reflection of the total population for most questions; for some questions, in fact, a smaller sample was adequate. This represented a sample size of just over 22% for this large school.

As nearly all surveys have been carried out on year groups that are much smaller than 450 (typically around 200), a sample size of 100 selected from these represents a much larger percentage sample than the 22% random sample found adequate in the pilot work. This, coupled with the attention paid to selecting a sample that reflects the academic profile of the year group, gives even more confidence in the extent to which the sample data reflects that of the total year group.*

The connection between the health of individuals and their socio-economic status is widely accepted (Townsend et al., 1992). Links between academic success at school and social background have also been established (Lawton, 1972). Therefore, to attempt to accommodate this factor in the sampling method, the stated instruction in the survey planning documentation is to select the sample to 'reflect the academic profile of the year group'.

Assuming that the participating schools have selected the recommended sample of the year group, the total effective population represented in, for example the 1998 figures, will be considerably larger than the number of questionnaires processed — equivalent to about 45,000 pupils, which is a very large group.

Preparation for the survey

We support very careful preparation for the surveys by working with teams of personnel from health authorities linked with LEAs. We also recommend and support training seminars for the teachers that will collect the data in their own schools, and our manual *Collecting Good Data* contains precise instructions for supervisors to follow.

*Absent pupils will tend to be those who are ill or habitually miss school. Therefore some of the data recorded in the surveys may be too 'comfortable'. This will be a feature of any school-based survey. However, staff may already be more familiar with the characteristics of this absentee group than with those of the section of the school population that complete the questionnaire

It is particularly important that staff from the health authority consider the number and distribution of the schools approached to participate in the survey.

It is common practice for health authority representatives to meet the Unit's staff team to plan a programme of activities, starting well before the data collection and continuing well beyond it to include 'after-care' programmes in schools and the support of planning or report writing.

Importance to pupils

The manner in which the data are collected is also vital. The best possible sample and the best-researched enquiry instrument will not produce sound data if the respondents do not take the exercise seriously.

An HRBQ enquiry requires a substantial commitment by the school in terms of staff training and the need to make space for it in the timetable, which means that the collection of data is never casual. This commitment will readily communicate itself to the pupils taking part. The supervisor is also given guidance in explaining to the pupils how conscientious completion of the questionnaire is ultimately for their own benefit.

Atmosphere

From all the work that has gone into the development of the methodology, we know that in every school supervisors can be found who can generate an atmosphere of importance for the task, inspire trust in the confidentiality and anonymity of the exercise, and provide ideal support for the completion of the questionnaire. Such conditions offer the most favourable environment for the collection of valid data.

The information returned to the school is only as good as the way in which it was collected. In part this is the outcome of the quality of each question, but the

Year 10 Males (continued)

PUPIL'S PIN	EXERCISE H1	GENERAL HEALTH H2	DIET H3	SMOKING + DRINKING H4	HRA TOTAL
1703	4	17	9	0	30 ******
3391	24	16	5	25	70 **************
8728	23	20	3	25	71 **************
8946	24	20	6	23	73 **************
0296	11	16	0	0	27 *****
6108	17	21	8	24	70 **************
4164	23	20	21	24	88 *****************
2114	16	16	6	19	57 ***********
0992	24	21	5	23	73 **************
6001	15	23	4	25	67 *************
4237	25	20	9	25	79 ***************
3599	15	17	6	21	59 ***********
6500	3	13	16	25	57 ***********
5760	25	18	9	25	77 ***************
3241	23	16	3	22	64 ************
9999	25	22	8	23	78 ***************
3489	24	16	6	25	71 **************
1710	12	16	7	25	60 ************
1818	17	17	7	23	64 ************
0558	12	18	9	25	64 ************
4072	24	17	8	25	74 **************
6666	7	21	0	25	53 **********
2020	25	21	0	24	70 **************
9999	9	20	22	25	76 ***************
6160	25	21	22	0	68 *************
5667	9	20	5	22	56 ***********
7159	24	22	16	25	87 *****************
2226	15	19	12	0	46 *********
9999	21	18	0	24	63 ************
6969	11	17	10	25	63 ************
6819	13	22	0	0	35 *******
2523	24	22	0	19	65 *************
Average	17.3	18.4	7.7	18.2	61.6

H1 to H4 are measured on a scale of 0-25, to TOTAL is out of 100.
H1 is a measure of how much exercise is taken.
H2 is a measure of general attitude to health.
H3 is a measure of the quality of the diet.
H4 deducts points from 25 for smoking, for more than moderate drinking, and for trying other drugs.

Part of the printout showing the Health Risk Appraisal (HRA) scores for a group of Year 10 males. Each asterisk represents 5 points. The HRA score is computed for all pupils, so that the school derives its own mean for each gender and year group. Those pupils who did not supply a confidential number for identifying their score are coded 9999.

manner and atmosphere in which the data were collected will have the greatest effect on their validity.

Commitment

In our experience, participating schools take a lot of trouble to follow the prescribed method of data collection. This includes careful preparation for the survey both outside and within the school, together with planned programmes of follow-up work.

Confidentiality

If the children know that the questionnaires are completely anonymous, that they will immediately be sealed in envelopes to be sent away for processing, and that the results will be returned only as a summary in which no individuals can be identified, their motivation to be honest will be reinforced.

7 Returning the data to schools and health organisations

A routine part of the service to schools is to return tabulated data in bound, indexed volumes together with guidelines to the interpretation of the results. In addition, each pupil's Health Risk Appraisal or HRA score is calculated by awarding or deducting points for health-related aspects of their responses (see illustration). Each school participating in a group project receives its separate written report. The aim is to return each school's results within 4–6 weeks.

The data can additionally be returned in graphical form. This is necessarily less detailed compared with most tables, as only a restricted number of response options can be presented on a diagram. However, the visual impact and simplicity of a histogram or pie chart can be invaluable for certain purposes.

The Health Risk Appraisal (HRA) option uses a computer program to select each respondent's answers to key questions and bestow 'healthy' points or deduct 'unhealthy' ones. The pupils can discover their HRA scores by using a confidential method involving a PIN, which preserves anonymity.

A health organisation or LEA organising a survey of the schools in its care may request an analysis broken down by geographical location or any other division that is required.

Computer analysis

An attractive option is for schools to have their data returned in computer-readable form. This can be done in two ways:

(1) As analysed data, representing the content and labels of the tables returned in the bound report. Pupils can use these to create their own tables, pie charts or histograms.

(2) As the punched raw data, accompanied by a file of variable names and value labels. This can be used in conjunction with suitable software to create tables and graphs, but also permits more sophisticated analysis, for example looking for correlations between different behaviours.

These collections of data offer the opportunity to investigate lifestyles and challenge prejudices regarding young people's behaviours.

It is also ideally suited to resourcing the Mathematics Attainment Target 4 — *Handling data.* Questions that might allow individuals to be identified (for example height, weight, and family type and number) are excluded from these compilations.

These data files are available in a form suitable for use on almost all commercially-available software analysis packages.

Comparing individual schools with district results

In addition, we can offer a *Community Profile Report.* This compares a school's results with the average for all the schools in a district survey, and lists those questions where the results for the pupils sampled differ by 10% or more from this average. This is helpful to the school in signalling areas for further examination. It can also bring school staff and Public Health staff together to plan health care provision at community level.

Seminars

Many group projects have a post-survey seminar to help teachers examine and interpret their data, and to study them in the light of results from other schools in their area. A typical programme would include *Interpretation of the data, Dissemination to colleagues in school, Curriculum planning from the data, Dissemination to pupils, and Use of combined area data.*

Workshops

We have developed a series of workshops to help schools respond to their Health Related Behaviour Questionnaire data. Different workshops support curriculum development, work in the classroom, or parents' evenings. Titles *include Write a letter to the Head* (for pupils), *Parents + schools and alcohol* (for parents), and *Do we stigmatise asthma sufferers?* (for staff discussion).

Teaching materials

We have extended the support we can offer to users of the primary-age questionnaire, which can be used in tandem with the HRBQ to profile secondary schools and their feeder primaries. A set of 5 books in the *Healthy Schools Series* contains teaching plans alongside the relevant worksheets under different titles: *Safety, Drugs Education, Emotional Health & Well Being, Physical Activity* and *Healthy Eating.* Several of the exercises have also been found suitable for Key Stage 3 pupils.

8 Health Related Behaviour survey results and 'research/project' models

The publicity associated with our work has resulted in the Unit being widely reported as 'doing surveys', which suggests a 'research model' or a 'project model' based within the Unit. This is misleading, since the individual surveys are most commonly directed by health organisations. Models of best practice in the use of the survey method come from health organisations where the Unit's survey has been carefully set within a programme of preparation and follow-up activities (for example, intervention programmes). These activities may extend over a considerable period of time.

The reasons for doing the survey and the responsibility for the quality of the outcome rests with the regional or district co-ordinators and the members of their teams. Typically programmes do run productively, and when re-run they are even better.

It is clear from the history of the evolution and development of the HRBQ survey service that there have been many authorities who (a) have used the survey method on more than one occasion (b) been enthusiastic about the outcomes and used them to considerable advantage.

Across so many years of use, we have come to expect high levels of satisfaction in the outcome of a particular survey. As a staff we are particularly delighted when stimulus of the survey outcome leads into a fruitful after-care programme in a district. We have long since recognised that we can support the collection of very good-quality data from young people in schools when supervised by experienced teachers who are well known to the pupils contributing to the enquiry. The method has been practised thousands of times.

For the health authority team, the particularly hard work starts when the survey data are returned to them, typically as:

(a) Printed tables

(b) Draft reports for joint revision and refinement

(c) Refined data on computer disc to match local hardware and software requirements, and to enable database interrogation to meet local needs.

Very occasionally users of the survey have been disappointed when they have failed to plan effectively. The service the Unit provides is access to an established method with a history of over 25 years of use. The quality of the survey method in each district depends upon the commitment to the process and to the after-care programme planned around the survey. The Unit's staff always try to provide an abundance of ideas and case histories of successful use to health authority personnel prior to their first use of the methodology.

We try to spend a lot of time in support of the planning stages for surveys with health authority/LEA teams; we often quote:

The easiest part of the process is the survey. We know how to get good-quality data. The hard work commences when the data are returned. Have you planned appropriately for the variety of people who could usefully have access to the data to be involved, and stimulated them to anticipate ways in which they might use the data?

We observe that the most profitable and extensive outcomes arise from those health teams who make the most extensive enquiries beforehand into the opportunities for use of the resulting survey details. Commitment to the project within the district together with consistent co-ordination from the same person(s), without change of local ownership throughout, are of paramount importance in determining a successful outcome.

The quality of the data is only as good as the way in which they have been collected. In today's climate, posts do not last long and jobs started are too often not completed.

Typically the attention to the detail of the methodology is meticulous and the motivation in the schools supporting the health authority's invitation to be involved is very high. Health organisations and schools can get very good-quality data (both honest and consistent) from the young population surveyed. The accumulation and compilation of all the surveys over the years has resulted in a vast sample of information, although it is 'only as good as the way in which it was collected'. This quality depends upon the performance of the local co-ordinators and their colleagues, and usually this is committed, perceptive and resourceful, co-operative and exciting.

For our part, we have always faithfully recorded and explained:

(a) The questionnaire content and method of data collection.

(b) The sample on which results are based.

We also comment on our knowledge of the quality of the data and present our reservations where they exist.

The purpose of each individual survey is for the data to be examined by those who collected them in schools, and even by those who provided them. Planning can then be taken forward with an active and objective participation. Our feedback to the users of the survey method, not only of results and clarification of their method of presentation but also of commentary on insight into quality of data and any potential bias, is vital to planning.

This continuous process over more than a decade has prompted changes in questions to strengthen the process. From a research point of view interesting discoveries are made.

Unfortunately, we have very occasionally encountered projects where repeated delegation of responsibility and change of staff in charge of the programme has happened, resulting in a large amount of frustration and aggravation. Consistency in the core of the team of people promoting and co-ordinating the programme is enormously important, and the presence of an advisory teacher often enhances the work.

9 Data consistency: annual comparisons and cohort study use

How representative is the the Unit's annual compilation of those surveys taking place in any one year of the country as a whole?

We can point to the consistency between data collected in successive years from different nationwide samples. On page xix of *Young People in 1994* we presented a table of data demonstrating how similar these can be between annual compilations, and also how consistent one year group of pupils' results can be with respect to the levels recorded in the same calendar year of age groups above and below it. Version 16 of our questionnaire was used continuously throughout the two years. Both samples are very large —29,000 in 1993 (Balding, 1994), 48,000 in 1994 (Balding, 1995) — but the representation of different parts of the country is not the same. Despite this, similarities between the two sets of figures are widespread through the reports, and can be investigated further by comparing these tables with the corresponding ones in *Young People in 1993*. The 10-year presentation on pages 66 and 67 of *Young People in 1994* shows the comfortable and predictable fit for trends in smoking levels.

However, another chance of testing the representative nature of the data occurred with some surveys that were carried out in Yorkshire a few years ago.

The percentage that drank some alcohol during the previous 7 days

MALES

	1991	1993	1995
Year 9 (13–14)	**45%**	50%	–
Year 11 (15–16)	63%	**63%**	–
Year 13 (17–18)	–	–	**79%**

FEMALES

	1991	1993	1995
Year 9 (13–14)	**37%**	45%	–
Year 11 (15–16)	56%	**61%**	–
Year 13 (17–18)	–	–	**77%**

Comparison of data from three surveys, *revealing changes across five calendar years of the same 'cohort' (bold type). Changes between 1991 and 1993 within pupils in Years 9 and 11 can also be seen.*

See 'Yorkshire surveys, 1991–1995'

Yorkshire surveys, 1991–1995

Under Tony Goodall's supervision, and largely inspired by him, a 3-stage study was set up to track a cohort of males and females from selected schools across the Yorkshire Region, as it was known in 1991. All of the 17 DHAs then in existence were involved, and three schools within each one were funded by the RHA to be included in the survey. Some districts expanded the survey to involve more schools and thus have a larger database against which to identify priorities and plan their own programmes.

The plan was to follow as many as possible of the 1991 Year 9 cohort into their GCSE year (1993, stage 2) and then to survey as many of them as could be tracked again in 1995 (stage 3). For stages 1 and 2, the Unit prepared databases for Yorkshire Health and also prepared comparative tables and reports to support their monitoring requirements both at regional and at district levels.

The table shows in simplified form the 1991, 1993 and 1995 responses by young people in Years 9 –13 to one of the bank of questions on consumption of alcohol. The data show, among other things:

- The proportion of males that reported drinking during the previous 7 days was in all cases greater than that of the females.
- The percentage of 'drinking' females in Years 9 and 11 showed an increase from 1991 to 1993; the males in Year 9, but not Year 11, also showed an increase.
- The 'cohort' groups (black type) showed an increase in the proportion of 'drinkers' each time they were re-surveyed after a 2-year interval.

These trends are typical of HRBQ survey findings across the country, such as the ones presented in this report. Nevertheless, the discovery of marked changes across the 2-year and 4-year periods were cause for interest, and in some cases concern, such as the increased level of smoking and exposure to illegal drugs. Following the Unit's provision of comparative summaries, as in the table just examined, we were rapidly contacted to check whether some of the more worrying changes registered in Yorkshire health authorities were out of step with other parts of the country.

The Unit checks revealed that the comparable data from our databanks were a good predictor of Yorkshire, and vice versa; where any differences were indicated, they suggested lower levels of increase in 'undesirable' behaviours among the youngsters in the Yorkshire sample than elsewhere; this may have had some calming effect on the anxious health authority personnel!

It would appear from this structured study emanating from Yorkshire Health that, for many behaviours, the large annual summary of the numerous separate surveys taking place across the UK is a good predictor of many other parts of the country not involved in surveys in that year.

But if that were all, then health-care professionals might reasonably ask: *Why not save money and use the Unit's annual 'Young People' compilation?*

Percentage of Ward Respondents who are Current Smokers

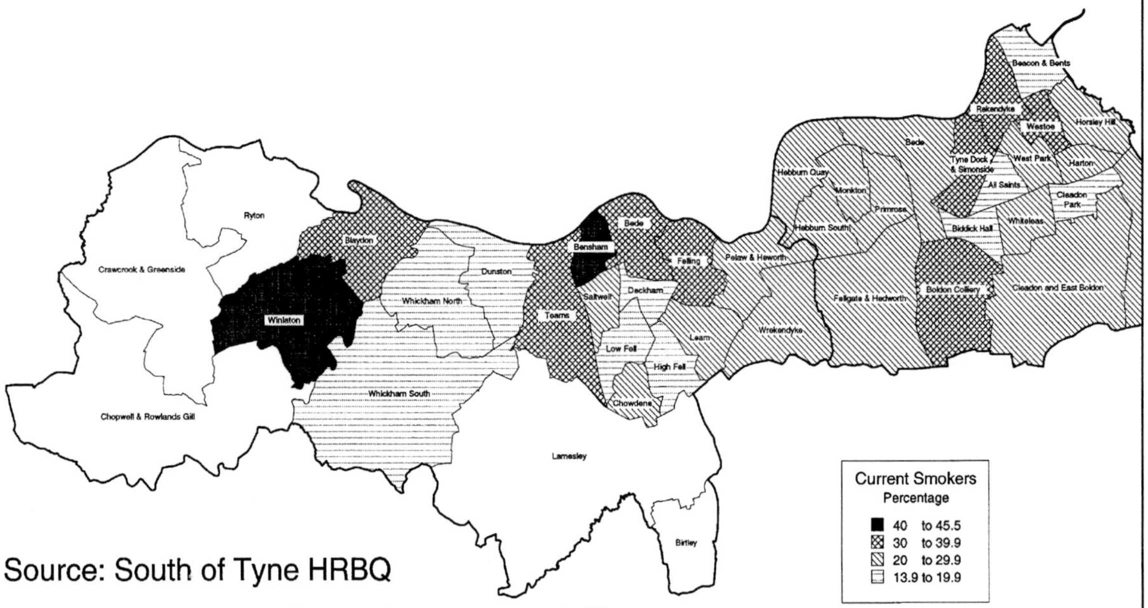

Source: South of Tyne HRBQ

No ward level analysis available for Birtley, Chopwell & Rowlands Gill, Crawcrook & Greenside, Lamesley or Ryton.

This graph shows the detailed mapping of health-related behaviours — in this case, the level of smoking — that is possible when the HRBQ respondents identify the ward in which they live.

Health Care provision is delivered at community level

What the compilations disguise, however, is the wide variation of behaviours that can and does exist between neighbourhoods and communities. Health care action is delivered at community level by primary care trusts.

Sensible intervention or education programmes delivered in schools must be cognisant of the nature of the particular and relevant levels of behaviour in the population that they serve, if a programme is to be effective. 'Global' summaries do not meet specific community needs (Balding, 1991).

Stimulated by City Challenge initiatives, and particularly by Drs John Harvey (Newcastle), Kevin Kelleher (Wolverhampton), Peter Bundred (Wirral), and Ruth Wallace (Lewisham), we developed methods to associate behaviour with locality of the home of the respondent. Successful models have been developed in Newcastle upon Tyne and Liverpool, and very particularly in Dudley, where links with National Census survey data have been achieved. The illustration is taken from the 1995 Newcastle upon Tyne survey.

Bullying: an example of variation between schools

For most recorded behaviours there is wide variation between the results from different schools. Our report Bully Off (Balding, 1996) showed that this is certainly true for the levels of fear of bullying. The histogram and table opposite present the number of schools within the sample in which different percentages of Year 8 pupils feared bullying.

It will be seen that the percentages for the males' responses accumulate towards the left of the histogram, and those for the females towards the right. This distribution reflects the overall difference in the percentage of males (24.6%) and females (34.6%) reporting fear of bullying.

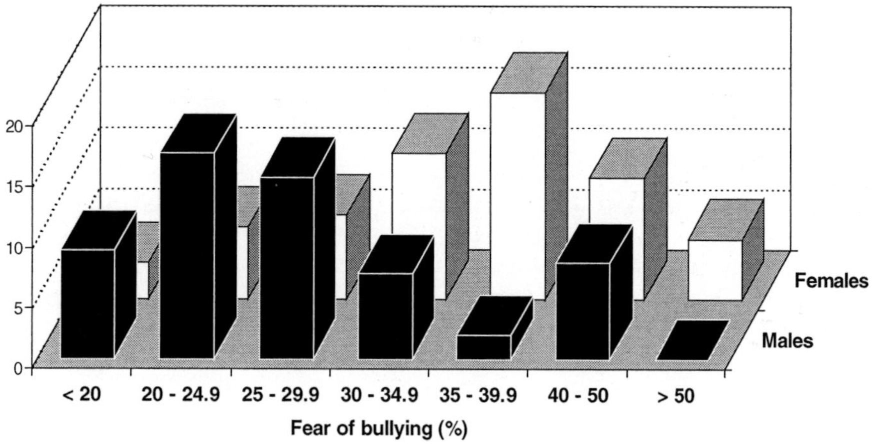

% that fear bullying	Number of schools Males	Females
<20%	9	3
20-24.9%	17	6
25-29.9%	15	7
30-34.9%	7	12
35-39.9%	2	17
40-50%	8	10
>50%	0	5
Schools	58	60

Results from a total of 60 secondary schools were analysed in the 'Bully Off' study. The numbers of schools with different percentages of Year 8 pupils that fear going to school at least sometimes are shown here. These schools represent 7 different area health authorities, and show the wide variation in levels that go to form the nationwide 'average'. The greater vulnerability of the females is clearly seen.

10 The 2003 sample

The first report of this series was published in 1986. We have maintained a continuous annual series since that time, and this is the 18th volume in the *Young People* sequence.

The year groups represented

Because of strategic sampling by the health organisations that commissioned most of the 2003 surveys, the sample is heavily concentrated on Years 6, 8 and 10, and we do not present results from the other years.

Areas and groups represented

Altogether, data from 15,526 young people in 196 schools are represented in this report. The largest contributing region was West Midlands followed by the North West.

The sample size

The available sample in each gender and year group is as shown in the following table.

Year group	Males	Females	Total
6 (10–11)	2422	2300	4722
8 (12–13)	3064	2865	5929
10 (14–15)	2450	2425	4875
Totals	***7936***	***7590***	***15526***

The concentration on Years 6, 8 and 10 reflects a strategy that many surveyors adopt in their anticipation of collecting serial data. This is promoted through the use of the survey in alternate years, and, provides an accumulation of data to examine for behaviour trends and the effects of intervention programmes in individual districts.

European Union regions represented in the 2003 data, showing the percentage of the 196 schools (primary and secondary combined).

	%
West Midlands	45
North West	15
East Anglia	10
East Midlands	8
South East	6
South West	5
Northern	4
Yorkshire and Humberside	4
Wales	3

School parameters

This information, together with other general data, is collected from each school carrying out an HRBQ survey.

	% of schools	
Type of school	***Sec***	***Pri***
Comprehensive	91	
Independent	3	
Primary		77
Junior		19
Other	5	1
Middle	1	1
Combined		2
Gender of school population		
All-male school	5	0
All-female school	3	0
Mixed school	92	100
Percentage of ethnic-minority children in the school		
0–1%	30	27
2–5%	23	20
6–10%	7	19
11–15%	5	5
16–20%	5	5
21–30%	13	4
31–40%	5	5
41–50%	2	3
>50%	9	11
School lunch provision		
Cafeteria	64	22
Set lunch	1	58
Packed Lunch	1	6
Both	4	3
Other/missing	16	10
None	1	1

	% of schools	
Percentage of children in the school qualifying for a free meal	***Sec***	***Pri***
0–1%	7	6
2–5%	18	11
6–10%	14	15
11–15%	11	9
16–20%	16	5
21–30%	25	22
31–40%	7	20
41–50%	0	5
>50%	2	7
Percentage of children in the school being transported by school bus		
0–10%	58	92
11–20%	9	3
21–30%	6	3
31–40%	4	0
41–50%	9	1
51–60%	6	0
61–70%	6	0
71–80%	2	2
>80%	0	0
Catchment area		
100% r	8	8
75% r, 25% s	2	2
50% r, 40% s, 10% u	4	1
100% s	17	21
75% s, 25% u	10	4
40% s, 50% u, 10% i	0	1
100% u	38	40
75% u, 25% i	4	1
25% u, 75% iu	19	23

r = rural, s = suburban, u = urban, i = inner urban

II The Unit's databanks

Data from the various questionnaires listed on page vii are stored in our data banks. In the majority of years more than one version of the questionnaire was in operation, and the version numbers are indicated in parentheses. The numbers of schools and respondents published in the annual reports from 1986 onwards are tabulated here, together with the contents of earlier but unpublished databanks. Until 1992 it was possible to present the results from only one version (indicated in bold type), but since that date it has been possible to merge the results from different versions. The total number of respondents in all surveys to date is over 640,000. (School and pupil numbers were revised in 2003 to coincide with our annual figures of schools surveyed.)

1983 (version 8)
Number of schools = 71
Number of pupils = 10,674

1984 (versions 8 & 10)
Number of schools = 43
Number of pupils = 8,834

1985 (versions 8 & 10)
Number of schools = 49
Number of pupils = 12,618

1986 (version 10)
Number of schools = 88
Number of pupils = 18,002

1987 (versions 10 & 11)
Number of schools = 116
Number of pupils = 18,407

1988 (versions 10 & 11)
Number of schools = 222
Number of pupils = 33,459

1989 (versions 11 & 12)
Number of schools = 104
Number of pupils = 15,672

1990 (versions 11, 12 &15)
Number of schools = 131
Number of pupils = 18,941

1991 (version 15)
Number of schools = 142
Number of pupils = 23,928

1992 (versions 15 & 16)
Number of schools = 141
Number of pupils = 20,218

1993 (version 16)
Number of schools = 171
Number of pupils = 29,074

1994 (version 16)
Number of schools = 279
Number of pupils = 48,297

1995 (versions 16 & 17 combined)
Number of schools = 108
Number of pupils = 16,711 [Plus Year 6 data]

1996 (versions 16, 17 & 18 combined)
Number of schools = 130
Number of pupils = 22,067

1997 (versions 18 & 19 combined)
Number of schools = 122
Number of pupils = 28,756 [Plus Year 5 & 6 data]

1998 (version 19)
Number of schools = 112
Number of pupils = 18,221

1999 (versions 20 & 21)
Number of schools = 181
Number of pupils = 31,182 [Plus Year 6 data]

2000 (version 21)
Number of schools = 389
Number of pupils = 42,073 [Including Year 6 data]

2001 (version 21)
Number of schools = 334
Number of pupils = 15,881 [Including Year 6 data]

2002 (version 22)
Number of schools = 499
Number of pupils = 37,150 [Including Year 6 data]

2003 (version 22)
Number of schools = 196
Number of pupils = 15,526 [Including Year 6 data]

The quality of the survey data

1 How reliable are the percentages?

Reliability and validity

We are often asked whether the answers are 'trustworthy' — can we really believe these figures? Ideally, any differences between answers given by two people about their behaviour should be due only to differences in their behaviour.

In practice, differences also arise because of

- *Differences in their recollection of their behaviour.*
- *Differences in their understanding of the question.*
- *Differences in their willingness to report their behaviour accurately.*

So to some extent, the trust we place in the data depends on the trustworthiness of the young people answering — that is, whether they are likely to try and mislead us or not. We have described elsewhere the various steps we have taken to try and reduce or eliminate the temptation to mislead, by getting the atmosphere for collecting data right. But the questions also need to be appropriate, and understood in the same way by different people. We have also recorded above the care we take over question design and development.

These issues can be seen in consideration of a question we no longer ask, namely *When did you start smoking?* Answers to this question seemed internally consistent and reliable, and young people in interview were convincing in their efforts to report their behaviour honestly. We did, however, notice a curious feature of the data: the average age when respondents said that they started smoking tended to be about two years younger than they were now, no matter what their age was. Here we seem to have raised a problem of memory: the length of time since they started smoking may have 'felt' about two years for the longer-standing smokers, but could have been longer.

We identify here two separate aspects to the 'trustworthiness' of the data:

Reliability: *Are the answers 'well-behaved' in their pattern?*

Validity: *Do the answers accurately represent the behaviours or beliefs of the respondents?*

Researchers have a high regard for questions of trustworthiness, and have developed a whole apparatus of language and standards for investigating questionnaire quality. We discuss these standards below, and how we might know when things are going astray.

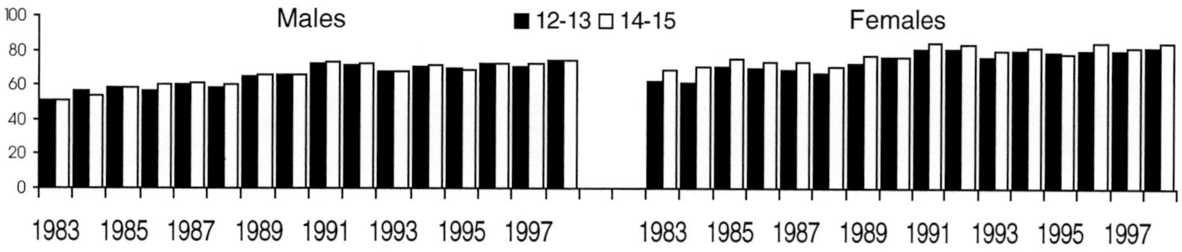

Above: The percentage that wash their hands 'whenever possible' after visiting the toilet, in the annual samples from 1983 to 1998. Below: A breakdown of the percentages within the principal health authorities (A-G) contributing to the 1998 sample.

Health	12-13		14-15	
authority	*M*	*F*	*M*	*F*
	%	%	%	%
A	70	80	71	81
B	73	80	72	82
C	-	-	73	85
D	73	83	73	92
E	79	83	81	89
F	72	81	78	81
G	74	84	77	87
Average	73.7	81.3	73.8	84.1

Reliability

Reliability is the measure of whether the same question is answered in the same way on each occasion. For example, a person might be asked *What do you think of the price of eggs?* Because it is not something they think about a great deal, they might give a completely different (though equally honest) answer next week, or even elsewhere in the same questionnaire. The consistency between answers given by the same people is known as internal reliability.

It is also important to know whether another person will answer the question in the same way: the so-called external reliability. Two different groups of people, asked *Are you a vegetarian?* may have different views as to what a vegetarian is. The people in one group, who eat dairy products, may see themselves as vegetarians, but those in another group, who also eat dairy products, may see vegetarianism as being stricter than this and so not describe themselves as such. So although honest and consistent within themselves, the two groups will answer the same question in different ways. These questions of reliability are perhaps less pressing in the case of behaviours as opposed to attitudes.

Internal reliability

A scale is said to be internally reliable if a person's answers on one part of the scale are correlated well with answers to other items in the scale. For example, we have a block of questions on self-esteem, and we know that answers to each item are highly predictive of answers to other items. So we can say that this scale is internally reliable.

This notion of internal reliability was developed in connection with scales of this sort, and not for disparate questions in ones and twos. We can apply the idea to the questionnaire as a whole, and look for consistency between items that overlap in content. Where overlap exists, we see that the items are highly consistent. For example, an early question on spending habits mentions spending money on cigarettes and alcohol, which can be related to answers many pages away which ask specifically if any cigarettes or alcohol have been consumed recently. From the 1998 data we found that of those Year 10 pupils saying they spent *any of their own money on cigarettes*, 95% reported that *they smoked last week*. Similarly, of those saying they *spent any of their own money on alcohol*, 95% said they *drank alcohol* last week.

External reliability

Questions are externally reliable if they give consistent results when used with different populations. Part of the aim of doing surveys in different populations is to see if they are different, so what we are looking for here are results that are similar in range, distribution and so on. Some of our questions are typically very stable from population to population — for example, the question about washing hands after visiting the lavatory.
The histogram reproduces a chart from *Young People in 1998* (Balding, 1999). It can be seen that the year-to-year variations are not large enough to mask a general rising trend. However, within the 1998 sample the question records a range of values exceeding 10% when the larger contributing health authority results are examined (see table).

Test-retest reliability

This is a special sort of reliability which is particularly useful to enquire into with respect to topics that are suspected of not being stable in the mind of the subjects. For example, while washing habits may be expected to be stable from week to week, opinions may not. We have very few data on this sort of reliability for our questions, and the questions on self-esteem, or attitudinal topics, would be interesting to look at in terms of their stability over time. Such studies as we and others have done suggest that scores on the self-esteem scale are indeed tolerably stable over time.

Validity

The notion of validity is what people usually have in mind when looking at a question — does this question really measure what you say it does? Validity is perhaps the critical issue: do the answers mean what they appear to mean? Are the respondents honest? Does the question mean anything to the respondents? If people were asked whether they would prefer to go on holiday to Flaunce or to Gzornenplatch, they may reliably give a preference for Flaunce, perhaps because of its earlier position or its more mellifluous sound. The fact that people have never heard of either resort cannot be detected from the reliability of their written responses.

Whether the answers to our questions mean what we think they mean must therefore be investigated in other ways, for example by interviews. There is a common-sense approach to this: namely, does it look as though it works? For example, one might be hesitant about accepting *How much do you like pop music?* as a measure of extroversion, but be more convinced by *Do you generally like loud, fast music, or is the music you prefer more often quiet and slow?* This sort of 'looks right' validity is called face validity. Other sorts of validity are described in the literature, but these are not readily applied to the HRBQ.

Other aspects of the data which might reassure us about the data's quality are the distribution of responses between pupils. Typically there are highly regular and consistent age-related trends, and often differences between the sexes. Where this pattern is seen and is consistent with expectations, we have more confidence in the data. In these annual compilations we can see age-related trends even when year groups are composed of young people from different parts of the country.

Also, we can look for associations between items in our questionnaire that have been found elsewhere — for example, there are a number of known correlates of smoking in young people, such as drinking alcohol, dating, school attainment and other variables such as self-esteem and locus of control. All these associations can be found in our data, which firstly reassures us that our data are valid, and secondly suggests that new associations can be sought in the wider range of topic items held in the databanks.

Finally, the interview and other work described above in piloting new questions, and the thousands of sheets of supervisors' feedback relating to established ones, provide a solid foundation for our confidence in the validity of the answers.

2 Statistical analysis of the data

Expected errors

Toss a coin ten times, and you might expect to get five heads and five tails. However, you could end up with anything but this proportion, and this reflects the problem of sampling: knowing what proportion you expect, you know that if you try to assess it by a sample, you are probably going to be a little way out, and you might be a long way out. Fortunately we can strictly define limits of doubt and uncertainty, and calculate how likely it is that a sample is going to be a certain degree 'out' from the expected result. We can also work backwards: given the result in a sample, we can say how likely it is that the 'real' population result is within a certain range. This is precisely the problem we face here.

We will adopt a standard symbol set:

n = sample size

p = proportion of sample reporting given behaviour

N = population size (whole school, or whole area sample)

The usual approach to estimating confidence limits and differences in proportions, given a sample of size n and proportion p, is to derive the standard error of proportion using Equation 1:

$$\sqrt{\frac{p(1-p)}{n}}$$

Eq. 1

95% confidence limits for a proportion are assumed to be twice this figure (technically 1.96 times). So, for a sample of 100 females, if the observed proportion is 8% (0.08), the standard error is $\sqrt{0.08(0.92)/100}$, i.e. 0.027 (3%). The 95% limits are therefore ±2 × 0.027, which is about ±5%. So we are 95% confident that the true figure is between 8% – 5% and 8% + 5%, i.e. 3%–13%.

The following points should be made:

- *For larger samples, the confidence limits grow narrower (i.e., improve)*
- *For proportions nearer 50%, the confidence limits are wider (i.e., less precise) than for smaller or larger proportions observed in samples of the same size*
- *Confidence increases as the range increases. For the example quoted, we would be 99.75% confident that the proportion lies between 8% ±7.5% (0.5%–15.5%).*

There are other connections we need to make, because this calculation assumes that N is many times larger than n. In a school, though, 50 males may be 50 out of 75 in the whole year group — see below.

Statistical models

Most methods of statistical analysis assume that the samples taken from a population are *(a)* gathered randomly, reducing the likelihood of sampling bias, and *(b)* that the size of the total population is many times larger than the size of the sample.

Our approach is rather different to this standard method.

Randomness

There is usually no attempt to randomise sampling within or between schools, and instead groups (usually classes or tutor groups) are selected to reflect the range (academic and social) of pupils within a school. Typically, schools are selected by health authority or health board personnel. Often there is a negotiation between volunteer schools and an area co-ordinator who wishes to select a representative range. This makes usual assumptions underlying statistical testing less valid, although it may be that analysis can still proceed.

Size

If we consider to what extent the school sample is representative of the school year group, it may be that 50 males have been taken from a total of 150 males on the school roll. Here the sample is 1/3 of the total, and is so large that it reduces the theoretical error that can arise through chance (i.e. that we happen to have included more of the smokers in the year in the 50 sampled than might have been expected). If the sample is a fair proportion of the population — and this can equally apply within area-wide samples, where a large proportion of the year group across the county are in schools that are surveyed — then the expected sampling errors are reduced.

Independence of pupils

The fact that each set of pupil data is not independent of others — pupils of similar lifestyles may cluster in certain schools, or in certain classes within the school — increases the uncertainty in behavioural estimates. The ONS have used a multiplication factor for confidence limits for use with their system of quota sampling within randomly-selected schools.

Confidence limits

These revised assumptions can act to make estimates based on the Health Related Behaviour methodology more accurate. In fact, the improvement can itself be calculated, and we are grateful to Dr. Ken Read of the University of Exeter's Department of Mathematics and Operational Research for his guidance in this matter.

For statistical purposes the total population from which the sample is taken is often very much larger than the sample. For Health Related Behaviour data the population is usually not so large — in fact, in some cases the sample is the whole school year group. In this case, barring absentees, there is no sampling error to estimate! Similarly, the proportion of schools sampled within an authority's control may be high — for example, eight out of a possible 20 schools (40%). If these eight include the largest schools, the proportion of the total population which is in fact sampled may be nearer 50%. In many districts, over half and in some cases all of the schools in the area covered by an Authority have been surveyed.

In these cases the sampling error is much reduced. This expected reduction can be calculated, as in Equation 2, which gives the standard error of proportion with known population size.

$$\sqrt{\frac{p(1-p)}{n}\,\frac{N-n}{N-1}}$$

Eq. 2

Depending on the size of the actual school year, this can have a very significant effect in reducing the theoretical sampling error. For each school we record the sample sizes and the school roll for the different year/gender groups: in 1998 the average sample size for both Years 8 and 10 was 52 , and the average representation of those on the roll in both years combined was 66%. Even for an observed proportion of 50% (which as stated above gives the poorest confidence limits), this means that the expected error is reduced to ±4% for a typical school.

For sample sizes of a thousand or more, as the following table shows, the expected errors and confidence limits are of the order of a few percentage points.

Sample (N)	*Standard error for proportion of 50%*	*95% confidence limits*
1000	1.6	±3.2% (46.8%–53.2%)
4000	0.4	±0.8% (49.2%–50.8%)

	86	87	88	89	90	91	92
Age	%	%	%	%	%	%	%
MALE smokers							
11–12	5		2		5		5
	2	**2**	**2**	**5**	**3**	**-**	**3**
12–13	6		5		7		8
	5	**5**	**4**	**6**	**5**	**6**	**7**
13–14	11		10		11		11
	12	**8**	**9**	**9**	**12**	**10**	**14**
14–15	13		16		21		26
	18	**15**	**13**	**20**	**19**	**18**	**20**
FEMALE smokers							
11–12	2		3		2		4
	2	**2**	**2**	**2**	**3**	**-**	**4**
12–13	5		4		8		8
	6	**4**	**5**	**7**	**6**	**8**	**8**
13–14	13		9		16		17
	15	**13**	**12**	**17**	**16**	**14**	**16**
14–15	25		21		25		26
	26	**20**	**20**	**26**	**24**	**25**	**28**

This table compares 'regular + occasional' smokers in ONS data for England 1986–1992 (Thomas et al., 1993) with those smoking 'any cigarettes last week' in the Unit's annual data collations (Balding 1987-93).The Unit's data in **bold** *type. The data have been adjusted to take account of (a) combined age groups and (b) time of year. (Further details are given in Balding, 2000). ONS annual samples are typically about 300 per gender/year group; the Unit's are typically over 2000.*

The figures assume that the population being surveyed is many times larger than the sample, as is the case with, for example, nationwide opinion surveys.

However, if we assume that the population is only about twice the size of the sample, then these error estimates are much reduced. As stated above, in 1998 66% of the schools' Year 8 and 10 populations were sampled.

This explains why we are so confident that the data effectively represents the population from which the samples are drawn. However, the extent to which that population represents the national picture cannot be derived from these formulæ.

3 Comparison of the Unit's data with other surveys

There are some areas of the Health Related Behaviour instrument for which national data are directly available for comparison, and it is of interest to study these.

There are several differences between the way our data are collected and the methods used by other sources — for example, the uneven sampling across regions — but if we found large differences between the behaviours reported using the different methods, which were consistent for different regions sampled in our surveys, this could indicate problems with methodology.

Conversely, if we found a good match between our data and other representative surveys for which comparison data are available, we have some optimism that the remaining topics in our data are also to some extent representative of the national picture. (In the case of certain topics we know of no other work, in this or any other country, where the behaviours in question have been examined.)

It is not uncommon to find our work cited by other researchers (e.g. Plant et al., 1990, and Brannen et al., 1994).

We obviously believe that the data are of sufficient quality and interest to be worthy of attention, and some of the evidence for this is collated below.

Smoking

The ONS has had a succession of biennial surveys with which our data can be directly compared: it uses a system of quota sampling within randomly-selected schools (although, as noted on pages xii–xiii, there is a level of non-co-operation by schools and by pupils).

The ONS studies define 'occasional' and 'regular' smokers using a combined diary + self-description definition, whereas we use only retrospective self-reports of consumption. If memory is accurate, this should yield similar figures to the ONS diary data from the same subjects.

The smokers (regular and occasional) in ONS include some regular smokers that did not smoke during the previous week, and some subjects that did smoke but did not describe themselves as smokers. Their figures resulting from this approach are very similar to our own (see table).

Note how the low 1988 figures are supported in the annual the Unit's sampling by the 1987 data; biennial sampling may fail to give sufficiently close 'markers' to interpret such rapid changes with confidence.

The following charts are displayed in order to show comparisons between ONS surveys and data from the Unit.

Below is a chart of the serial data from the ONS/OPCS surveys of young people's smoking: the figures are for 14-15 year-old females.

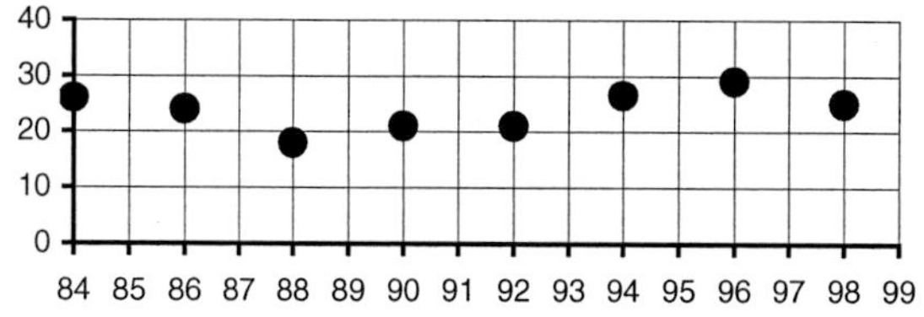

There is an apparent drop in the smoking prevalence in these Year 10 girls between 1986 and 1988, and another ten years later. Without the intermediate years being represented, it's not clear whether the figures are aberrant or in keeping with a more general trend.

The next chart shows the equivalent figures from the Unit's databanks, corrected for time of year.

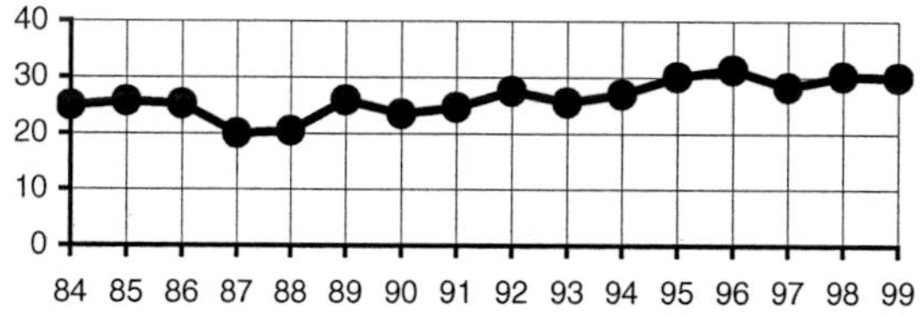

The figures are tolerably similar to the ONS figures, but that is not all that we wish to show here. The pattern of the figures is as interesting as the levels: the low in 1988 and the high in 1996 seem confirmed as such, and the figures from the neighbouring years suggest that these were not years out of keeping with general trends at the time.

Other drugs

The most recent ONS surveys have included a section on illegal drugs. How do these data compare with those from the Unit's surveys? The Unit's data were described in *Young People and Illegal Drugs on 2000* (Balding, 2000).

The data are derived from different questions and presented in different ways in our respective reports, but the patterns are similar and the differences are in the directions expected — for example, some differences in drug use are consistent with known differences in the age composition of the samples.

1998 DRUG DATA

	Age	Gender	ONS	The Unit
Ever offered				
All drugs	11-15	M+F	34%	
	12-15	M+F		25%
	11-15	M	36%	
	12-15	M		25%
	11-15	F	32%	
	12-15	F		24%
	11	M+F	15%	
	12-13	M+F		10%
	15	M+F	61%	
	14-15	M+F		37%
Cannabis	11-15	M+F	26%	
	12-15	M+F		20%
Ever taken				
All drugs	11-15	M+F	13%	
	12-15	M+F		16%
	11	M+F	1%	
	12-13	M+F		6%
	15	M+F	33%	
	14-15	M+F		25%
Taken in past year				
All drugs	11-15	M+F	11%	
	12-15	M+F		12%

Note that the ONS surveys sampled young people in year groups 7-11 (age range 11-15). The Unit's survey data were derived from year groups 8 and 10 only (ages 12-13 and 14-15).

There is a difference in drugs use by gender in the ONS surveys which has also seen in other studies (as Eileen Goddard points out in her review); however, differences between males and females in drug use in our 1998 figures are smaller or absent. It is interesting to note that in the 2001 data set, when we look at the Year 10 figures males report use more often than females.

Visiting the doctor — local data

At one point an opportunity arose to check young people's reports of GP attendance. A practising doctor from Barnham was presented with results of the West Sussex survey at a meeting, and thought that the rates shown for Year 8 and Year 10 pupils visiting the doctor were implausibly high. He immediately organised a check on his figures, and a colleague searched the computer files from the group practice. He was astonished to find that in his practice the GPs had seen 40% of their patients aged between 13 and 19 in the past three months, which fitted within the summary data for the whole DHA (Wallis, 1993).

Alcohol

Although we spend a long time looking at comparisons between our data and figures from other studies, usually we are reassured by this exercise. However, it must be noted that our figures for the frequency of reported alcohol use in the previous week are higher than are seen in other studies. The levels of consumption, however, are not higher. The questions about alcohol used in our surveys and the ONS studies look and feel very different, it is not clear to us why they produce such different results.

4 Looking for trends: a 'health warning'

Because of the way we collect our data (see pages x-xii), we have to be more than usually careful about interpreting our statistics. Any changes we see between successive calendar years may be due to a change in the behaviour of the whole UK population of children, which is thus reflected in our data and in surveys by others. On the other hand, the changes may be apparent, not real, due to interference from a number of other factors. These are discussed below.

Changes in the question

We occasionally make changes to the wording or layout of a question in response to feedback from schools. These changes sometimes appear to make differences to the proportions that choose different options.

This is a well-known phenomenon, but some of our discoveries about questionnaire design we have not seen reported elsewhere (e.g. the 'order effect', *Young People into the Nineties, Book 1, Doctor and Dentist*).

Changes in the context of a question

In designing new versions of the questionnaire we occasionally make changes to the order of questions and their context. So although the question and prompts may be identical, if a question is placed with new neighbours this may affect the responses; see p. 13 below. Again, this effect has been noted in the literature (e.g. Budd & Spencer, 1986).

Changes in the sample

1. Distributional

The compilation of schools taking part in surveys across the country may be very different from year to year. Usually we cannot see any major effects of these differences, but occasionally we see rather clear associations with the sample.

For example, in 1993 we had an unusually large representation of Scottish schools in year groups 7-9, and these regional biases were detectable in the newspapers taken in the home (in this case the Scottish *Daily Record*).

	92	93	94
Daily Record taken	%	%	%
Year 7	22.8	39.2	7.2
Year 8	6.0	26.2	1.0
Year 9	10.8	36.4	14.8

However, the 'Scottish factor' does not not appear to have had any influence on the smoking data that can be recognised within the expected fluctuations between successive samples.

	92	93	94
Smoked last week	%	%	%
Males			
Year 7	2.7	4.3	3.6
Year 8	6.9	6.1	7.1
Year 9	14.0	12.8	11.9
Females			
Year 7	4.2	4.2	2.1
Year 8	7.9	7.8	9.2
Year 9	15.9	17.5	17.9

It can be seen from p. *xviii* that this year's sample featured an unusually high number of Scottish schools: 36% of all schools sampled this year were Scottish. However, this has not so big an effect as one might suppose, for most of these schools are very small primary schools. The proportion of the pupils who are Scottish is just 12%, and if we look at the proportion of *Daily Record* readers in the Family and Home chapter (p.50) it is not very great at all.

2. Temporal

The 1997 sample was unusual, not in its regional distribution but its timing; most of the largest surveys took place in the autumn, and so the pupils in each year group were in the first term of their school year. We did notice that for some of the behaviours that are strongly age-related, like smoking, the levels reported were unusually low. If we corrected for age as an influence, the levels returned to previous normal levels: see Balding (1998 & 1998a).

Confidence

We have more confidence in attributing real significance to a change if:

- it is not associated with major changes in the wording or placing of the question;
- it persists as either a long-term change from one level to another, or part of an upward or downward trend carrying over several years.

(See also Section 9 of the Introduction: *Yorkshire surveys*, 1991-1995.)

5 Conclusion

We hope that this account will provide some insight into the work we have done on the important questions of reliability and consistency. Over the years we have brought a number of lines of enquiry to bear on these issues, and hope by discussing them here to allow a more informed assessment of the quality of the data presented on the following pages.

References

Balding, J. W. (1987). *Young People in 1986*. Exeter: University of Exeter, Schools Health Education Unit.

Balding, J. W. (1989). *Young People in 1988*. Exeter: University of Exeter, Schools Health Education Unit.

Balding, J. W. (1991). *Young People in 1990*. Exeter: University of Exeter, Schools Health Education Unit.

Balding, J. W. (1992). *Young People in 1991*. Exeter: University of Exeter, Schools Health Education Unit.

Balding, J. W. (1994). *Young People in 1993*. Exeter: University of Exeter, Schools Health Education Unit.

Balding, J. W. (1995). *Young People in 1994*. Exeter: University of Exeter, Schools Health Education Unit.

Balding, J. W. (1996). *Young People in 1995*. Exeter: University of Exeter, Schools Health Education Unit.

Balding, J. W. (1996). *Bully Off*. Exeter: University of Exeter, Schools Health Education Unit.

Balding, J. W. (1996a). *Cash and Carry*. Exeter: University of Exeter, Schools Health Education Unit.

Balding, J. W. (1998). *Young People and Illegal Drugs in 1998* (revised 2nd edition). Exeter: University of Exeter, Schools Health Education Unit.

Balding, J. W. (1998a). *Young People in 1997*. Exeter: University of Exeter, Schools Health Education Unit.

Balding, J. W. (1999). *Young People in 1998: with a look back as far as 1983*. Exeter: Schools Health Education Unit

Balding, J. W. (2000). *Young People and Illegal Drugs in 2000*. Exeter: Schools Health Education Unit.

Balding, J. W. & Shelley, C. (1989). Catchment area and health-related behaviour. *Education and Health*, 7, 1, 17–22.

Balding, J. W., Foot, G. & Regis, D. (1991). *The Assessment of Health Needs at the Community Level: a Guide for District Health Authorities*. Exeter: University of Exeter, Schools Health Education Unit.

Balding, J. W., Regis, D. & Wise, A. (1998). *No Worries? Young people and mental health*. Exeter: Schools Health Education Unit.

Brannen, J. et al. (1994). *Young People, Health and Family Life*. Buckingham: Open University Press.

Budd, R. J. & Spencer, C. P. (1986). Lay theories of behavioural intention: a source of response bias in the theory of reasoned action. *British Journal of Social Psychology*, 22, 109-117.

Coleman, L. & Cater, S. (2003) What do we know about young people's use of alcohol? *Education and Health*, 21: 3, 50-55.

Devon County Council (1999). *Travelwise survey*. Prendergast,W., Exeter.

Dobbs, J. & Marsh, A. (1983). *Smoking among secondary schoolchildren*. London: HMSO.

DOH (1992). *Health of the Nation*. London: HMSO.

Flood, S. (2000). Drug misuse among the young may have peaked. *Education and Health*, 18: 2, 41-42.

Goddard, E. (2001) *Evaluation of various data sources on drug use, smoking and drinking by children of secondary school age*. Located at http://www.homeoffice.gov.uk/rds/pdfs/drugsuse.pdf

Griffiths, M. (1998). Children and the Internet: issues for parents and teachers. *Education and Health*, 16: 1, 9-10.

Griffiths, M. (2002). The educational benefits of videogames. *Education and Health*, 20: 3, 47-51.

Griffiths, M. (2003). Videogames: Advice for parents and teachers. *Education and Health*, 21: 3, 48-49

HEA/MORI, (1992). *Tomorrow's Young Adults: 9-15-year-olds Look at Alcohol, Drugs, Exercise and Smoking*. London: Health Education Authority.

Hackett, A., Gibbon, M. & Lamb, L. (2003). Eating habits of children in Liverpool: a need for health education? *Education and Health*, 21:1, 3–8.

Lawrence, D. (1981). Development of a self-esteem questionnaire. *British Journal of Educational Psychology*, 51, 245–251.

Lawton, D. (1972). *Social Class, Language, and Education*. London: Routledge & Kegan Paul.

MacGregor, I., Balding, J. W. & Regis, D. (1994). *Toothbrushing in Adolescence*. Exeter: University of Exeter, Schools Health Education Unit.

Masters, B. (2003). Sport as a health risk. *Education and Health*, 21: 3, 43-47.

Morris, B. & Trimble, N. (1991). Promotion of bicycle helmet and use among school children: a randomised clinical trial. *Canadian Journal of Public Health*, 82, 92-94.

Nelson, S. C. et al. (1985). The Avon prevalence study: a survey of cigarette smoking in secondary schoolchildren. *Health Education Journal*, 44, 12–15.

OFSTED. (2002). Bare Facts of Life are not enough. *Education and Health*, 20: 2, 38-39.

Olweus, D. (1989). *Bully/victim problems among school children: basic facts and effects of a school-based intervention program*. In Rubin, K.H. & Pepler, D. (eds.), *The Development and Treatment of Childhood Agression*. Hillsdale, N.J. Erlbaum.

O'Neill, M. & O'Donnell,D. (2003). Smart Snacks Scheme: A healthy breaks initiative for the school environment. *Education and Health*, 21:1, 9–13.

Plant, M. et al., 1990. Young people and drinking — results of an English national survey. *Alcohol and Alcoholism*, 25, 6, 685–690.

Raw, M., McNeill, A. & West, R. (1998). Smoking Cessations Guidelines and their cost effectiveness. *Thorax*, 53, 5.

SHEU (2003). *Trends-Young People's Food Choices:Attitudes to healthy eating and weight control 1983-2001*. Exeter. SHEU

SHEU (2003). *Trends-Young People and Smoking:Attitudes to cigarettes 1983-2001*. Exeter. SHEU

SHEU (2003). *Trends-Young People and Alcohol:Attitudes to drinking 1983-2001*. Exeter. SHEU

SHEU (2004). *Trends-Young People and Emotional Health and Well-Being 1983-2003*. Exeter. SHEU

Thom, B., Herring, R., Judd, A. (1999). Identifying alcohol-related harm in young drinkers: The role of accident and emergency departments. *Alcohol and Alcoholism*, 34, 910-915.

Thomas. M. et al., (1993). *Smoking among secondary schoolchildren in 1992*. London: HMSO (SS1349).

Townsend, P., Davidson, N. & Whitehead, M. (1992). *Inequalities in Health*. Harmondsworth, UK: Penguin Books.

Tunstall, J. (1980). *The British press in the age of television*. In Christian, H. (ed.), *The Sociology of Journalism and the Press*. Stoke on Trent: University of Keele.

Wallis, P. (1993). For the record. *Education and Health*, 11: 1, 13.

Willemsen, M.C. & De Zwart, W.M. (1999). The effectiveness of policy and health education strategies for reducing adolescent smoking: a review of the evidence. *Journal of Adolescence*, 22, 587-599.

Woodroffe, C. et al. (1993). *Children, Teenagers and Health: the Key Data*. Oxford: Oxford University Press.

Index to questions

1. Food choices and weight control

2. Doctor & Dentist

3. Health & Safety

4. Family & Home

5. Legal & Illegal Drugs

How the information is arranged

We attempt to present the information as accurately and helpfully as possible. The 2003 responses are summarised as percentages, in tabular form. The question wording, and the wording of the responses, are presented as accurately as space will permit. We like to indicate *Valid responses* rather than *Sample size*, as *Valid responses* excludes respondents that did not answer the question. However, some presentations combine responses to several questions or sub-questions. In this case there is no single value for *Valid responses*. Instead, we give the *Sample size* and indicate the percentage of *Missing data*. In some charts we also include *None of the these* or *None of the above* which also includes on most pages *Missing data*. The proportion of *Missing data* might be estimated by reference to adjacent questions; where it has been considered important to distinguish *None of the these/ None of the above* and *Missing data* e.g. participation in sport p.98, this is noted on the chart.

Schoolday breakfast

22% of the Year 10 females have *nothing at all* for breakfast

The main observation

The question and number

What did you have for breakfast this morning? (19) (Pri.6)

Observations on the data

1. Seeking the breakfast 'missers', we find more Year 10s than Year 8s, and more Year 10 females than Year 8 females.
2. *Cereal* is the most commonly reported breakfast item, particularly for Year 6 pupils (43%), Year 8 males (40%) and Year 10 males (37%).
3. *Just a drink* is reported by 17% Year 8 females and 19% Year 10 females.
4. *A cooked breakfast* is taken by few and mainly the males.

The 2003 data

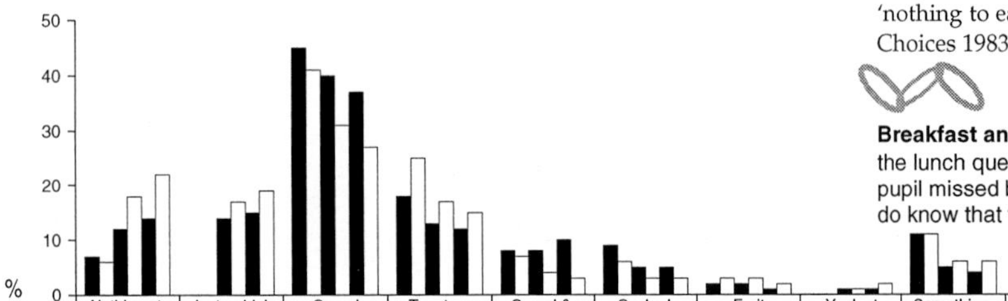

'Rounded' percentages

	Nothing at all	Just a drink	Cereal	Toast or bread	Cereal & toast/ bread	Cooked breakfast	Fruit	Yoghurt	Something else	Valid responses
■ Yr 6 M	7	0	45	18	8	9	2	0	11	2015
□ Yr 6 F	6	0	41	25	7	6	3	0	11	1918
■ Yr 8 M	12	14	40	13	8	5	2	1	5	1941
□ Yr 8 F	18	17	31	17	4	3	3	1	6	1879
■ Yr 10 M	14	15	37	12	10	5	1	1	4	1505
□ Yr 10 F	22	19	27	15	3	3	2	2	6	1565

Comments

Comments on the data

1. Is the high percentage of those having nothing at all or just a drink cause for concern?
2. We do not know if missing breakfast is an undesired omission (e.g. through lack of organisation, time or effort) or a deliberate decision to reduce food intake. In 'Young People in 1997', (Balding, 1998a), we found a substantial number of 9-11 year olds were eating shop bought snack-type food before school although it was not related to lack of breakfast. Hovever, programmes, such as the 'Smart Snacks Scheme', show that pupils can be encouraged to eat more healthily by the development of school policies on healthy snacks (O'Neill & O'Donnell, 2003).
3. Data since 1983 reveal an upward trend, for all groups, of those having 'nothing to eat for breakfast' (SHEU, 2003, 'Trends-Young People's Food Choices 1983-2001').

Comments on linked data

Breakfast and lunch: The breakfast question is about this morning, and the lunch question is about yesterday, so we cannot demonstrate that any pupil missed both breakfast and lunch on the same day. Nonetheless, we do know that the two options are related. For example, among Year 10 females: those missing breakfast are nearly twice as likely to have missed lunch the previous day:

Proportion having nothing for breakfast this morning: 22%

Proportion missing lunch yesterday: 20%

Proportion of those having nothing for breakfast this morning who had nothing for lunch yesterday: 26%

1

1 Food choices and weight control

This section of the Health Related Behaviour Questionnaire has passed through more revisions than any other. In earlier versions, attempts were made to derive quality and quantity measurements from the respondents' account of 'yesterday's intake', but the vagueness about amounts and quality made it impossible to do more than note the apparent presence or absence of certain important nutrients. The 2003 questionnaire (version 22) contains a checklist of 16 common food items against which the pupils indicate typical levels of consumption. It is hoped that classroom discussion of these results will raise levels of awareness regarding 'healthy' and 'unhealthy' foods. The health-related aspect of diet, as well as attitude to personal weight, is also included in this section.

Question

Schoolday breakfast

22% of the Year 10 females have *nothing at all* for breakfast

What did you have for breakfast this morning? (19) (Pri.6)

1. Seeking the breakfast 'missers', we find more Year 10s than Year 8s, and more Year 10 females than Year 8 females.
2. *Cereal* is the most commonly reported breakfast item, particularly for Year 6 pupils (43%), Year 8 males (40%) and Year 10 males (37%).
3. *Just a drink* is reported by 17% Year 8 females and 19% Year 10 females.
4. *A cooked breakfast* is taken by few and mainly the males.

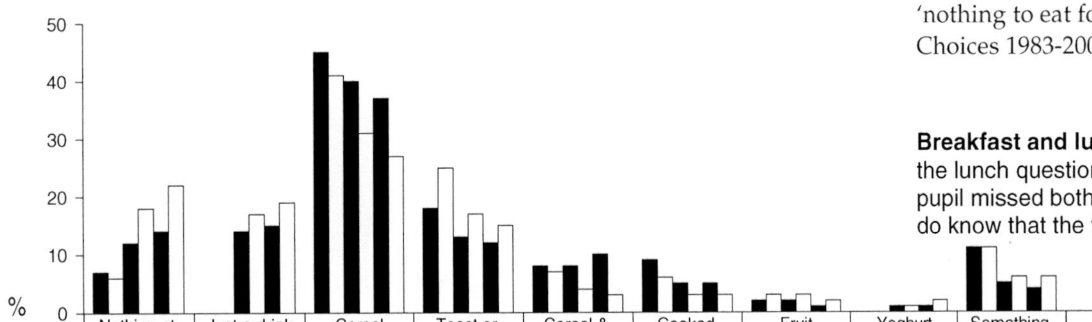

	Nothing at all	Just a drink	Cereal	Toast or bread	Cereal & toast/ bread	Cooked breakfast	Fruit	Yoghurt	Something else	Valid responses
■ Yr 6 M	7	0	45	18	8	9	2	0	11	2015
□ Yr 6 F	6	0	41	25	7	6	3	0	11	1918
■ Yr 8 M	12	14	40	13	8	5	2	1	5	1941
□ Yr 8 F	18	17	31	17	4	3	3	1	6	1879
■ Yr 10 M	14	15	37	12	10	5	1	1	4	1505
□ Yr 10 F	22	19	27	15	3	3	2	2	6	1565

Comments

1. Is the high percentage of those having nothing at all or just a drink cause for concern?
2. We do not know if missing breakfast is an undesired omission (e.g. through lack of organisation, time or effort) or a deliberate decision to reduce food intake. In 'Young People in 1997', (Balding, 1998a), we found a substantial number of 9-11 year olds were eating shop bought snack-type food before school although it was not related to lack of breakfast. Hovever, programmes, such as the 'Smart Snacks Scheme', show that pupils can be encouraged to eat more healthily by the development of school policies on healthy snacks (O'Neill & O'Donnell, 2003).
3. Data since 1983 reveal an upward trend, for all groups, of those having 'nothing to eat for breakfast' (SHEU, 2003, 'Trends-Young People's Food Choices 1983-2001').

Breakfast and lunch: The breakfast question is about this morning, and the lunch question is about yesterday, so we cannot demonstrate that any pupil missed both breakfast and lunch on the same day. Nonetheless, we do know that the two options are related. For example, among Year 10 females: those missing breakfast are nearly twice as likely to have missed lunch the previous day:
Proportion having nothing for breakfast this morning: 22%
Proportion missing lunch yesterday: 20%
Proportion of those having nothing for breakfast this morning who had nothing for lunch yesterday: 26%

Schoolday lunch

20% of the Year 10 females did not have any lunch

What did you do for lunch yesterday? (18)

1. A cafeteria lunch was the most popular option including up to 39% of the Year 8 pupils.
2. Up to 33% had a packed lunch.
3. Figures for a school set lunch are low; around 5% reported having this type of lunch.
4. 20% of the Year 10 females had no lunch.

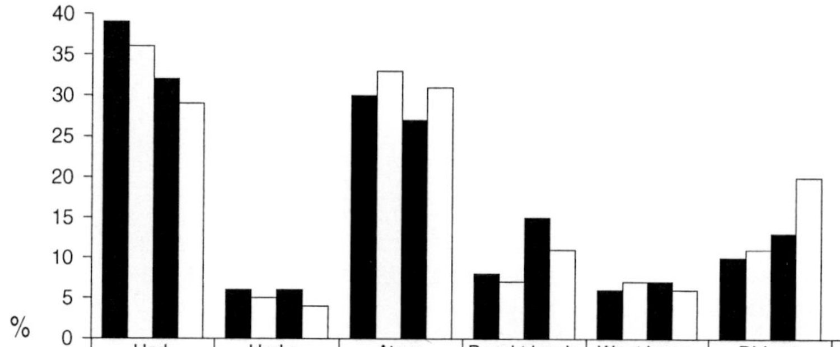

	Had cafeteria lunch	Had a set lunch in school	Ate a packed lunch	Bought lunch from shop	Went home for lunch	Did not have any lunch	Valid responses
■ Yr 8 M	39	6	30	8	6	10	3006
□ Yr 8 F	36	5	33	7	7	11	2832
■ Yr 10 M	32	6	27	15	7	13	2408
□ Yr 10 F	29	4	31	11	6	20	2399

Comments

1. The 'packed lunchers' form an interesting group. Basic analysis of data from the 1990s suggested that this group were likely to enjoy a more balanced overall diet than those choosing other lunch options – not necessarily because of what was in the lunch box as parents are less likely to put items in the lunch box that their child will not eat. However, those supplying a packed lunch tended to give more thought to what pupils eat at lunchtime and throughout the day. Data since 1985 show a fluctuating trend of 'packed lunchers'. Data from recent years show that younger pupils and females more than males are 'packed lunchers' (SHEU, 2003, 'Trends-Young People's Food Choices 1983-2001').
2. Are those who are buying their lunch from a shop allowed to leave the school premises at lunchtime or are they off-site without permission? 22% of the Year 10 males either went home for lunch or bought their lunch from a shop. Why are they chosing this option above the option of lunch at school?
3. Data since 1983 reveal an upward trend, for all groups, of those not having schoolday lunch (SHEU, 2003, 'Trends-Young People's Food Choices 1983-2001').
4. We have seen on the previous page that there is a relationship between those who missed lunch and those who missed breakfast. Are there connections between pupils who miss meals and their attitudes to losing weight? [See over]

Attitude to personal weight

58% of Year 10 females and
54% of Year 8 females would like to lose weight

Your weight — which statement describes you best? (21)

1. Many more females than males want to lose weight.
2. 58% of the Year 10 females and 54% of the Year 8 females would like to lose weight.
3. More of the younger males would like to lose weight, as opposed to more of the older females.
4. Only 36% of the Year 10 females said they were happy with their weight as it is.

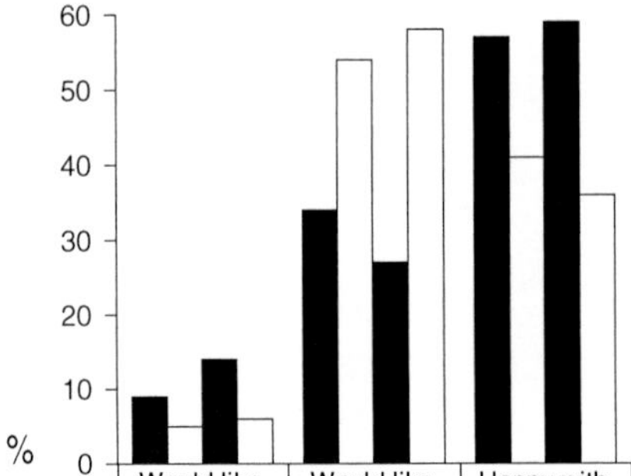

	Would like to put on weight	Would like to lose weight	Happy with weight as it is	Valid responses
■ Yr 8 M	9	34	57	3010
□ Yr 8 F	5	54	41	2838
■ Yr 10 M	14	27	59	2417
□ Yr 10 F	6	58	36	2399

Comments

1. It is easy to understand why more females than males want to lose weight, but the age differences are interesting:
The slight preponderance of younger males could mean that they feel more self-conscious, or that weight seems more of a disadvantage — it could also be because more are overweight.
Conversely, the preponderance of older females suggests the opposite.
2. An analysis of the characteristics of the Year 10 females shows that most of those wanting to lose weight are within the limits of 'healthy' weight, and some are already underweight (see page 6).
3. Data since 1991 reveal an increasing trend of desire for weight loss for all groups (SHEU, 2003, 'Trends-Young People's Food Choices 1983-2001').
4. We have a problem of sending appropriate messages to a population of young people, many of whom are overweight, and yet more seem overanxious about their weight.

Year 10 females were more likely to miss breakfast and lunch if they desired to lose weight:
Proportion who had nothing for breakfast today: 22%
Proportion who missed lunch yesterday: 20%
Proportion of those who want to lose weight who missed breakfast: 25%
Proportion of those who want to lose weight who missed lunch: 25%
In earlier books in this series we also showed that a desire to lose weight could be linked to food choices.

Weight

Up to 50% were unsure of their weight

Do you know your weight? (17)

1. There are some unsurprising age and sex differences here: older males are the heaviest, which fits well with the data relating to height.
2. We do not ask the question in the primary version of the questionnaire because of the work that would be involved for teachers in the collection of accurate data. In the secondary surveys, schools are asked to prompt pupils to check their height and weight before completing the questionnaire.

Comments

1. Unusually high or low responses reported to us may be due to difficulties of converting. [Answers may be given in imperial or metric units, although schools have encouraged use of metric measures for years. We also provide conversion charts in the survey support materials.]
2. The following percentages of missing values provides an indication of those who did not know or were unsure of their weight:

   Y8M: 47% Y8F: 48% Y10M: 30% Y10F: 50%
3. There is little evidence in our data that those young people who are unhappy with their weight are significantly less likely to report their weight to us than the rest of the sample.
4. However, not all areas using our survey chose to include the height/weight questions, and so the sample used here is much smaller and regionally restricted. Nonetheless the figures are of interest.

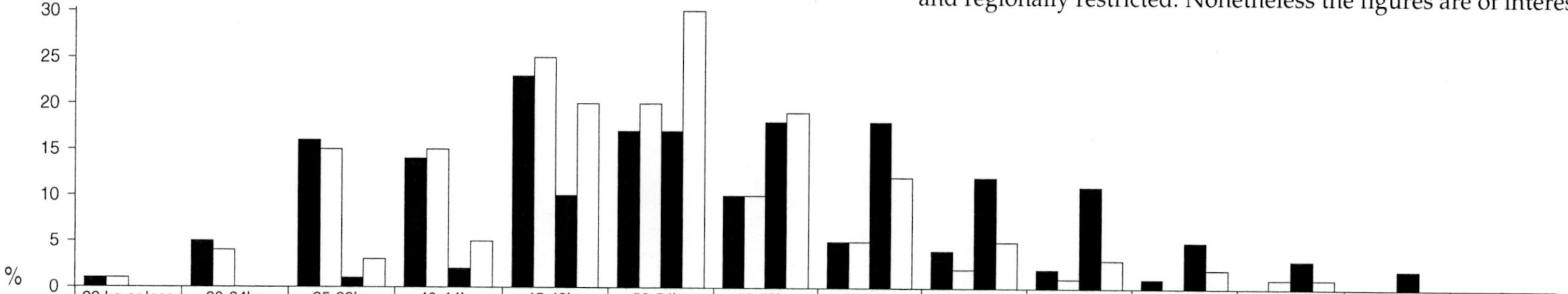

	29 kg or less	30-34kg	35-39kg	40-44kg	45-49kg	50-54kg	55-59kg	60-64kg	65-69kg	70-74kg	75-79kg	80-84kg	Over 85kg	Valid responses
■ Yr 8 M	1	5	16	14	23	17	10	5	4	2	1	0	0	1601
□ Yr 8 F	1	4	15	15	25	20	10	5	2	1	0	1	0	1313
■ Yr 10 M	0	0	1	2	10	17	18	18	12	11	5	3	2	1420
□ Yr 10 F	0	0	3	5	20	30	19	12	5	3	2	1	0	1216

Height

Males start 'growing away' from females in Year 10

Do you know your height? (16)

1. Again, we see that older males are the tallest. Females appear to be taller than the males in Year 8, but by Year 10 the males are clearly taller than the females.
2. Height and weight are 'continuous' measures, which show the classical pattern of a 'bell curve': a heap in the middle with two tapering ends.

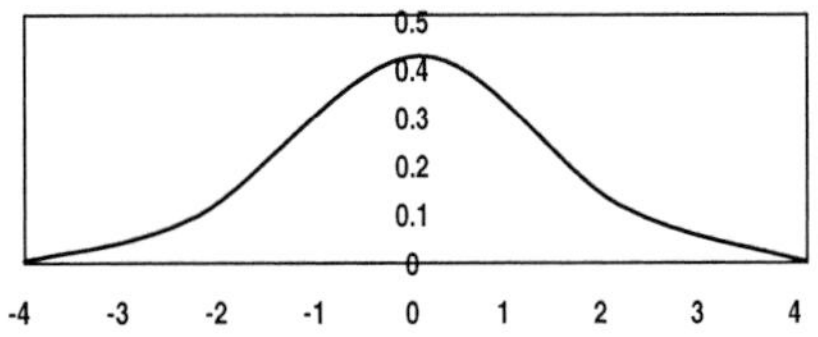

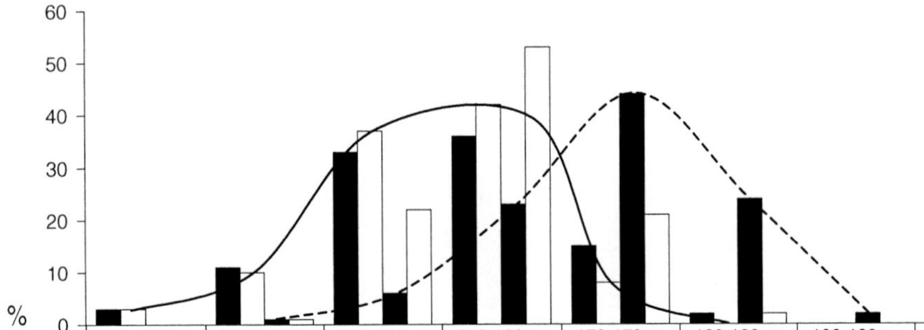

	Up to 139cm	140-149cm	150-159cm	160-169cm	170-179cm	180-189cm	190-199cm	Valid responses
■ Yr 8 M	3	11	33	36	15	2	0	1391
□ Yr 8 F	3	10	37	42	8	0	0	1395
■ Yr 10 M	0	1	6	23	44	24	2	1403
□ Yr 10 F	0	1	22	53	21	2	0	1437

Comments

1. Many of the comments we made about weight above also apply here.
2. A higher proportion of young people are sure of their height than their weight.
3. A comment from many primary school teachers is that youngsters, particularly girls, are getting taller at an earlier age. If this is combined with theories about better diet and lack of exercise producing taller individuals then it will be interesting to see if the average heights observed increase in our data in the years to come.
4. Is height a health issue? In fact, poverty and poor diet may still contribute to a failure to grow as well as possible. But beyond this, it may have more subtle effects. For example, taller young people may find it easier to purchase age-restricted material.
5. However, not all areas using our survey chose to include the height/weight questions, and so the sample used here is much smaller and regionally restricted. Nonetheless the figures are of interest.

Weight analysis

Around 12% need to lose weight

Derived body mass measurement

All 14-15y males: 2nd and 91st Percentiles of BMI

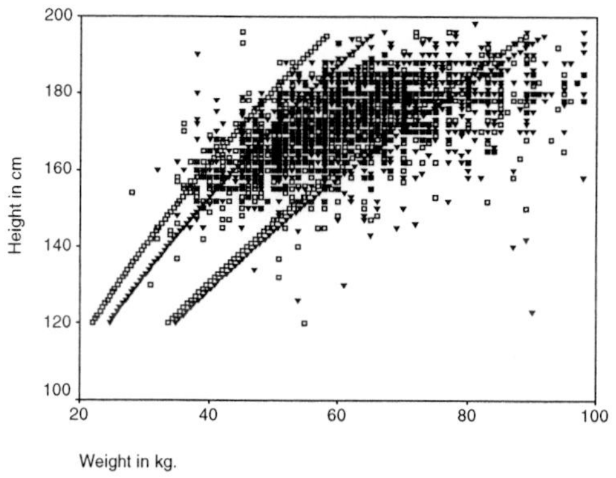

Males: 2nd and 91st Percentiles of BMI for those who would like to lose weight

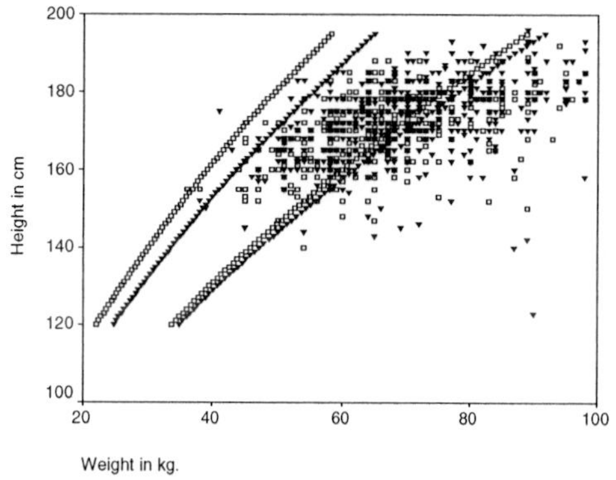

All 14-15y females: 2nd and 91st Percentiles of BMI

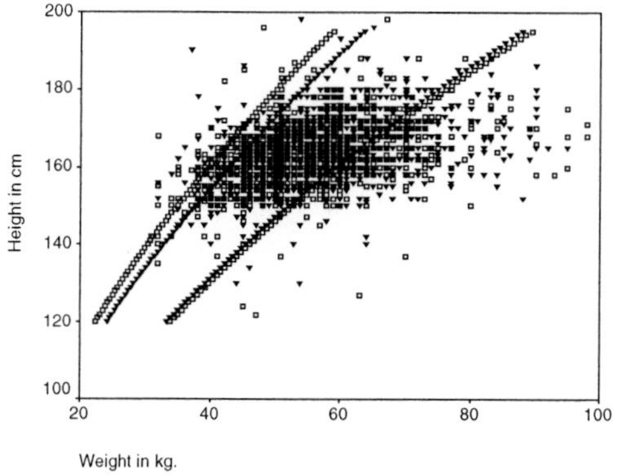

Females: 2nd and 91st Percentiles of BMI for those who would like to lose weight

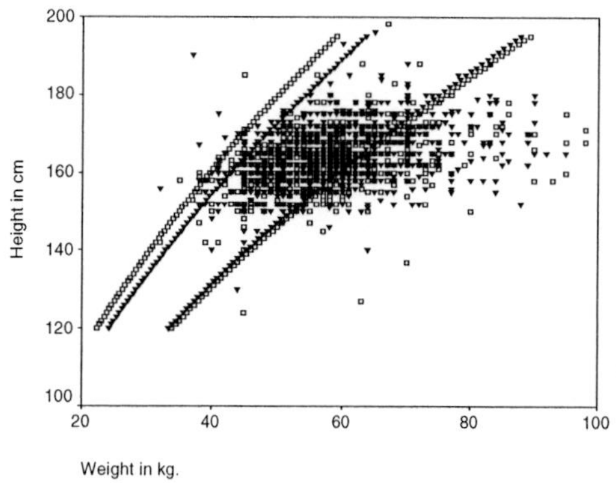

The Overweight group

1. The Year 10 group of respondents contained 14-year-olds and 15-year-olds. In order to relate their recorded weight to published guidelines regarding 'desirable' weight, we separated the children of different ages. This is because the Body Mass Index (BMI) formula for young people takes their age as well as their height into account.
2. Of this sample, 14% of the males and 11% of the females were 'overweight' according to the Child Growth Foundation charts used in this presentation. This compares with the 27% of all Year 10 males and 58% of all Year 10 females in the survey that would have liked to lose some weight.
3. The scattergrams presented here include two lines representing the upper and lower limits of 'satisfactory' weight. The left-hand diagrams plot all the 14-year-olds; the right-hand diagrams show only those who want to lose weight.
4. Examining the 'want to lose weight' diagrams, it is seen that less than half of those males are above the guidelines for healthy weight, and the rest are concentrated in the upper part of the 'safe' band.
5. However, the pattern for females is almost indistinguishable from that in the left-hand diagram for the whole sample, confirming that their desire to lose weight bears little correlation with their actual weight.
6. We also note, in the right-hand diagrams, that some individuals wishing to lose weight are already at or below the 'safe' weight limit.
7. As noted on previous pages, the sample size for this analysis is much smaller than in previous because not all the regions using the survey chose to include these questions.

The weight guidelines on this page were derived using a UK-reference group for Body Mass Index adjusted for age (Child Growth Foundation).

Year 10	*Males*	*Females*
Underweight	7%	5%
Satisfactory	79%	83%
Overweight	14%	11%
Valid responses	*1115*	*989*

Protein

64% of 14-15 year old males have dairy produce *on most days*

Protein items in their diet (22a) (Pri.8)

Responses to eaten 'on most days'.

Please note that all the 'diet' items are offered as a single list, and are not subdivided by content as we have done here.

1. *Meat* is more popular with males than females.
2. *Dairy products* are more frequently eaten than *meat* and *fish.*
3. There is a marked age gradient for *meat* and *dairy products*, with older pupils reporting eating them with higher frequencies. In Year 8, 33% of males and 29% of females report eating *meat* on most days but by Year 10, 45% of the males and 36% of the females report the same.

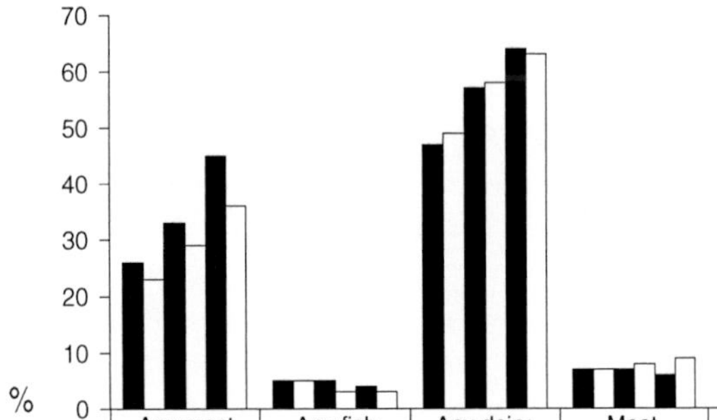

	Any meat	Any fish	Any dairy produce	Meat substitute e.g. soya	Available sample
■ Yr 6 M	26	5	47	7	2422
□ Yr 6 F	23	5	49	7	2300
■ Yr 8 M	33	5	57	7	3064
□ Yr 8 F	29	3	58	8	2865
■ Yr 10 M	45	4	64	6	2450
□ Yr 10 F	36	3	63	9	2425

Comments

1. The age differences are interesting: is it that the older age groups are better at recognising when a food item is present? For example, do primary school pupils recognise that 'cottage pie' is a meat dish? Of course, the differences may well be genuine. Is this a deliberate plan by older pupils to increase intake of protein, either by the young people or their parents, or is it a reflection of personal preference and enhanced spending power that comes with age and opportunities e.g. to eat burgers?
2. The small sex differences also demand an explanation. It may be that more girls than boys avoid meat products, either because they are uncomfortable with the way animals are raised, or because these high-protein foods may also be rich in fats.
3. Foods that are not normally thought of as being high in protein, like cereals and pulses, also contribute significantly to the amount of protein eaten.

Starchy foods

As they get older,
fewer eat sugar-coated cereals

Starchy items in their diet (22b) (Pri.8)

Responses to eaten 'on most days'.

Please note that all the 'diet' items are offered as a single list, and are not subdivided by content as we have done here.

1. The males show no age-related rise in the consumption of chips/roast potatoes.
2. Where sex differences are found, the males are usually ahead of the females, especially sugar-coated cereals.
3. As they get older, fewer eat sugary cereals.

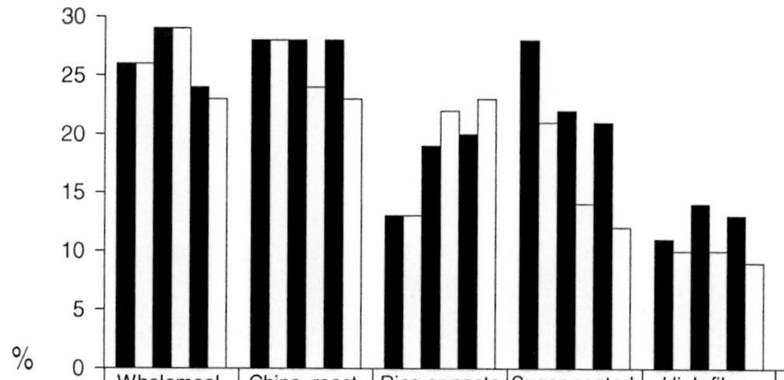

	Wholemeal bread	Chips, roast pots	Rice or pasta	Sugar-coated cereals	High-fibre cereals, muesli	Available sample
■ Yr 6 M	26	28	13	28	11	2422
□ Yr 6 F	26	28	13	21	10	2300
■ Yr 8 M	29	28	19	22	14	3064
□ Yr 8 F	29	24	22	14	10	2865
■ Yr 10 M	24	28	20	21	13	2450
□ Yr 10 F	23	23	23	12	9	2425

Comments

1. Slightly more males more than females are inclined to choose chips, does this reflect the increased diet-consciousness of the females? The age-related drop in the responses of females suggests that this is the case.
2. Data since 1990 reveal an overall increase of those choosing chips/roast potatoes 'on most days'. These figures are consistent with last year's data (SHEU, 2003, 'Trends-Young People's Food Choices 1983-2001').
3. The avoidance by older females of sugar-coated cereals may be part of a general avoidance of calorific foods, but there may be some specific attitudes at play here - perhaps a greater sensitivity to dental risks than the older males, or that fewer females eat breakfast by comparison.
4. The slight excess of males over females eating high-fibre cereals is interesting and counter to our expectations. More females than males skip breakfast (page 2) but when we select only for those pupils having breakfast the difference persists.

In earlier books in this series we showed that the frequency of eating chips could be linked to the type of lunch eaten e.g. those eating a packed lunch were less ikely to eat chips.

Fruit and vegetables

Less fresh fruit but more vegetables eaten as pupils get older

Fruit and vegetables in their diet

(22c) (Pri.8)

Responses to eaten 'on most days'.

Please note that all the 'diet' items are offered as a single list, and are not subdivided by content as we have done here.

1. Less fresh fruit but more vegetables eaten as pupils get older
2. 50% of 10-11 year olds females report eating fresh fruit 'on most days' but this has dropped to 40% by the time they are 14 years old.
3. By contrast, 33% of 10-11 year olds females report eating vegetables 'on most days' which has increased to 44% by the time they are 14 years old.

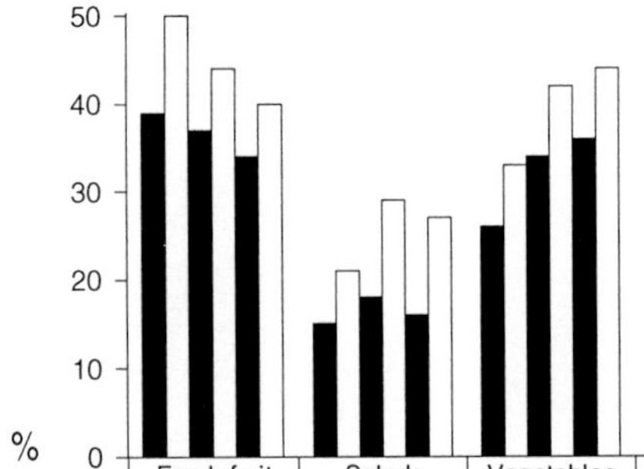

	Fresh fruit	Salads	Vegetables	Available sample
■ Yr 6 M	39	15	26	2422
□ Yr 6 F	50	21	33	2300
■ Yr 8 M	37	18	34	3064
□ Yr 8 F	44	29	42	2865
■ Yr 10 M	34	16	36	2450
□ Yr 10 F	40	27	44	2425

Comments

1. Gender differences are most marked in this section: we may speculate about differences in health and diet consciousness.
2. Up to 29% of the females in secondary school eat salad and over 42% of them eat vegetables on most days. Is this because they are keen to have a balanced diet or are they choosing food items that have lower calorific content?
3. There is an increase with age in the consumption of vegetables for both genders. Perhaps this is a sign of youngsters approaching adult tastes rather than the juvenile abhorrence of certain vegetables.
4. Data from 1990-1998 reveal a downward trend of pupils eating fresh fruit 'on most days' From 1999-2001 there was a reversal of this decline which may be associated with changes to the questionnaire (SHEU, 2003, 'Trends-Young People's Food Choices 1983-2001'). This year's figures suggest a downward trend similar to 2002.
5. There are Government initiatives to promote consumption of fruit and vegetables in young people's diet. We find that the young people who report eating fresh fruit are more likely to eat other healthy items like fish, wholemeal bread and vegetables.

Drinks and snacks

Crisps remain popular particularly for Year 6 females

Drinks and snacks they enjoy (22d) (Pri.8)

Responses to eaten 'on most days'.

Please note that all the 'diet' items are offered as a single list, and are not subdivided by content as we have done here.

1. Males have a taste for fizzy drinks, and females for low-calorie drinks.
2. There is little gender difference in the appeal of sweets and crisps although 47% of the Year 6 females eat crips 'on most days.'
3. Many of these high-calorie foods show high values in Year 6.

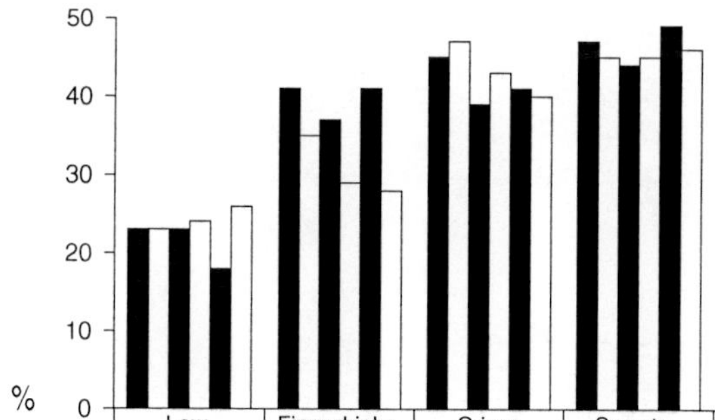

	Low cal.(diet) drinks	Fizzy drinks (not low-cal.)	Crisps	Sweets, chocs./bars	Available sample
■ Yr 6 M	23	41	45	47	2422
□ Yr 6 F	23	35	47	45	2300
■ Yr 8 M	23	37	39	44	3064
□ Yr 8 F	24	29	43	45	2865
■ Yr 10 M	18	41	41	49	2450
□ Yr 10 F	26	28	40	46	2425

Comments

1. The greater health-consciousness of the females is reflected in their choice of drinks, but not in other highly calorific or dentally-doubtful snacks.
2. Are the high figures here related to items that youngsters find in their packed lunches? Do more primary school pupils than secondary school pupils have a packed lunch? Figures from secondary pupils generally show an upward trend since 1995 in those eating packed lunches, although this year the figures decline with age (see page 3).
3. Figures from 1987 suggest a slightly downward trend in the popularity of crisps with secondary pupils (SHEU, 2003, 'Trends-Young People's Food Choices 1983-2001'). However, around 41% of this age group report eating crisps 'on most days'. Young people aged 10-11 years show a higher percentage liking crisps, compared with the older pupils. Females have consistently remained higher than the males but the trend is downward:

Eating crisps on most days	Males (10-11 yrs.) %	Females (10-11 yrs.) %
1999	54	57
2000	51	54
2001	47	50
2002	48	51
2003	45	47

Dietary decisions

25% of the Year 10 males
never consider their health when choosing food

When choosing what to eat, do you consider your health? (20)

1. Most of the young people respond at least *sometimes.*
2. More females than males respond very often, and many more males than females respond *never*.
3. With respect to age, more of the older males respond *never*; the females show less change.

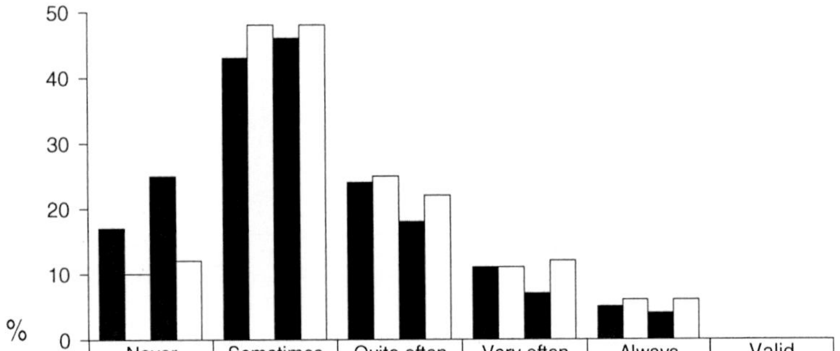

	Never	Sometimes	Quite often	Very often	Always	Valid responses
■ Yr 8 M	17	43	24	11	5	3014
□ Yr 8 F	10	48	25	11	6	2844
■ Yr 10 M	25	46	18	7	4	2431
□ Yr 10 F	12	48	22	12	6	2416

Comments

1. More than half of this sample 'never' or only 'sometimes' evaluate their diet from a health point of view. Figures from 1991 suggest a slightly increasing trend in those 12-15 year olds who do not 'consider their health' when eating pupils (SHEU, 2003, 'Trends-Young People's Food Choices 1983-2001').
2. The table bears out the evidence of the previous pages that the females are more health-conscious about food than the males. Has 'scare fatigue' particularly affected the Year 10 males? Evidence from 'Education and Health' suggests that the first years of secondary school may be crucial for implementing healthy eating initiatives and, in particular, influencing boys attitudes to food (Hackett et al., 2003).
3. Other figures support the view about the implementation of healthy eating intitiatives in the first years of secondary school. Data show that around 41% of 12-13 year olds found 'Healthy eating' lessons useful compared with around 29% of 14-15 year olds (see page 106).

Are they 'really' considering their health or just saying so? We looked in the dataset for correlations between positive responses to this question and more healthy dietary choices. We found that they are clearly present: the older males and females who say they often think about their health when choosing food are more likely to: eat salads, fruit, vegetables, fish and drink low-calorie drinks on most days than their peers, and they are less likely to eat chips, sweets, sugary cereals or drink sugary fizzy drinks on most days. This tells us that these global attitudes to food may be important, not being vague opinions but having a real effect on behaviour.

2 Doctor and Dentist

The 'doctor' questions are about the respondents' last visit to their GP. With respect to dental hygiene, the questions are about toothbrushing frequency and their last visit to the dentist.

Visiting the doctor

About half had visited the doctor within *the past 3 months*

How long ago did you last visit the doctor? (47)

1. Up to 29% visited within *the past month*. About 50% report having visited their GP within *the past 3 months* — a figure that rises to over 83% for *the past year*.
2. There is little age or gender difference, although slightly more older females (29%) report going to their GP in the past month compared with the older males (21%).

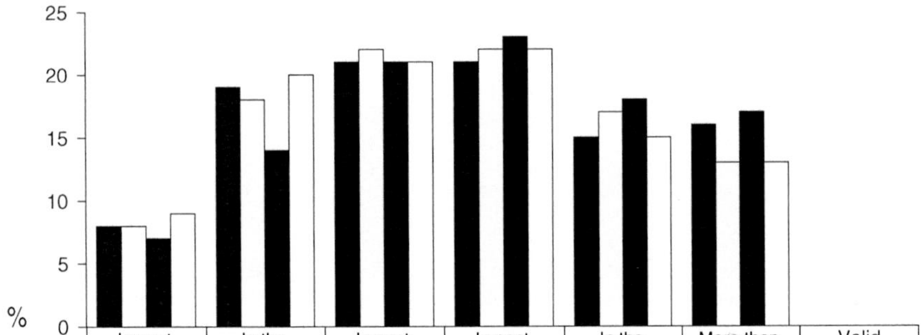

	In past 7 days	In the past month	In past 3 months	In past 6 months	In the past year	More than a year ago	Valid responses
■ Yr 8 M	8	19	21	21	15	16	2873
□ Yr 8 F	8	18	22	22	17	13	2781
■ Yr 10 M	7	14	21	23	18	17	2368
□ Yr 10 F	9	20	21	22	15	13	2377

Comments

1. Are GPs aware of these perhaps surprisingly high frequencies of attendance? In the 'Introduction' (page xxv), we reported how one GP was so disbelieving of the attendance figures reported locally that he checked his own practice records, and found them consistent with the rates recorded in the survey.
2. Are the numbers going up or down? Since 1999 the percentage of those visiting the doctor in the past month are:

Visit GP in past month	1999 %	2000 %	2001 %	2002 %	2003 %
Yr 8 Male	26	29	27	25	27
Yr 8 Female	28	30	28	27	26
Yr 10 Male	26	27	26	24	21
Yr 10 Female	31	29	29	29	29

Gender and age differences are generally consistent and females have usually been visiting more frequently than males. The differences are small with the exception of older pupils in 2003.

Talking to the doctor

Up to 27% of the females felt *quite uneasy* or *very uneasy*

On this last visit, did you feel at ease with the doctor? (48)

1. More males than females felt *at ease* on their last visit.
2. Up to 27% of the females felt *quite uneasy* or *very uneasy* with the younger females reporting higher figures.
3. As they get older, young people feel more at ease talking to the doctor.

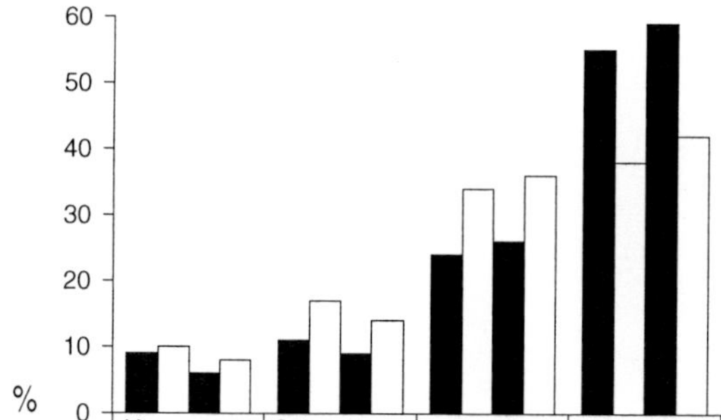

	Very uneasy	Quite uneasy	A little uneasy	At ease	Valid responses
■ Yr 8 M	9	11	24	55	2794
□ Yr 8 F	10	17	34	38	2718
■ Yr 10 M	6	9	26	59	2339
□ Yr 10 F	8	14	36	42	2352

Comments

1. This question has been asked since 1981. Earlier surveys recorded the gender of the GP last visited, and suggested that both boys and girls were more likely to be at ease with female doctors, who are of course in the minority.
2. The level of ease with the doctor could reflect general confidence with adults, or concern about the reason for the visit.
3. A less trusting interpretation is that males are less likely to admit to unease.

In *Young People in 1997* we have shown that those young people who say they were at ease with their GP on their last visit were also likely to have visited their GP more recently:

At ease (whole sample) : 50%
At ease (visited last week) : 55%
(visited last year) : 48%

Cleaning teeth

Up to 26% of the males brush *only once*

How many times did you clean your teeth yesterday? (44) (Pri.34)

1. More than 72% of males and at least 85% of females brushed their teeth at least twice.
2. Up to 26% of the males brush only once.
3. Across the three age groups represented, more girls consistently report brushing their teeth at least twice on the previous day.

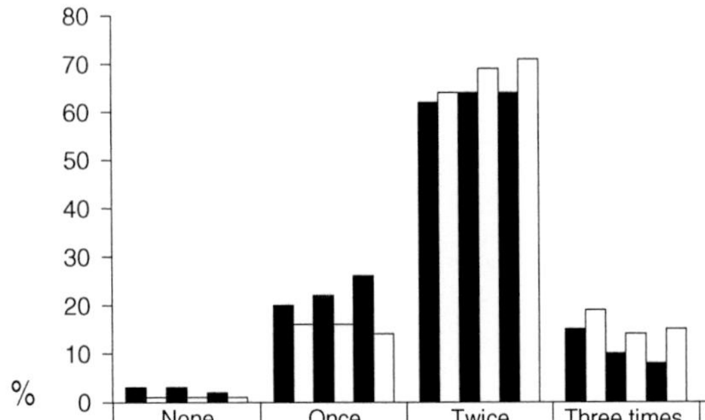

	None	Once	Twice	Three times or more	Valid responses
■ Yr 6 M	3	20	62	15	2312
□ Yr 6 F	1	16	64	19	2246
■ Yr 8 M	3	22	64	10	2916
□ Yr 8 F	1	16	69	14	2796
■ Yr 10 M	2	26	64	8	2374
□ Yr 10 F	1	14	71	15	2377

Comments

1. Twice-daily brushing is recommended, and the majority of young people are achieving this.
2. The females are recording higher average brushing levels than the males, but these may be linked to having their teeth looking nice, and general concern about their appearance, rather than to 'health' issues.
3. Despite the improvement in children's dental health, decay remains a significant problem. This is most often caused by the frequent consumption of foods and drinks containing sugar (DOH, 1989).
4. As well as toothbrushing, the use of floss or other inter-dental cleaning aids can be discussed with young people.

Toothbrushing frequency, as we have demonstrated over the years, is related to several other aspects of lifestyle, including birth order, ease with the opposite sex, region of the country, self-esteem and smoking.

Visiting the dentist

Most had been within the past six months

How long ago did you last visit the dentist? (45)

1. About 82% of all the groups state that they have been within the past 6 months, which is the recommended interval.
2. The females' average frequency of visits is slightly higher than the males', and the Year 8 pupils tend to have been a little more recently than those in Year 10.

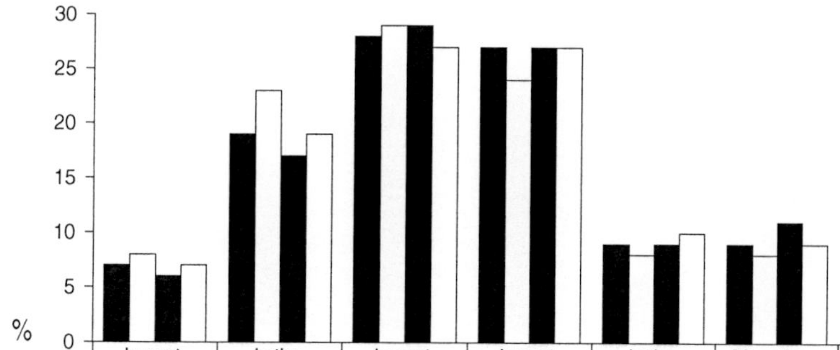

	In past 7 days	In the past month	In past 3 months	In past 6 months	In the past year	More than a year ago	Valid responses
■ Yr 8 M	7	19	28	27	9	9	2874
□ Yr 8 F	8	23	29	24	8	8	2775
■ Yr 10 M	6	17	29	27	9	11	2367
□ Yr 10 F	7	19	27	27	10	9	2379

Comments

1. The '6-month rule' is only a recommendation, and we are advised has no strictly scientific basis. This doesn't mean it should be ignored!
2. Are the Year 8 respondents better at going to the dentist because they are more biddable, more conscientious, or suffer from more dental problems? Are they more likely to share a 'joint booking' with a parent, at least for the initial check-up?

3 Health and Safety

Many of the questions in this group reflect a traditional view of health — physical cleanliness, use of medicines, and common ailments. We also have questions about accidents, and the vulnerability of young cyclists is also a major concern.

(51a):

Safety helmets

36% of the Year 10 males
don't have a safety helmet

When you cycle do you wear a safety helmet? (94) (Pri.24)

1. Most of the respondents cycle, although by Year 10 this figure is down to 61% for the females.
2. With age the percentage of cyclists who at *most times* wear a safety helmet is seen to fall, e.g. from 16% of females in Year 6 to 6% of females in Year 10.
3. 36% of Year 10 males *do not have a safety helmet.*

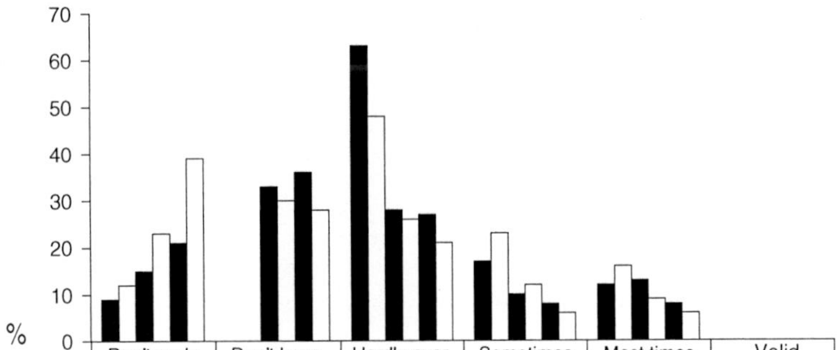

	Don't cycle	Don't have a safety helmet	Hardly ever or never	Sometimes	Most times	Valid responses
■ Yr 6 M	9	*	63	17	12	2363
□ Yr 6 F	12	*	48	23	16	2263
■ Yr 8 M	15	33	28	10	13	2179
□ Yr 8 F	23	30	26	12	9	2138
■ Yr 10 M	21	36	27	8	8	1988
□ Yr 10 F	39	28	21	6	6	2000

* Year 6 not given this option

Comments

1. Head injuries are the commonest cause of accidental death among young people.
2. Cycling seems to be currently fashionable, but does this extend to wearing a helmet? Over the years we have seen changes between years large enough to suggest that helmet-wearing may be a 'volatile' behaviour, sensitive to publicity campaigns and the opinions of others.
3. Cycling is environmentally friendly and promotes fitness, but it presents dangers to young people and is a cause of anxiety to their parents. Efforts to promote the wearing of cycle helmets have shown mixed results. The Royal Society for the Prevention of Accident's website refer to some research papers about cycle safety helmets: http://www.rospa.com/pdfs/road/cycle_helmets_2003.pdf

In an earlier book in this series we showed that young people who reported having been on a cycle training course were more likely to report wearing a cycle helmet at least most of the time.

Toilet hygiene

Few pupils *never* or *almost never* wash their hands

How often do you wash your hands after visiting the lavatory? (42) (Pri.33)

1. More than three quarters of the males and over 85% of the females do wash *whenever possible*. This gender difference is consistent across the three age groups.
2. The percentage that *never* or *almost never* wash is very small.

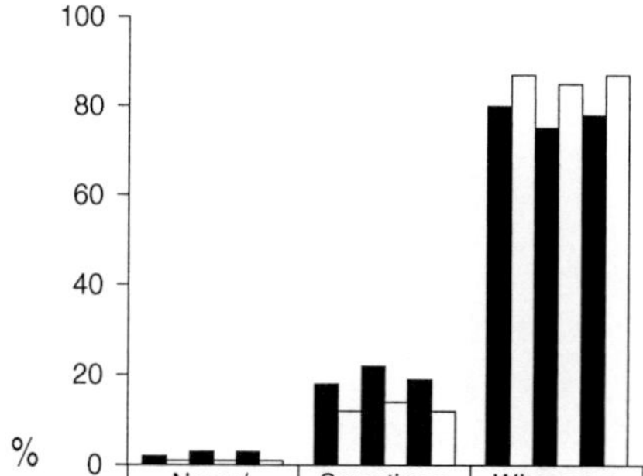

	Never/ almost never	Sometimes	Whenever possible	Valid responses
■ Yr 6 M	2	18	80	1642
□ Yr 6 F	1	12	87	1532
■ Yr 8 M	3	22	75	2923
□ Yr 8 F	1	14	85	2805
■ Yr 10 M	3	19	78	2381
□ Yr 10 F	1	12	87	2386

Comments

1. Since 1999, the figures for washing hands *whenever possible* have remained consistent.

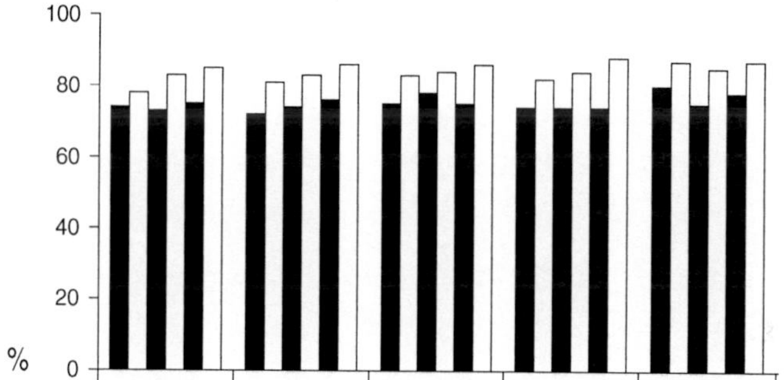

	1999	2000	2001	2002	2003
■ Yr 6 M	74	72	75	74	80
□ Yr 6 F	78	81	83	82	87
■ Yr 8 M	73	74	78	74	75
□ Yr 8 F	83	83	84	84	85
■ Yr 10 M	75	76	75	74	78
□ Yr 10 F	85	86	86	88	87

2. Gender and age differences are consistent across the three age groups and percentages from the females remain higher than males. This is particularly noticeable for the Year 10 group (14-15 year olds) where around 10% more females than males report washing hands after visiting the lavatory.

Baths and showers

More males than females,
report having seven baths or showers

How many baths or showers have you had in the past week? (43)

1. About half the males and females in each year group report having had at least six baths or showers in the previous week.
3. For the first time in recent years, more males than females, report having seven baths or showers in the past week and, more 14-15 year old males (32%) compared with 12-13 year old males (27%).
4. Around 23% of the 14-15 year olds had eight or more baths or showers in the past week

Comments

1. We have seen a general increase in the mean number of baths or showers taken in the week from 1986.

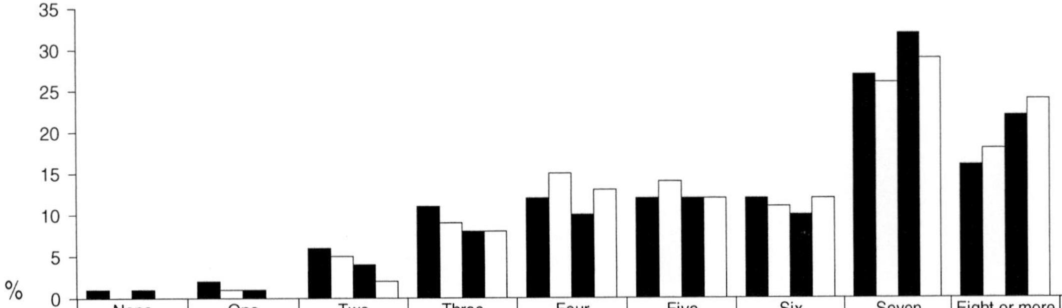

	None	One	Two	Three	Four	Five	Six	Seven	Eight or more	Valid responses
■ Yr 8 M	1	2	6	11	12	12	12	27	16	2681
□ Yr 8 F	0	1	5	9	15	14	11	26	18	2570
■ Yr 10 M	1	1	4	8	10	12	10	32	22	2205
□ Yr 10 F	0	0	2	8	13	12	12	29	24	2180

Asthma

Up to 19% of pupils say *yes*

Do you have asthma? (49) (Pri.29)

1. Up to 19% of the year-gender groups report *yes*, with a similarity of responses between the two genders.
2. With age there is a slight increase in the percentage of females who report not knowing if they have asthma.

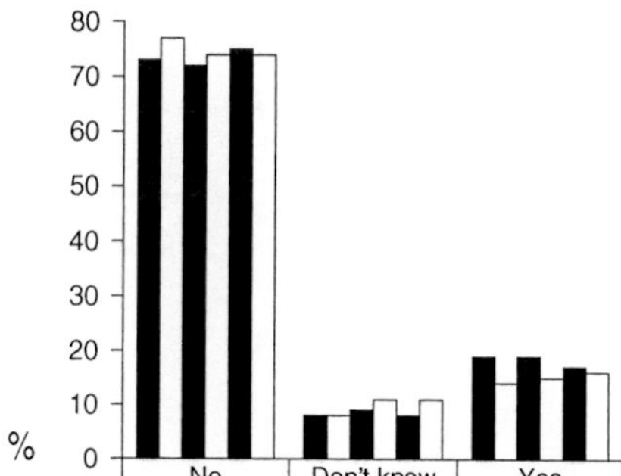

	No	Don't know	Yes	Valid responses
■ Yr 6 M	73	8	19	2179
□ Yr 6 F	77	8	14	2152
■ Yr 8 M	72	9	19	2855
□ Yr 8 F	74	11	15	2771
■ Yr 10 M	75	8	17	2365
□ Yr 10 F	74	11	16	2371

Comments

1. The young people may 'have asthma' but be free from symptoms.
2. There are several stages from the presence of symptoms to confirmation of asthma (e.g. *have symptoms* ➔ *notice symptoms* ➔ *report to parents* ➔ *see GP for diagnosis* ➔ *child reports this in survey*). It is not clear if the observed differences relate mainly or only to having asthma symptoms, as the young people's own reports are all we have to go on.
3. The frequency records of asthma medication taken in the previous week are shown on page 24.
4. Earlier reports on young people and mental health (*No Worries?* Balding, 1998), describes a high level of connection between general levels of worry and asthma and its symptoms. Figures for 2003 are shown below.

Asthma medication		Count	Percentage who worry about 5 or more topics
Males:	No	4365	7%
	Yes	544	10%
Females:	No	4377	13%
	Yes	523	17%

Remedies and medication

51% of 14–15 year old females report taking painkillers in the past week

On how many days, in the last week, have you used remedies or medications? (50) (Pri.30)

1. The 'remedies and medication' options now show *Painkillers* remaining the most frequently used remedy followed by medications for *Skin problems* and up to 26% report taking *Vitamin tablets* 'at least one day in the last week'.
2. In almost all cases, more females than males report having used these remedies and medications, the exception being *Asthma*.

Remedies/medications taken at least one day

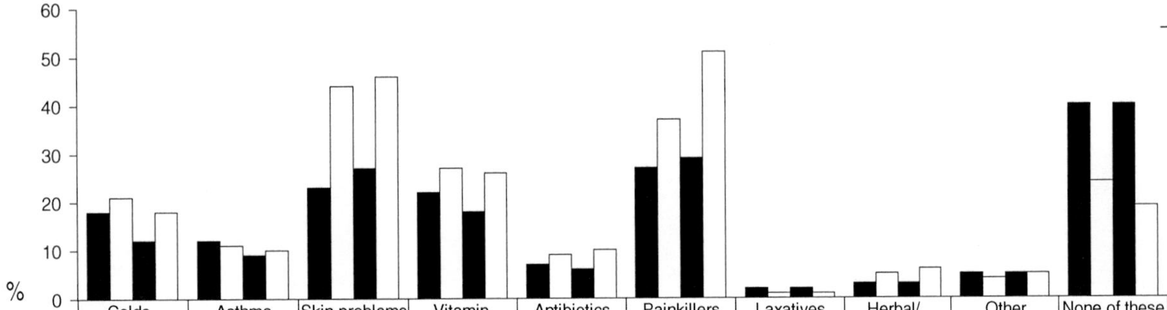

	Colds. coughs, flu	Asthma	Skin problems	Vitamin tablets	Antibiotics	Painkillers	Laxatives	Herbal/ homeopathic	Other	None of these	Available sample
■ Yr 8 M	18	12	23	22	7	27	2	3	5	40	3064
□ Yr 8 F	21	11	44	27	9	37	1	5	4	24	2865
■ Yr 10 M	12	9	27	18	6	29	2	3	5	40	2450
□ Yr 10 F	18	10	46	26	10	51	1	6	5	19	2425

Comments

1. This is the second time this question has been asked using the options shown below which were previously covered by two questions.
2. 51% of the 14-15 year old females are taking *Painkillers,* but they cannot all be suffering from period pains during the week before the survey. Assuming that up to a quarter are, the remaining 26% must be taking them for other reasons, closely matching the proportion of males that are doing so.
3. Worries may literally prove to be a headache: when we look at the number of significant worries against painkiller use, there is a clear association:

Painkillers		Count	% who worry about 5 or more topics
Males:	No	3423	7%
	Yes	1472	8%
Females:	No	2692	12%
	Yes	2206	16%

'Wheezers'

Around 60% of females have had trouble breathing

When you run, do you 'wheeze' and have trouble breathing (not just feel out of breath)? (46)

1. More females than males report some degree of discomfort.
2. Between 13% to 18% of each group exhibit these symptoms *quite often* or *very often*.

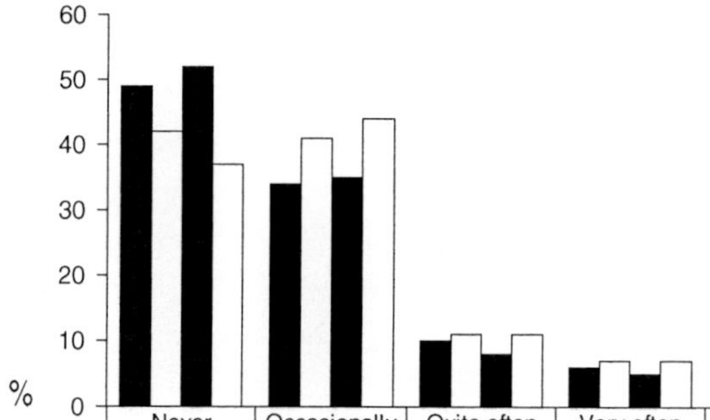

	Never	Occasionally	Quite often	Very often	Valid responses
■ Yr 8 M	49	34	10	6	2891
□ Yr 8 F	42	41	11	7	2790
■ Yr 10 M	52	35	8	5	2370
□ Yr 10 F	37	44	11	7	2382

Comments

1. This question is valuable because of its use as a marker for asthma. It is a belief among many paediatricians that there is a degree of under-diagnosis of asthma, and thus also a population of young people who, if they sought medical support to manage their symptoms, could have a better quality of life. (See the medication question, page 24.)
2. The wheezy noise of asthma is characteristic; however, the difference between 'wheezing' and 'breathlessness' may not always be clear to young people, and this question is probably picking up some young people who are just unfit.
3. Good asthma control may reduce wheeziness, even during exertion.
4. The perceptible fall with age in the percentage reporting *quite often* and *very often* could be linked to (a) improvement in their asthmatic condition, (b) less running and vigorous activity generally, or (c) greater understanding among older pupils of the difference between wheezy breathlessness and just lack of fitness.

Community safety

Up to 24% of over 10,000 young people say that safety after dark is *poor* or *very poor*

How do you rate your safety when going out during the day, and after dark, in the area where you live? (52a, 52b)

1. Males are more likely to feel safe than females, and in general there is little difference in the perception of safety between the two age groups. Females report consistently for the 'OK' categories and similarly, males for the 'Very good' categories.
2. The perception of safety after dark is far lower than during the day for both age and gender groups.

Comments

1. Whether perceived safety is related to actual safety, we do not know, but it is likely that perceived safety has an effect on young people's quality of life.
2. Are individual differences in perceived safety related to other attitudes and anxieties? We might expect those more anxious about safety to worry more about other matters.

Safety outside after dark

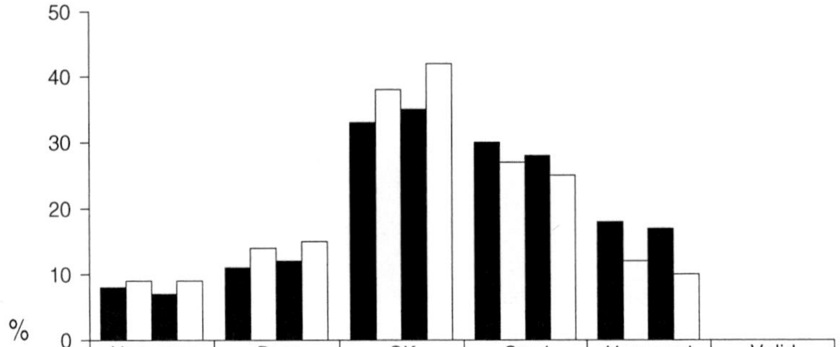

	Very poor	Poor	OK	Good	Very good	Valid responses
■ Yr 8 M	8	11	33	30	18	2858
□ Yr 8 F	9	14	38	27	12	2761
■ Yr 10 M	7	12	35	28	17	2349
□ Yr 10 F	9	15	42	25	10	2359

Safety outside during the day

Note different scale

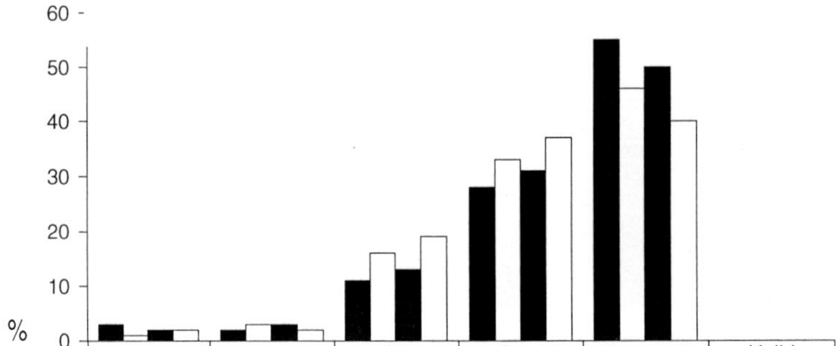

	Very poor	Poor	OK	Good	Very good	Valid responses
■ Yr 8 M	3	2	11	28	55	2812
□ Yr 8 F	1	3	16	33	46	2745
■ Yr 10 M	2	3	13	31	50	2325
□ Yr 10 F	2	2	19	37	40	2354

Carrying weapons

27% of 14-15 year old males are 'fairly sure' or 'certain' that friends carry weapons

Do you have friends who carry weapons for protection when going out? (53)

1. 27% of 14-15 year old males responded they were 'fairly sure' or 'certain' that friends did carry weapons.
2. Up to 25% of the sample, were 'not sure' if their friends carried weapons for protection.
3. There are clear gender and age differences with males reporting higher percentages across the 'fairly sure' or 'certain' options.

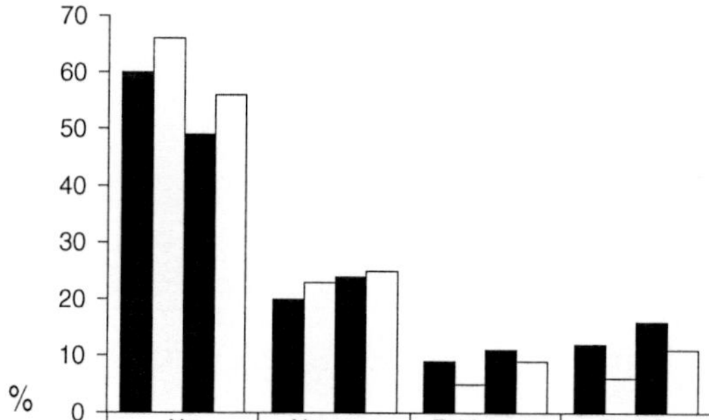

	No	Not sure	Fairly sure	Certain	Valid responses
■ Yr 8 M	60	20	9	12	1790
□ Yr 8 F	66	23	5	6	1807
■ Yr 10 M	49	24	11	16	1489
□ Yr 10 F	56	25	9	11	1557

Comments

1. This is the second time we have asked a question, about friends carrying weapons, since 1996. A question in 1996 also contained an option - 'no friends carry weapons' (*Cash and Carry*, Balding 1996). The following show the question, option and percentage responses:

   Do any of your friends carry some protection, if so what?

No friends carry weapons	%	Count
Yr. 8 M	70%	2709
Yr. 8 F	75%	2780
Yr. 10 M	57%	2146
Yr. 10 F	70%	2147

2. Given that the 1996 and 2002/2003 questions are worded differently and their placement in the questionnaire are not the same we have not drawn conclusions about differences but included the earlier data for comparison. In 1996, 57 % of older males specified that friends didn't carry some protection, suggesting 43% did. We also found that those who had friends that carried protection were more likely to be 'armed' themselves. We have no reason to think that this association has changed and view the current figures in this context.
3. However one interprets the current figures from those who were 'not sure', over 44% of 14-15 year olds suggest that their friends may carry weapons when going out.

Fear of being bullied

40% of the 10-11 year old females fear bullying at least *sometimes*

Do you ever feel afraid of going to school because of bullying? (57) (Pri.11)

1. 40% of the Year 6 females fear bullying at least *sometimes.*
2. The females are more fearful than the males, and the older they get the less afraid they become.

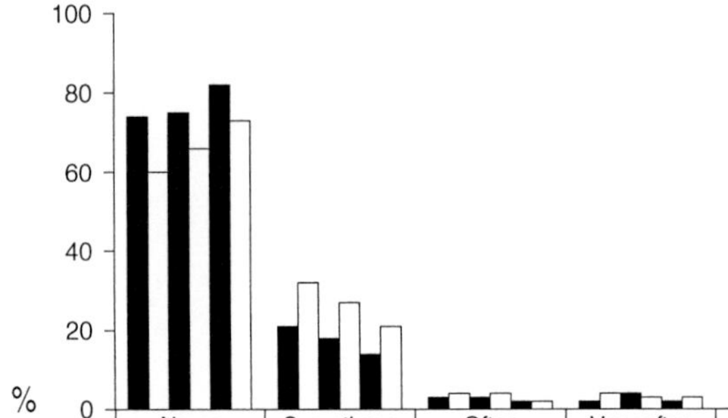

	Never	Sometimes	Often	Very often	Valid responses
■ Yr 6 M	74	21	3	2	2395
□ Yr 6 F	60	32	4	4	2282
■ Yr 8 M	75	18	3	4	2772
□ Yr 8 F	66	27	4	3	2691
■ Yr 10 M	82	14	2	2	2303
□ Yr 10 F	73	21	2	3	2306

Comments

1. We have shown elsewhere, (*Young People in 1998*, Balding, 1999), that the proportion fearing bullying in different schools varies widely. Many items in the survey have been linked with fear of bullying, most notably low self-esteem and poor perceived control, but also asthma, eczema and birth order (*Bully Off*, Balding 1996).
2. Since 1999, the figures for fear of being bullied, at least *sometimes*, are:

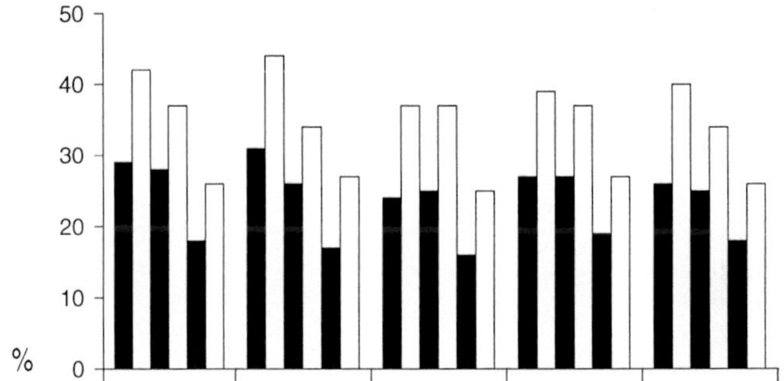

	1999	2000	2001	2002	2003
■ Yr 6 M	29	31	24	27	26
□ Yr 6 F	42	44	37	39	40
■ Yr 8 M	28	26	25	27	25
□ Yr 8 F	37	34	37	37	34
■ Yr 10 M	18	17	16	19	18
□ Yr 10 F	26	27	25	27	26

Percentages from the females remain higher than males. This is particularly noticable for the Year 6 females (10-11 year olds) – in this group, up to 14% more females than males report feeling afraid of going to school because of bullying. (see also pages 29, 134-136.)

Bullying

Slightly more males than females say *Yes*

Do you think others may fear going to school because of you? (58)(Pri.12)

1. The percentage of pupils that report they are the cause of why others may fear going to school ranges from 2%-5%.
2. There are clear gender and age differences seen from those reporting 'No'. The older they get, more pupils report they may cause others to fear going to school.
3. Slightly more males than females report being bullies.

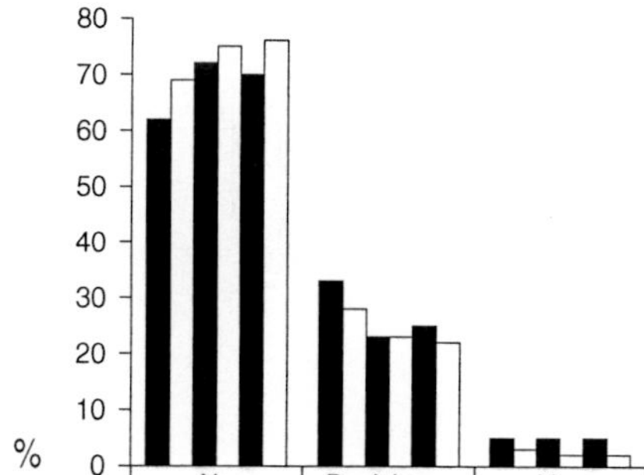

	No	Don't know	Yes	Available sample
■ Yr 6 M	62	33	5	2381
□ Yr 6 F	69	28	3	2276
■ Yr 8 M	72	23	5	2767
□ Yr 8 F	75	23	2	2691
■ Yr 10 M	70	25	5	2297
□ Yr 10 F	76	22	2	2306

Comments

1. This question has been asked of primary pupils for a number of years. Although we have asked older pupils this question since 1998 this is the second time it has been included in section 3 following the 'Fear of bullying ' question.
2. Figures for older pupils from previous years are shown below:

Do you think others may fear going to school because of you?	1998	1999	2000	2001	2002	2003
14-15 yr. Males – *Yes* response	5%	5%	5%	6%	5%	5%
14-15 yr. Females – *Yes* response	3%	3%	3%	3%	3%	2%

3. One might expect the older males to report higher percentages in the 'Yes' option but the differences between the genders is not great.
4. The 'don't know' responses could suggest honest lack of certainty or perhaps reluctance to admit a definite *Yes.*

Accidents (1)

Around 43% of the males had accidents

In the past 12 months, how many accidents have you had which were treated by a doctor or at a hospital?

(90) (Pri.26)

1. Up to 45% of the respondents reported having an accident that needed some sort of treatment by a doctor or at a hospital.
2. Consistently more boys than girls report involvement in such an accident.

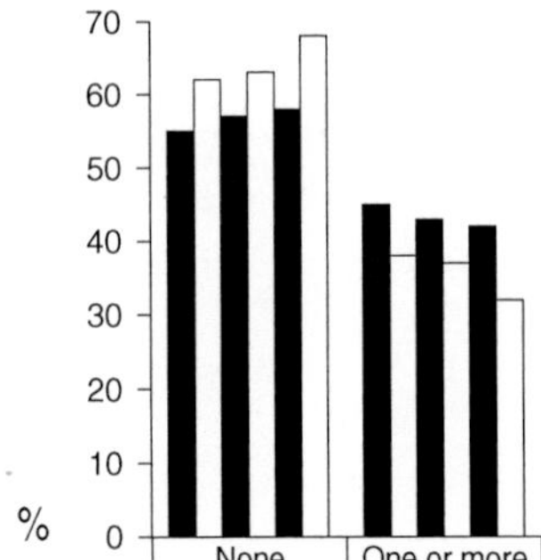

	None	One or more	Valid responses
■ Yr 6 M	55	45	2255
□ Yr 6 F	62	38	2187
■ Yr 8 M	57	43	1973
□ Yr 8 F	63	37	1911
■ Yr 10 M	58	42	1840
□ Yr 10 F	68	32	1819

Comments

1. Over half the fatal accidents in very young people occur at home, but once children reach school age there is an increase in deaths through road accidents, particularly head injuries.
2. Teenagers will always take risks: is it possible to take risks safely?
3. Males may well pursue activities with a higher risk of injury. Are older girls generally more risk-averse? Perhaps, but the picture is complex. Some health-risky behaviours, like smoking, are actually most frequent among older girls.
4. We can support other research (Thom et al, 1999) and show links between reported accidents and health-risky behaviours relating to substance use: for example, pupils reporting a recent accident are more likely to report smoking and drinking in the last week, or ever having used illegal drugs, and these difference apply in all age groups. The figures in the table below are for the year 10 males:

Accident in last year?	Smoked last week	Drank last week	Ever used drugs
No	13%	39%	22%
Yes	16%	52%	28%

Accidents (2)

Many accidents are age related although *broken bones* increase as males get older

Please think about the most recent accident within the last 12 months - what sort of accident was it? (91) (Pri.27)

1. The percentages on the table are of those that reported having an accident at all.
2. Percentages reporting that their most recent accident involved a *break* or a *cut* reveal higher percentages, consistently, for the males. For a *bruise/sprain* this gender pattern is reversed.
3. *Bruises, breaks* and *broken teeth* also show a marked age gradient.

Comments

1. The gender differences are striking and probably reflect the different activities pursued by males and females. (The activities being pursued at the time of the accident are reported overleaf.)
2. Other explanations are possible: for example, the different attitudes they and their carers have to injuries severe enough to require medical attention.
3. The age differences may be interpreted in similar ways.

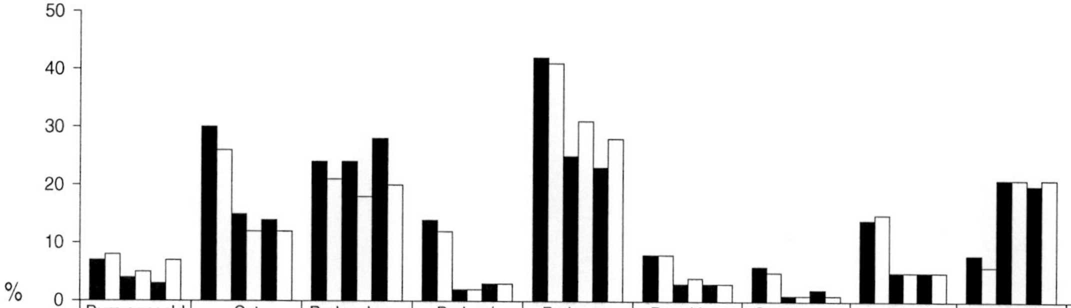

	Burn or scald	Cut	Broken bone	Broken/ damaged tooth	Bruise or sprain	Breathing problems	Swallowed something	Other	None of these	Available sample
■ Yr 6 M	7	30	24	14	42	8	6	14	8	1013
□ Yr 6 F	8	26	21	12	41	8	5	15	6	829
■ Yr 8 M	4	15	24	2	25	3	1	5	21	854
□ Yr 8 F	5	12	18	2	31	4	1	5	21	715
■ Yr 10 M	3	14	28	3	23	3	2	5	20	778
□ Yr 10 F	7	12	20	3	28	3	1	5	21	577

Accidents (3)

Most accidents occur while *playing sport*, for males, and *in my home* for females

What were you doing or where were you? (92) (Pri.28)

1. The main categories for females are: *walking or running outside* , *in my home*, and *in my school*. For males, the main options are *on a bicycle* and *playing sport*.
2. Many of these categories are strongly age-related. Accidents, that happen while *playing sport*, increase as males get older. However accidents, that happen while *in my school*, decrease as pupils get older.
3. Between 19%-27% of accidents, for the females, happen *in my home*.

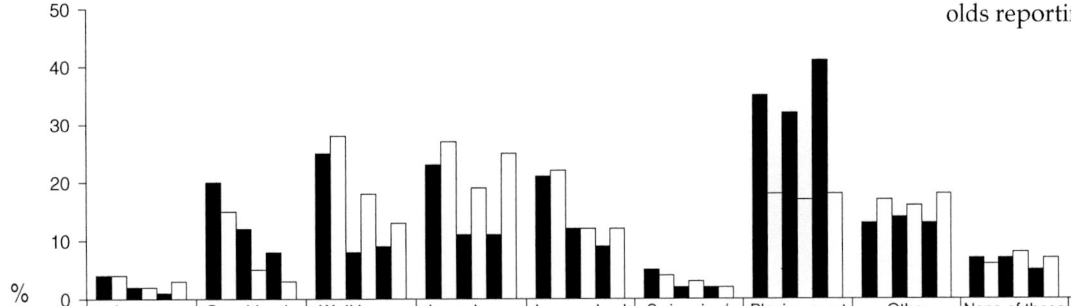

	In a car	On a bicycle	Walking or running outside	In my home	In my school	Swimming/ near water	Playing sport	Other	None of these	Available sample
■ Yr 6 M	4	20	25	23	21	5	35	13	7	1013
□ Yr 6 F	4	15	28	27	22	4	18	17	6	829
■ Yr 8 M	2	12	8	11	12	2	32	14	7	854
□ Yr 8 F	2	5	18	19	12	3	17	16	8	715
■ Yr 10 M	1	8	9	11	9	2	41	13	5	778
□ Yr 10 F	3	3	13	25	12	2	18	18	7	577

Comments

1. There are clear gender differences. For males, the most important cause of accidents from the list is through *playing sport*, naturally causing the question to be posed: 'Is exercise good for your health?' (see: Masters, 'Sport as a health risk', 2003). Unquestionably it is, but sports injuries are so common that we wonder if sufficient care is being taken. For females, the highest number of accidents happen *at home*.
2. Figures from the last four years show a similar pattern, up to 30% (2002) of accidents reported by the females happened *in my home* and, the 10-11 year olds reporting the highest percentages. Up to 41% (2003) of accidents reported by the males happened while *playing sport* and, the 14-15 year olds reporting the highest percentages.

Accidents at work (4)

11% of 14-15 year old males needed GP or hospital treatment

During the last 12 months have you had any accidents, which were treated by a doctor or at a hospital, while doing paid work?(93)

1. Figures range from 6% for the females up to 14% for the younger males that report having an accident, while at work, that required treatment by a doctor or at hospital.
2. The relatively low response rate is related to the numbers involved in paid work (see page 80) who also report having an accident.
3. Males report a slightly higher number of incidents of accidents than the females.

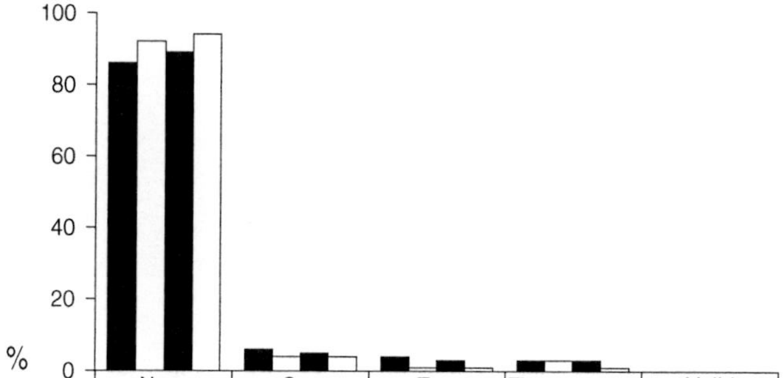

	None	One	Two	Three or more	Valid responses
■ Yr 8 M	86	6	4	3	774
□ Yr 8 F	92	4	1	3	649
■ Yr 10 M	89	5	3	3	743
□ Yr 10 F	94	4	1	1	543

Comments

1. This is the second time we have reported this question although it has been asked for a number of years. Work-related injury is a category with low frequency, but given the dangerous nature of many workplaces the injuries may be more serious. Figures from 1999-2003 show:

Accident at work: GP/hospital treatment	1999	2000	2001	2002	2003
14-15 yr. Males	4%	7%	9%	9%	11%
14-15 yr. Females	2%	3%	5%	4%	6%

2. We have seen (page 30) that 42% of the 14-15 year old males, compared with 32% of the females in the same age group,required GP or hospital treatment for an accident. Figures from those doing regular paid work (page 80) show that 36% of 14-15 year olds have a regular paid job. However, nearly twice as many older males (11%) report having treatment for accidents at work compared with the older females (6%).

Sunburn

As they get older fewer pupils 'always' try to avoid sunburn

Do you try anything to avoid sunburn? (54) (Pri.31)

1. Most respondents opt for 'usually' trying to avoid sunburn.
2. There is a noticable gender and age difference: as they get older, fewer report 'always' and, males more than females.
3. By the time they are 14-15 years of age nearly 10% more males than females report 'never' trying to avoid sunburn.

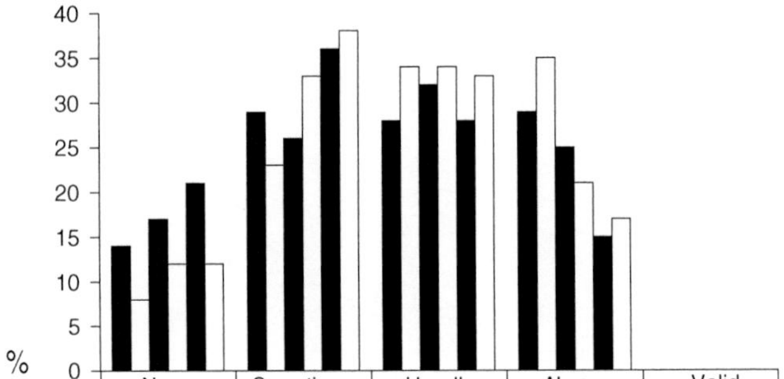

	Never	Sometimes	Usually	Always	Valid responses
■ Yr 6 M	14	29	28	29	924
□ Yr 6 F	8	23	34	35	919
■ Yr 8 M	17	26	32	25	932
□ Yr 8 F	12	33	34	21	838
■ Yr 10 M	21	36	28	15	801
□ Yr 10 F	12	38	33	17	738

Comments

1. This is an old question but has been rephrased this year. Previously pupils have responded to four options and 'putting on sun cream' was usually the favoured response.
2. Despite parental warnings, educational programmes and easily available sun protection products, up to 21% of males 'never' try to avoid sunburn.

4 Family and Home

Young people spend the majority of their time in and around the home. Relevant questions are scattered through the Health Related Behaviour Questionnaire, but the ones included here relate particularly to the kind of home they live in and the things they do when at home.

Question

Adults at home

Up to 63% of pupils live with both parents

Which adults do you live with? (2)

1. Up to 63% of the respondents live with *mother & father.*
2. If they live with just one parent their *mother* is more likely than their *father* to be present.

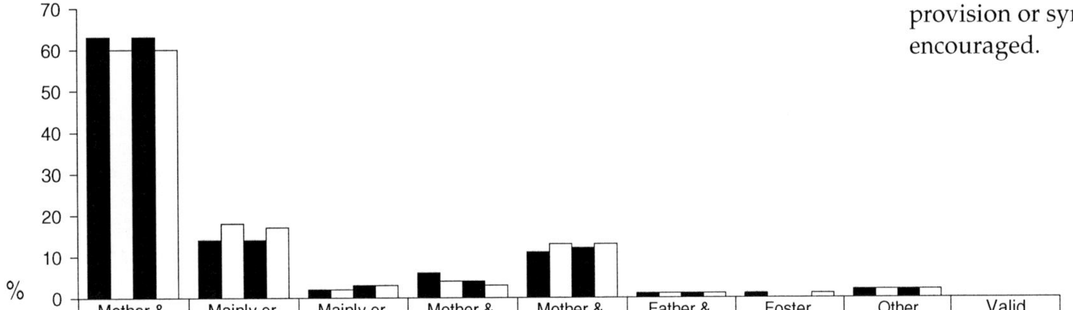

	Mother & father together	Mainly or only mother	Mainly or only father	Mother & father shared	Mother & stepfather/ partner	Father & stepmother/ partner	Foster parents	Other	Valid responses
■ Yr 8 M	63	14	2	6	11	1	1	2	3025
□ Yr 8 F	60	18	2	4	13	1	0	2	2843
■ Yr 10 M	63	14	3	4	12	1	0	2	2426
□ Yr 10 F	60	17	3	3	13	1	1	2	2405

Comments

1. In the case of the *mainly or only mother* category, some of these young people may have been brought up by a single parent from the beginning, while others may be with a parent who has separated.
2. The *other* category could include grandparents or other relations, as well as children in care homes.
3. It is often observed that the children of single or divorced parents fare worse, for example being more prone to depression, perhaps because of the trauma of the previous relationship, the likely poorer economic circumstances and other related factors. On the other hand, they may be in a better situation emotionally than if their parents had stayed together.
4. It is quite easy to demonstrate differences in the levels of health-risky behaviour between children with different family backgrounds, but we sometimes wonder if this helps anybody. If it was likely to improve provision or sympathy for disadvantaged groups we would be more encouraged.

Home population

Around 40% live in homes with five or more people

How many people live in your home (including yourself)? (3)

1. The most frequent value is 4, which is most likely to correspond to two adults and two children. Up to 61% report living in a home with at least 4 people. Up to 26% report living in a home with 5 people.

Comments

1. The community within the home may include friends and paying lodgers as well as family members.
2. Whilst larger family groups provide richer opportunities for interaction between young people and other individuals, the opportunity for seeking privacy is also important to youngsters. The bedroom question on page 40 can be used in conjunction with this question as an indicator of the amount of privacy available.

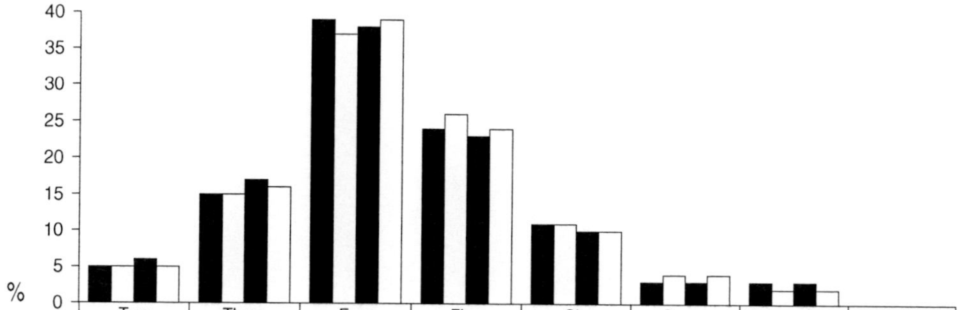

	Two	Three	Four	Five	Six	Seven	Eight or more	Valid responses
■ Yr 8 M	5	15	39	24	11	3	3	2981
□ Yr 8 F	5	15	37	26	11	4	2	2804
■ Yr 10 M	6	17	38	23	10	3	3	2401
□ Yr 10 F	5	16	39	24	10	4	2	2389

Younger and older siblings

Around 60% have at least one younger sibling

How many brothers and sisters are younger/older than you?
(4&5) (Pri.1 & 2)

1. Around 37% are the youngest, and up to 50% are the oldest. The ones who are neither youngest nor oldest (about 10%), must therefore be in a family of at least three, with at least one sibling older and one sibling younger than themselves.
2. Some individuals, who are 'only children', will appear in the 'none' columns on both charts.

Comments

1. The question specifies only those siblings living at home, and prompts for step-brothers and step-sisters if they are living at home. However, if the parents have separated and the children share time between them, the concept of 'home' may embrace more than one household.
2. We have been able to show that the frequency of tooth brushing declines with later children, as does the fear going to school because of bullying *Toothbrushing in Adolescence* (MacGregor et al., 1994) and *Bully Off (Balding, 1996)*.

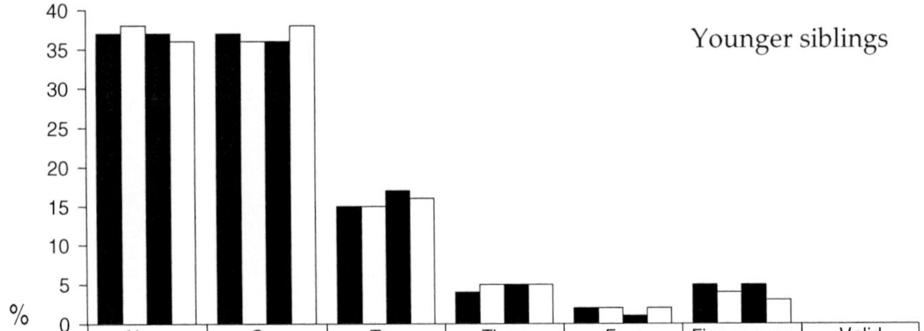

	None	One	Two	Three	Four	Five or more	Valid responses
■ Yr 8 M	37	37	15	4	2	5	3064
□ Yr 8 F	38	36	15	5	2	4	2865
■ Yr 10 M	37	36	17	5	1	5	2450
□ Yr 10 F	36	38	16	5	2	3	2425

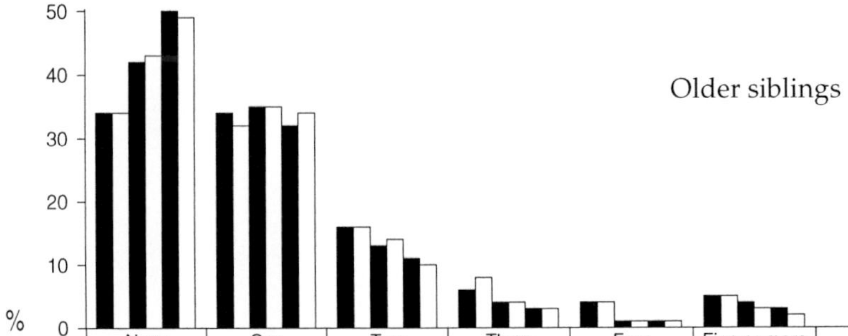

	None	One	Two	Three	Four	Five or more	Valid responses
■ Yr 6 M	34	34	16	6	4	5	2416
□ Yr 6 F	34	32	16	8	4	5	2296
■ Yr 8 M	42	35	13	4	1	4	3064
□ Yr 8 F	43	35	14	4	1	3	2865
■ Yr 10 M	50	32	11	3	1	3	2450
□ Yr 10 F	49	34	10	3	1	2	2425

Family size

Up to 20% of the 10-11 year olds live in a family with *five or more* children at home

Total number of children in the family living at home (4/5) (Pri.1)

1. In this sample, most pupils live in a family that has two children.
2. All age/gender groups record similar statistics, as would be expected.

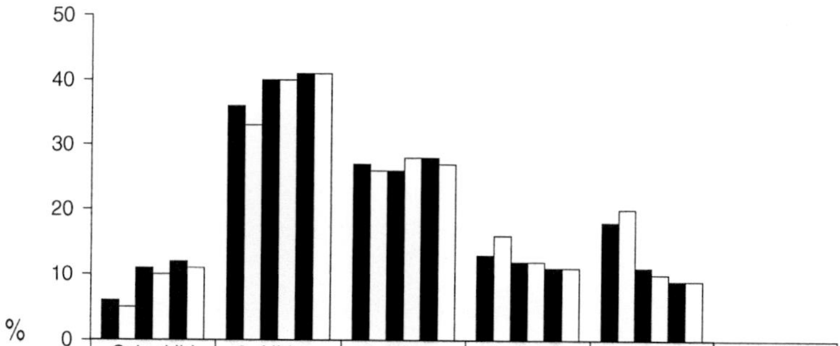

	Only child	2 children	3 children	4 children	Five or more	Valid responses
■ Yr 6 M	6	36	27	13	18	2396
□ Yr 6 F	5	33	26	16	20	2289
■ Yr 8 M	11	40	26	12	11	3031
□ Yr 8 F	10	40	28	12	10	2849
■ Yr 10 M	12	41	28	11	9	2416
□ Yr 10 F	11	41	27	11	9	2415

Comments

1. The secondary data refer explicitly to siblings living at home. This may be smaller than the total number of children, if some have moved away, but there could also be step-brothers and step-sisters from earlier marriages.
2. There is a slight inconsistency between this question in the primary and secondary questionnaires. The primary data include siblings that are not necessarily at home, hence the higher percentages recording large family numbers.
3. The mean family size, calculated from the secondary data, is 2.6 children. The widely-accepted figure of 2.4 may be consistent with this, as childless families are necessarily excluded.

Bedrooms

At least 54% of the sample live in a home with *three* bedrooms

How many bedrooms are there in your home? (6)

1. Up to 59% of these young people live in a three-bedroom home and up to 27% live in a four-bedroomed home.

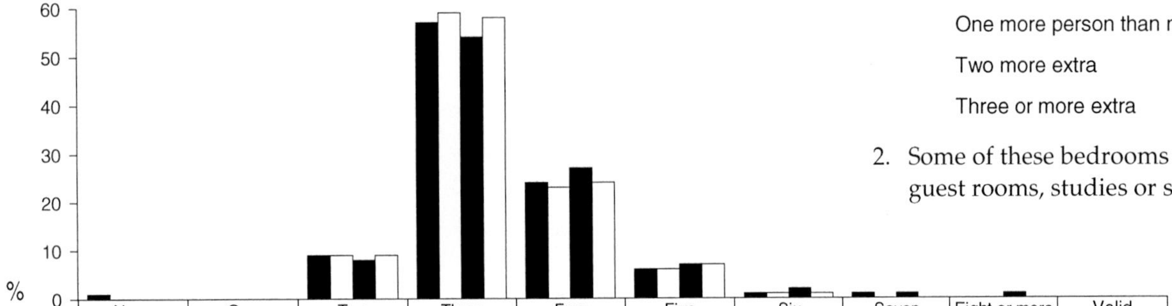

	None	One	Two	Three	Four	Five	Six	Seven	Eight or more	Valid responses
■ Yr 8 M	1	0	9	57	24	6	1	1	0	2966
□ Yr 8 F	0	0	9	59	23	6	1	0	0	2811
■ Yr 10 M	0	0	8	54	27	7	2	1	1	2380
□ Yr 10 F	0	0	9	58	24	7	1	0	0	2382

Comments

1. These data, in conjunction with those describing the home population on page 37, can be used as an indicator of the amount of privacy available. The table below shows the difference between the number of people and bedrooms in the home, obtained from the whole sample combined.

People/bedroom density

Crowding?	Percentage
Three extra bedrooms or more	0%
Two extra bedrooms	1%
One extra bedroom	6%
Equal number of people and bedrooms	22%
One more person than number of bedrooms	38%
Two more extra	19%
Three or more extra	11%

2. Some of these bedrooms may not be used for sleeping in: they may be guest rooms, studies or serve some other purpose.

Ethnic Group

A predominately white population is represented here

Ethnic group — which of the following most nearly describes you?
(7) (Pri.3)

1. Around 65% of 10-11 year olds and around 80% of 12-15 year olds in this sample reported being White, that is, *UK or European.*

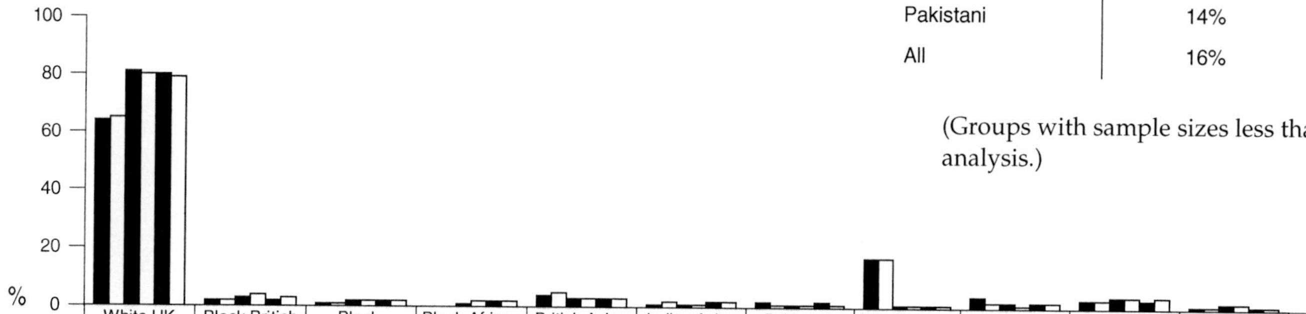

	White UK	Black British	Black Caribbean	Black African	British Asian	Indian Asian	Pakistani Asian	Bangladeshi Asian	Chinese	Mixed	Other	Valid responses
■ Yr 6 M	64	2	1	0	4	1	2	17	4	3	1	2381
□ Yr 6 F	65	2	1	0	5	2	1	17	2	3	1	2274
■ Yr 8 M	81	3	2	1	3	1	1	1	2	4	2	2855
□ Yr 8 F	80	4	2	2	3	1	1	1	1	4	2	2707
■ Yr 10 M	80	2	2	2	3	2	2	1	2	3	1	2356
□ Yr 10 F	79	3	2	2	3	2	1	1	2	4	1	2343

Comments

1. Some aspects of young people's lifestyles, such as diet and the use of legal and illegal drugs, are strongly influenced by cultural factors. For example, among Year 10 males, we see the following differences:

Ethnicity	Smoked in last week	Drank alcohol in the last week	Ever taken any illegal drugs
Black (either)	14%	21%	34%
UK or European	16%	48%	26%
Indian	2%	18%	9%
Pakistani	14%	4%	10%
All	16%	43%	25%

(Groups with sample sizes less than 30 have been excluded from this analysis.)

Journey to school

Around 23% go to school by *car*

How did you travel to school today? (14)

1. Over 20%, with more females than males, go at least part of the way to school by *car*.
2. About 14% go by *school bus*.
3. Up to 50% of males and females *walk* at least some of the way to school.

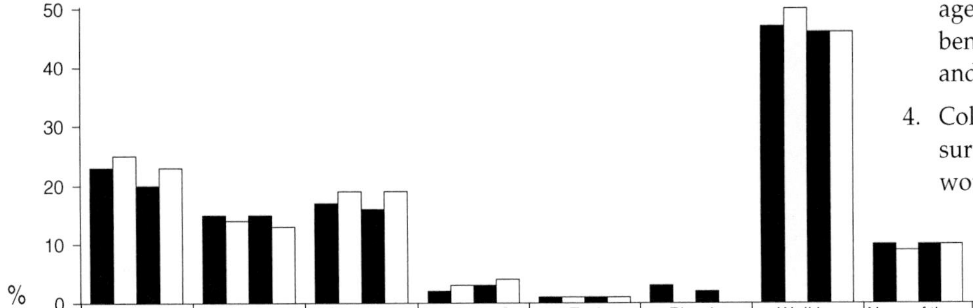

	Car/ van	School bus	Other bus	Train	Taxi	Bicycle	Walking	None of these	Available sample
■ Yr 8 M	23	15	17	2	1	3	47	10	3064
□ Yr 8 F	25	14	19	3	1	0	50	9	2865
■ Yr 10 M	20	15	16	3	1	2	46	10	2450
□ Yr 10 F	23	13	19	4	1	0	46	10	2425

Comments

1. Respondents were able to select more than one of these options, for instance if they travel part of the way to school by car and then walk the remaining part of their journey they were able to circle both these answers, hence row totals may add up to more than 100%.
2. The percentages of young people travelling to school by car represent a significant number of car journeys contributing to the congestion on our roads, the danger posed by traffic to pedestrians and cyclists and adding to pollution levels. Since 1999 we have seen similar percentages of pupils reporting car journeys to school. Some of these car journeys of course may occur where there are no suitable alternatives and indeed car-sharing arrangements may be operating.
3. It is comforting to note that at least half of males and females within these age groups still walk some of the way to school. These youngsters will benefit from this daily exercise as well as developing their independence and pedestrian skills.
4. Collaborative research by SHEU in Devon (P. Gimber: 'Travelwise' survey, Devon County Council, 2000) suggests that more young people would like to cycle to school than do so. (See also *safety helmets* page 20.)

Car ownership

Over 53% of families have *two or more cars*

How many cars/vans does your family own? (15)

1. At least 89% of households in this sample own at least one car.
2. Over 53% of families have *two or more cars.*

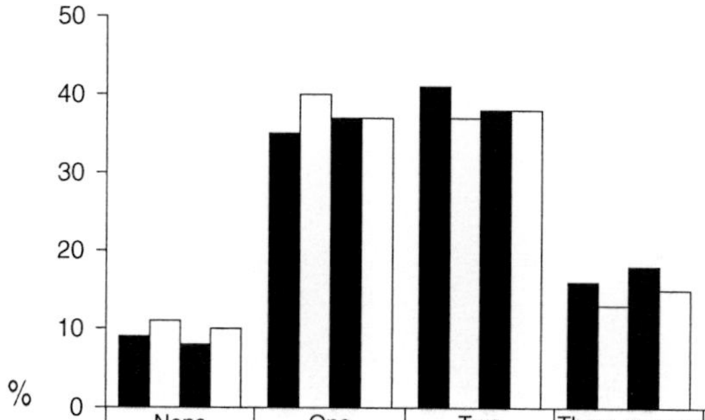

	None	One	Two	Three or more	Valid responses
■ Yr 8 M	9	35	41	16	2695
□ Yr 8 F	11	40	37	13	2573
■ Yr 10 M	8	37	38	18	2172
□ Yr 10 F	10	37	38	15	2154

Comments

1. The concept of 'family' may vary depending on young people's circumstances.
2. Ownership of a second car may encourage the 'school run'. These figures reveal that up to 18% of the families within this sample owned three or more cars.
3. Car ownership is another indication of family affluence and social background, although should not be interpreted glibly: some rural areas may be relatively deprived, but have high rates of car ownership, necessitated by the poor public transport available.

Television watching

At least 87% watched some TV during the evening prior to the survey

How long did you spend watching live or recorded TV programmes after school yesterday? (70a)

1. At least 17% watched for *more than 3 hours*, whilst 16% or fewer did not watch any at all.
2. 'Normal' gender differences are not apparent in this sample, with similar levels of males and females watching different amounts of TV.
3. At least 87% watched some TV during the evening prior to the survey

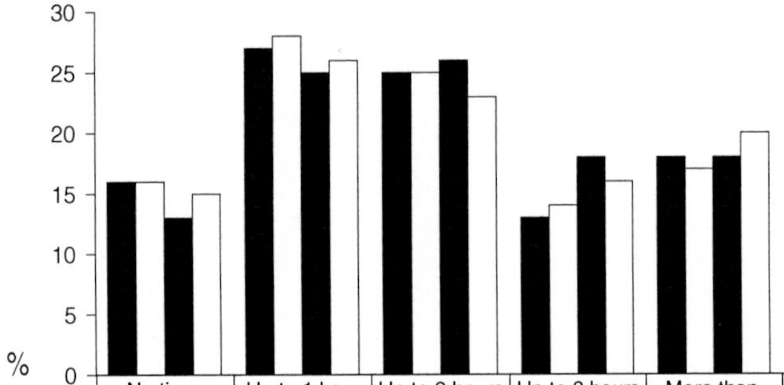

	No time at all	Up to 1 hour	Up to 2 hours	Up to 3 hours	More than 3 hours	Valid responses
■ Yr 8 M	16	27	25	13	18	2490
□ Yr 8 F	16	28	25	14	17	2454
■ Yr 10 M	13	25	26	18	18	2174
□ Yr 10 F	15	26	23	16	20	2206

Comments

1. Many people believe that television-watching is an incompatible activity with doing homework, although some pupils say they can do both at the same time. With computer games and the Internet as added possible distractions, perhaps young people today need to be more disciplined about their homework habits than ever before.
2. Time spent watching television, playing computer games and using the Internet will also prevent young people from taking part in any physical activity during these hours, thus encouraging a sedentary lifestyle.

Homework

Females spend more time

How long did you spend doing homework after school yesterday? (70b)

1. In general, more females than males did homework, and they tended to spend longer at it.
2. Fewer of the older pupils did any homework at all.

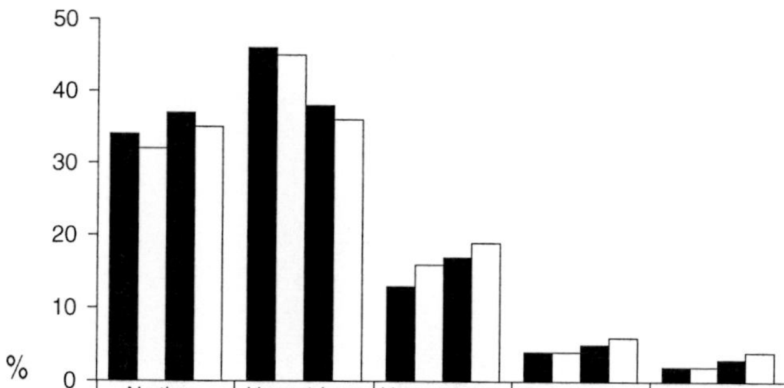

	No time at all	Up to 1 hour	Up to 2 hours	Up to 3 hours	More than 3 hours	Valid responses
■ Yr 8 M	34	46	13	4	2	2481
□ Yr 8 F	32	45	16	4	2	2437
■ Yr 10 M	37	38	17	5	3	2165
□ Yr 10 F	35	36	19	6	4	2197

Comments

1. The data refer to the evenings of Monday to Thursday only.
2. The slight increase in the percentages for *no time at all* with the older age group is perhaps the reverse of what may be expected.
3. The data appear to substantiate the view that females are more studious than males.
4. The average number of hours spent doing homework are calculated as follows:

Year 8 Males	0.9
Year 8 Females	1.0
Year 10 Males	1.0
Year 10 Females	1.1

Computer games

Up to 77% of males play computer games

How long did you spend playing computer games after school yesterday? (70c)

1. The much greater involvement of males than females is clear.
2. Up to 18% of males spent *more than 3 hours* on computer games.
3. Despite this male 'dominance', at least 32% of the females reported spending some time playing computer games after school, on the day prior to the survey.

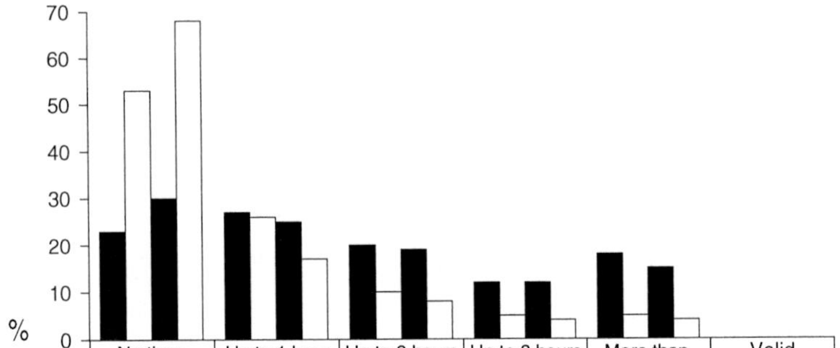

	No time at all	Up to 1 hour	Up to 2 hours	Up to 3 hours	More than 3 hours	Valid responses
■ Yr 8 M	23	27	20	12	18	2490
□ Yr 8 F	53	26	10	5	5	2443
■ Yr 10 M	30	25	19	12	15	2171
□ Yr 10 F	68	17	8	4	4	2190

Comments

1. The question lists Playstation, Gameboy and P.C. (Personal Computer) as examples.
2. The data reveal that significant percentages of males in this sample spent a considerable amount of time playing computer games during the evening before the survey. While there are benefits to playing some computer games, (Griffiths, 2002, 2003), it is easy to suppose that their time might be better spent.

Internet use

Up to 86% of Year 10 pupils access the Internet

Have you used the Internet in the last month? (72)

1. Between 56%-74% of the pupils accessed the Internet at school.
2. At least 56% of the pupils used the Internet at home.
3. The percentages of males using the Internet are slightly higher than those for females.
4. The *none of these* figures reveal that more than 75% of pupils in this sample do use the Internet.

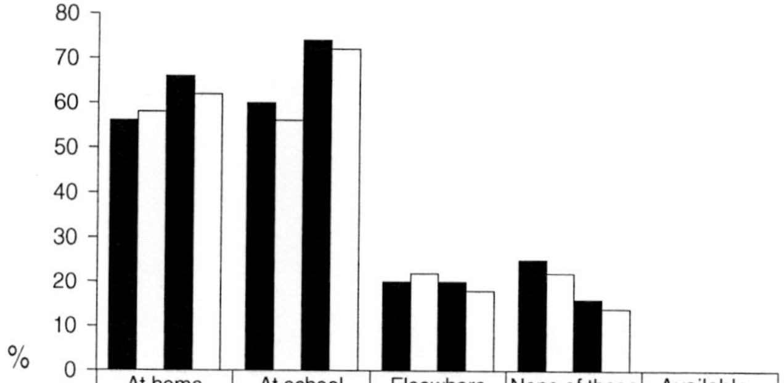

	At home	At school	Elsewhere	None of these	Available sample
■ Yr 8 M	56	60	20	25	3064
□ Yr 8 F	58	56	22	22	2865
■ Yr 10 M	66	74	20	16	2450
□ Yr 10 F	62	72	18	14	2425

Comments

1. The difference between males and females is apparent, however, it is not as great as the difference for playing computer games (see page 46). There may be marked differences in how members of each sex spend their time on the Internet.
2. Those pupils responding to the *none of these* category indicates that they have not used the Internet 'in the last month'. Since 2000, the *none of these* figures, (see below) show a sharp decline across age and gender. For example, in 2000, 44% of Year 8 females had not used the Internet 'in the last month'. This figure declines to 22% for the same group in 2003. Thus Internet use appears to have increased over the four year period from more than 56% in 2000 to more than 75% in 2003.

Those pupils **not** using the Internet *in the last month*

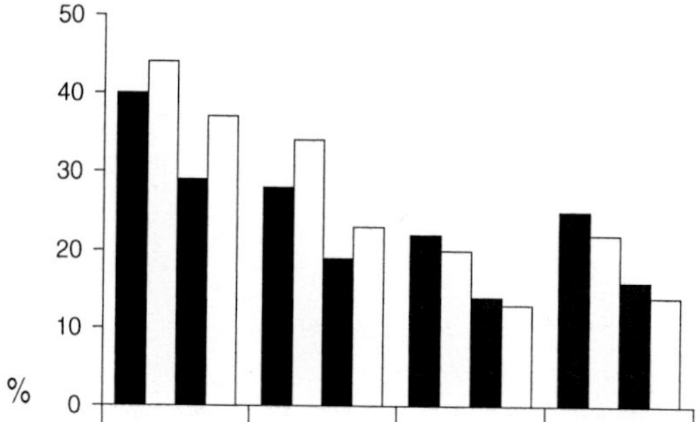

	2000	2001	2002	2003
■ Yr 8 M	40	28	22	25
□ Yr 8 F	44	34	20	22
■ Yr 10 M	29	19	14	16
□ Yr 10 F	37	23	13	14

Internet browsing

74% of Year 10 males browse without adult supervision

Are you able to 'browse' the Internet without adult supervision? (73)

1. Around three-quarters of young people are able to browse the Internet at least sometimes without adult supervision.
2. Slightly higher percentages of males than females are always able to browse the Internet without adult supervision.

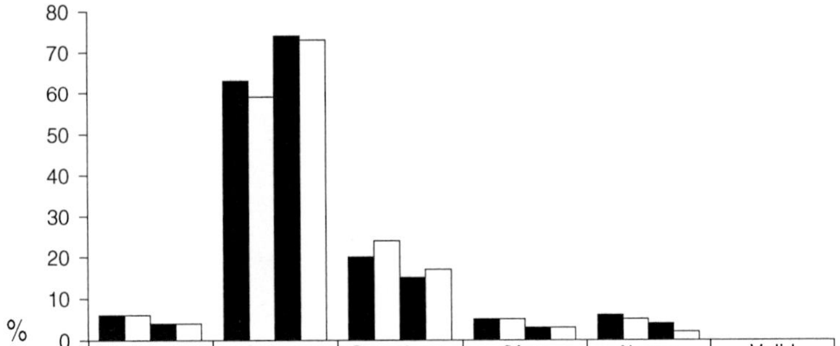

	Never use the Internet	Never supervised	Sometimes supervised	Often supervised	Always supervised	Valid responses
■ Yr 8 M	6	63	20	5	6	2489
□ Yr 8 F	6	59	24	5	5	2441
■ Yr 10 M	4	74	15	3	4	2166
□ Yr 10 F	4	73	17	3	2	2206

Comments

1. A number of news items have appeared in the recent past regarding young people accessing Internet 'chatrooms' and the associated potential dangers and subsequent risks of meeting undesirable adults. This is a major concern for parents and schools alike.
2. There is guidance for 'safe surfing' for parents and young people in a number of different publications, some of which is summarised in Mark Griffiths' article in *Education and Health*, Vol.22 No. 2.
3. Since 2000, we have seen a sharp rise (see below) in the percentages of young people that report browsing the Internet without adult supervision:

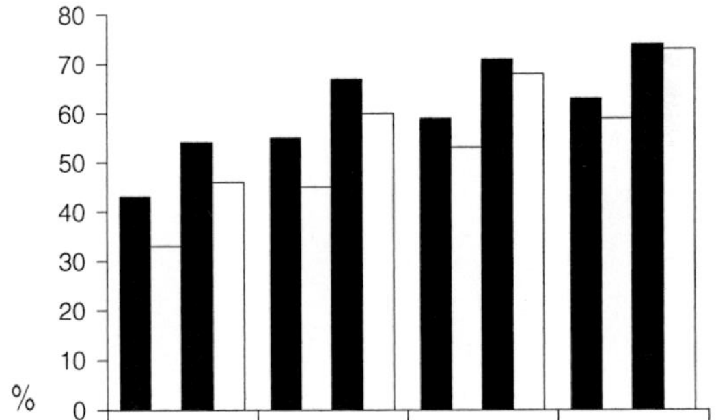

	2000	2001	2002	2003
■ Yr 8 M	43	55	59	63
□ Yr 8 F	33	45	53	59
■ Yr 10 M	54	67	71	74
□ Yr 10 F	46	60	68	73

After-school activities

Watching television is the most popular activity

Activities after school on the previous evening (71) (Pri.18)

1. More popular with males (5+% difference). All years: *Playing computer games, meeting with friends, playing sport.*
2. More popular with females (5+% difference). All years: *Reading a book.* Year 8: *Caring for pets.*
3. Age differences (5+% difference). Both genders: *reading books, meeting friends, computer games, sport.* Females only: *caring for pets.*

Comments

1. The fall in the percentage of 'readers' between Years 6, 8 and 10 implies a decline in the importance of books in the lives of children as they grow older.
2. The partial declining participation of females in sport seen for this question is mirrored in the later section on sport (page 95-97).
3. The use of computers, for a purpose other than playing games, is not markedly different between males and females but, clear differences are seen in relation to use of a computer for games.

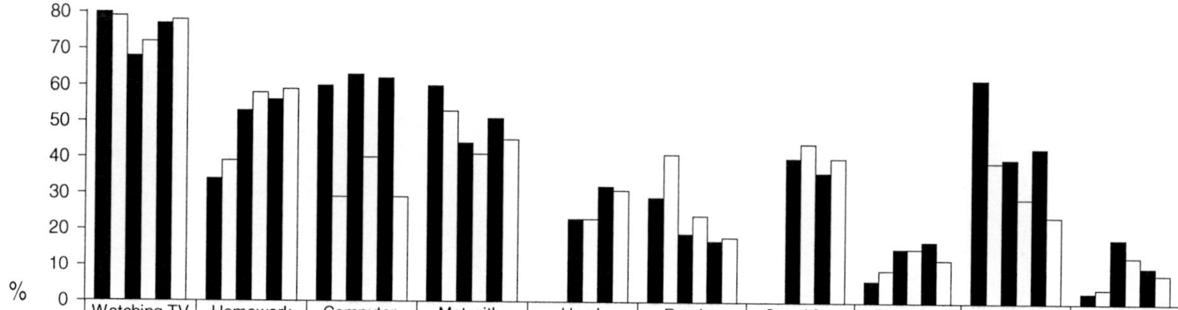

	Watching TV	Homework	Computer games	Met with friends	Used computer: school work	Read a book for enjoyment	Cared for pets	Played a musical instrument	Sport	None of these	Available sample
■ Yr 6 M	80	34	60	60	*	29	*	6	62	3	2422
□ Yr 6 F	79	39	29	53	*	41	*	9	39	4	2300
■ Yr 8 M	68	53	63	44	23	19	40	15	40	18	3064
□ Yr 8 F	72	58	40	41	23	24	44	15	29	13	2865
■ Yr 10 M	77	56	62	51	32	17	36	17	43	10	2450
□ Yr 10 F	78	59	29	45	31	18	40	12	24	8	2425

* Year 6 pupils were not asked about these activities

National newspapers

Up to 45% take *The Sun*

Which of the following newspapers are taken in your home on most days? (D) (Pri.5)

1. The order of popularity, based on this table, is: *The Sun, The Mirror, Daily Mail* and *The Times.*

Comments

1. For many years now we have classified these newspapers into *broadsheet, tabloid,* and *popular tabloid* groups, and used them as a broad socio-economic discriminator with which to match other behaviours, discovering some marked differences between groups, e.g. alcohol preferences.
2. The respondents often confuse local and national daily newspapers. Ambiguities can still occur despite the care we take to guide them through the questionnaire and also to obtain the names of the local newspapers found in a particular survey area.

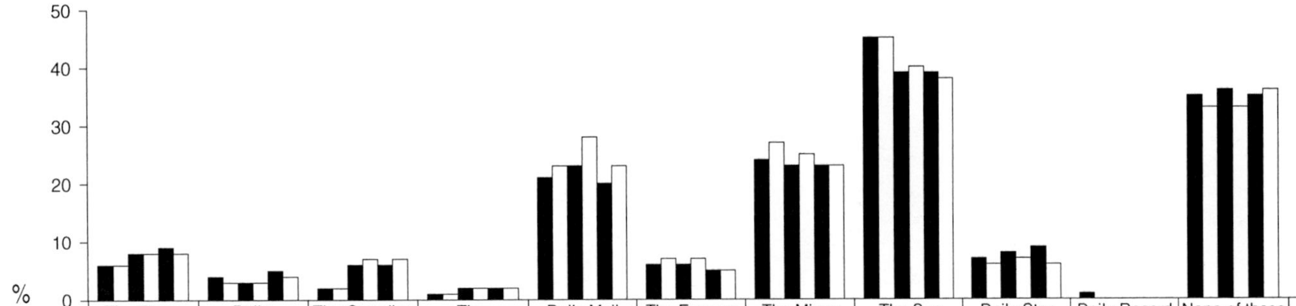

%	The Times	Daily Telegraph	The Guardian	The Independent	Daily Mail	The Express	The Mirror	The Sun	Daily Star	Daily Record	None of these	Available sample
■ Yr 6 M	6	4	2	1	21	6	24	45	7	1	35	2422
□ Yr 6 F	6	3	2	1	23	7	27	45	6	0	33	2300
■ Yr 8 M	8	3	6	2	23	6	23	39	8	0	36	3064
□ Yr 8 F	8	3	7	2	28	7	25	40	7	0	33	2865
■ Yr 10 M	9	5	6	2	20	5	23	39	9	0	35	2450
□ Yr 10 F	8	4	7	2	23	5	23	38	6	0	36	2425

5 Legal and Illegal Drugs

Information about the use of drugs, whether legal or illegal, is often sensationalised. It is an area where the teacher may feel handicapped by a lack of knowledge about people's degree of use, and a confidential questionnaire offers the best chance of deriving reliable information. Although tobacco and alcohol are in a general sense 'legalised', some of the questions reveal the extent of under-age purchase of alcoholic beverages. Information about personal and local use of 'illegal' drugs is presented, together with the perceived danger associated with their use. 'Young People and Illegal Drugs in 2000' (Balding, 2000) provides a more detailed analysis of the findings. See also 'Trends: Young People and Smoking 1983-2001' and 'Trends-Young People and Alcohol 1983-2001' (SHEU, 2003).

Question

5 Legal and Illegal Drugs

Alcoholic drinks

43% of the Year 10's had consumed *at least one drink*

During the last 7 days, have you had any of these alcoholic drinks? (30a) (Pri.39)

1. Wine is the most popular drink for the females, and beer or lager for the males. The table shows that more than 24% of the Year 8 pupils, and up to 44% of the Year 10 pupils, had consumed at least one of these drinks.
2. The inclusion of figures from Year 6 suggests that alcohol careers are established at an early age.
3. *Pre-mixed spirits* (Alcopops) are also popular, especially for the Year 10 females, who also have a taste for lager and spirits.

Comments

1. Canned shandy is barely alcoholic, but is recorded here to distinguish it unambiguously from mixed beer shandy.
2. Low-alcohol drinks have various strengths.
3. We note that more Year 10 females than males drank *alcoholic 'soft' drinks, pre-mixed spirits, wine* and *spirits*.
4. As noted in the introduction, the figures seen in our studies for the proportion of young people using alcohol in the previous week have been higher than those found in other research.

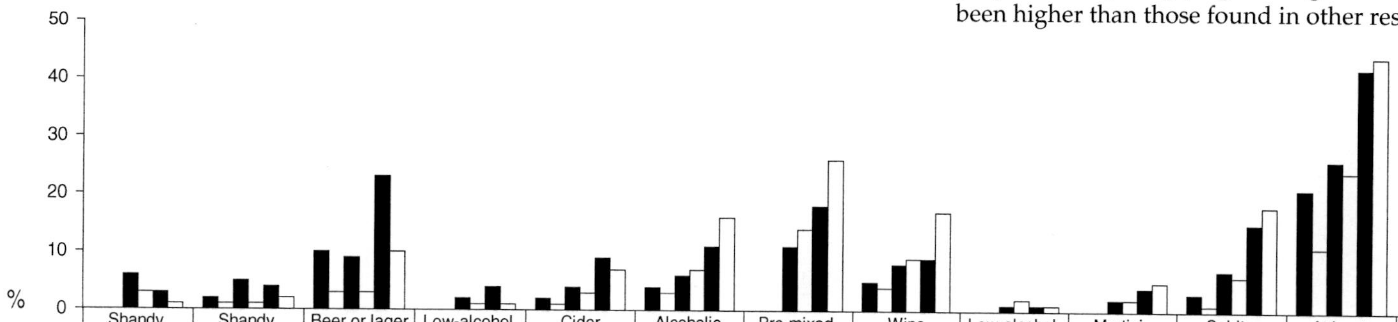

	Shandy (canned)	Shandy (mixed)	Beer or lager	Low-alcohol beer or lager	Cider	Alcoholic 'soft' drinks, e.g. Hooch	Pre-mixed spirits, e.g. Bacardi Breezer	Wine	Low-alcohol wine	Martini, cinzano, sherry, etc.	Spirits (gin, whisky, vodka, rum)	At least one drink	Available sample
■ Yr 6 M	*	2	10	*	2	*	0	5	*	0	3	21	2422
□ Yr 6 F	*	1	3	*	1	*	0	4	*	0	1	11	2300
■ Yr 8 M	6	5	9	2	4	6	11	8	1	2	7	26	3064
□ Yr 8 F	3	1	3	1	3	7	14	9	2	2	6	24	2865
■ Yr 10 M	3	4	23	4	9	11	18	9	1	4	15	42	2450
□ Yr 10 F	1	2	10	1	7	16	26	17	1	5	18	44	2425

* Options not available for Year 6

Canned shandy

A young males' drink

During the last 7 days, how many pints of canned shandy have you drunk? (30b)

One small can is counted as half a pint, and half-pints are rounded up to the next whole pint. Canned shandy is not included in total alcohol intake.

1. This drink appeals mainly to Year 8 males.

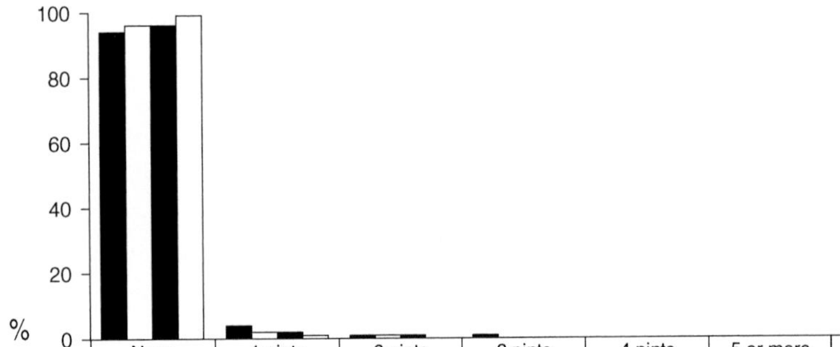

	None	1 pints	2 pints	3 pints	4 pints	5 or more	Valid responses
■ Yr 8 M	94	4	1	1	0	0	2631
□ Yr 8 F	96	2	1	0	0	0	2527
■ Yr 10 M	96	2	1	0	0	0	2169
□ Yr 10 F	99	1	0	0	0	0	2138

Comments

1. Canned shandy is not very alcoholic, but its associations with 'real' drink may make it appealing. It may also be less sweet than other canned drinks.
2. We have seen a decline in the popularity of both canned and mixed shandy, *Young People in 1998* (Balding, 1999). Have 'alcopops', which appeared at the beginning of shandy's decline, had anything to do with it?

Mixed shandy

A young males' drink

During the last 7 days, how many pints of mixed shandy have you drunk? (30c)

Half-pints are rounded up to the next whole pint. One pint is taken as one unit of alcohol when assessing total alcohol intake.

1. The Year 8 males are the principal drinkers of mixed shandy.
2. It is less popular with the females, and with the older pupils.

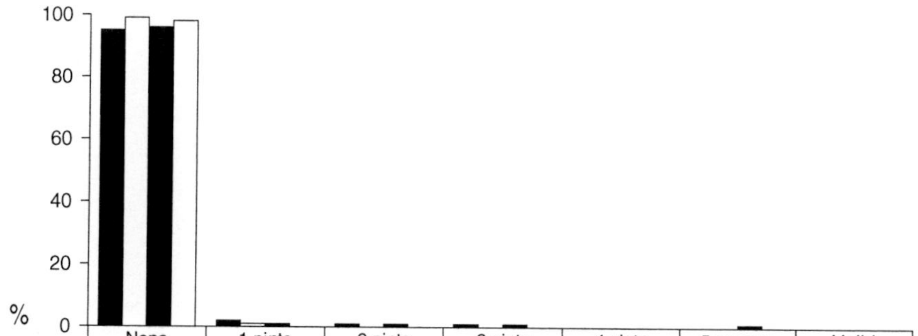

	None	1 pints	2 pints	3 pints	4 pints	5 or more	Valid responses
■ Yr 8 M	95	2	1	1	0	0	2846
□ Yr 8 F	99	1	0	0	0	0	2741
■ Yr 10 M	96	1	1	1	0	1	2338
□ Yr 10 F	98	0	0	0	0	0	2334

Comments

1. Beer and lemonade are needed to produce a mixed shandy. The message seems to be that the Year 10s are less keen to dilute their beer with lemonade.
2. As suggested previously with canned shandy and supported by the decline with age, the mixing of shandy with lemonade may serve as an introduction to the taste of beer to the younger age group.

Beer or lager

24% of the Year 10 males
drank at least 1 pint

During the last 7 days, how many pints of beer or lager have you drunk? (30d)

One pint is counted as two units of alcohol when assessing total alcohol intake, and half a pint is counted as one unit.

1. The attraction of beer or lager is much greater to the Year 10s, and to the males in particular, although 10% of the Year 10 females report drinking beer or lager in the last 7 days.

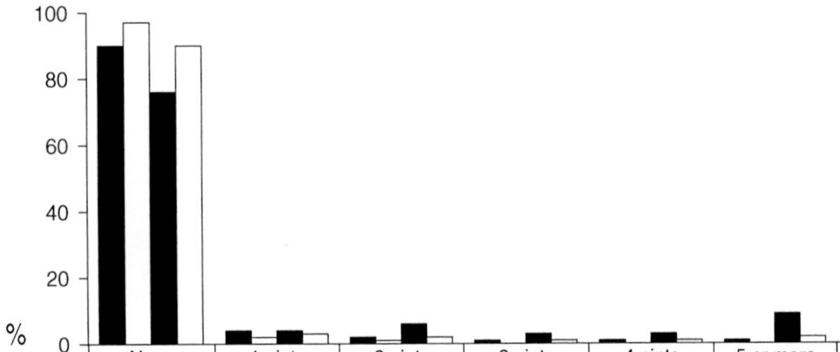

	None	1 pints	2 pints	3 pints	4 pints	5 or more	Valid responses
■ Yr 8 M	90	4	2	1	1	1	2846
□ Yr 8 F	97	2	1	0	0	0	2733
■ Yr 10 M	76	4	6	3	3	9	2322
□ Yr 10 F	90	3	2	1	1	2	2331

Comments

1. Beer or lager is a predominantly male type of drink, although in 1995 a quarter of the females had drunk some — we suspect that this may have been lager rather than beer.
2. Data from 1983 (SHEU, 'Trends-Young People and Alcohol. 1983-2001'), show there is an overall downward trend in 12-15 year olds drinking beer or lager 'in the last 7 days'. However, the following table shows a comparison between 1991 and 2003 of those 14-15 year old males that drank at least 1 pint 'in the last 7 days':

During the last 7 days, how many pints of beer or lager have you drunk?	None	1 pint	2 pints	3 pints	4 pints	5 pints+
Males 14-15yrs. (2003)	76%	4%	6%	3%	3%	9% (33%)
Males 14-15yrs. (1991)	66%	16%	7%	4%	2%	4% (12%)

Direct comparisons between years are misleading. However to guage a trend the data suggest that fewer report drinking in 2003 (76%). Of those 24% that drank in 2002, 33% are drinking 5 or more units compared with 12% in 1991. It would thus appear that fewer are drinking but 'drinkers' are consuming more.

Low-alcohol beer or lager

Very moderate appeal

During the last 7 days, how many pints of low-alcohol beer or lager have you drunk? (30e)

One pint is counted as two units of alcohol when assessing total alcohol intake, and half a pint is counted as one unit.

1. These beverages have very moderate appeal, which is more to the males.

	None	1 pints	2 pints	3 pints	4 pints	5 or more	Valid responses
■ Yr 8 M	96	2	1	0	0	0	1929
□ Yr 8 F	98	1	0	0	0	0	1905
■ Yr 10 M	94	2	2	0	1	1	1546
□ Yr 10 F	98	1	1	0	0	0	1603

Comments

1. Perhaps these drinks become more important to young people when they need to worry about drinking and driving.
2. We wonder if all the respondents recognise what is meant by low-alcohol beer or lager. They should not be confused with non-alcoholic drinks from which alcohol has been removed.

Cider

Up to 9% of the Year 10 group drank one or more pints

During the last 7 days, how many pints of cider have you drunk? (30f)

One pint is counted as two units of alcohol when assessing total alcohol intake, and half a pint is counted as one unit.

1. Cider appeals to both genders.

	None	1 pints	2 pints	3 pints	4 pints	5 or more	Valid responses
■ Yr 8 M	96	2	1	1	1	0	2850
□ Yr 8 F	97	1	1	0	0	0	2738
■ Yr 10 M	91	3	2	1	1	2	2338
□ Yr 10 F	93	2	2	1	1	1	2332

Comments

1. We have noticed from our regional surveys that cider consumption does vary across the UK.

'Alcopops'

24% of Year 10 females drank at least *1 can/bottle*

During the last 7 days, how many cans/bottles of 'alcopops' have you drunk? (30g)

One can/bottle is taken as half a pint, and half-pints are rounded up to the next whole pint. One can/bottle is taken as one unit of alcohol when assessing total alcohol intake,

1. Alcopops has an appeal to Year 10 females and 24% drank at least *1 can/bottle.*

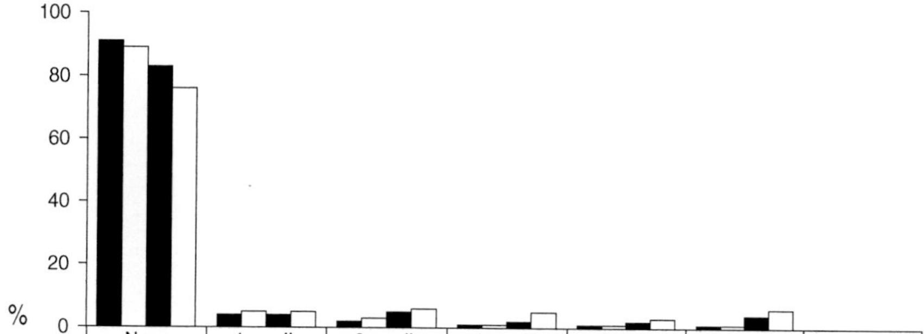

	None	1 small can/ bottle	2 small cans/ bottles	3 small cans/ bottles	4 small cans/ bottles	5 or more	Valid responses
■ Yr 8 M	91	4	2	1	1	1	1922
□ Yr 8 F	89	5	3	1	1	1	1902
■ Yr 10 M	83	4	5	2	2	4	1544
□ Yr 10 F	76	5	6	5	3	6	1597

Comments

1. These controversial drinks were launched with a lot of publicity, and were immediately added to the 'Young People...' questionnaire checklist in 1995.
2. A fear was voiced that 'alcopops' would be a gentle way of developing a taste for alcohol, and may have been marketed in part with that intention. In a detailed discussion of the place of 'alcopops' in young people's drinking patterns, ('Young People and Alcohol', Balding, 1997), we concluded that the consumers of alcoholic soft drinks tended also to consume a wider variety of other alcoholic drinks, which did not argue the case either way. However, we also discovered that the 'alcopoppers' were more likely to drink alcohol in places away from home compared with the others.
3. Figures, from 1996, for Year 10 females range from 18% (1998/99) to 30% (1997/2001), (SHEU, 'Trends-Young People and Alcohol 1983-2001'). 'Alcopops' have now replaced wine as the favourite drink for older females.

Wine

18% of older females drank at least one glass

During the last 7 days, how many glasses of wine have you drunk? (30h)

One glass is taken as one unit of alcohol when assessing total alcohol intake.

1. There is little gender difference in Year 8, but in Year 10 significantly more females than males had drunk some wine in the last 7 days.

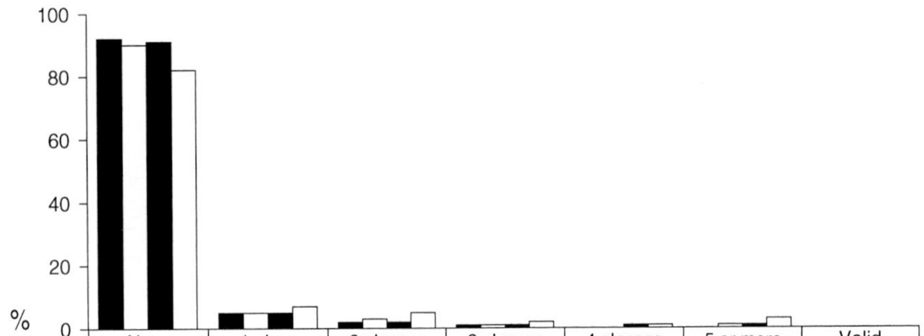

	None	1 glass	2 glasses	3 glasses	4 glasses	5 or more	Valid responses
■ Yr 8 M	92	5	2	1	0	0	2850
□ Yr 8 F	90	5	3	1	0	1	2728
■ Yr 10 M	91	5	2	1	1	1	2336
□ Yr 10 F	82	7	5	2	1	3	2324

Comments

1. Our surveys have usually shown wine to be a 'female' drink'; page 53 shows that it was drunk by more females than males.
2. We suspect that most wine-drinking goes on at home — a big change in UK drinking habits is buying wine from supermarkets with the family shopping. Drinking with meals is one way of introducing children to alcohol 'responsibly'.

Low alcohol wine

Not much appeal for young people

During the last 7 days, how many glasses of low-alcohol wine have you drunk? (30i)

One glass is taken as 0.3 unit of alcohol when assessing total alcohol intake.

1. This is not a popular beverage, with only about 3% of the respondents having drunk any.

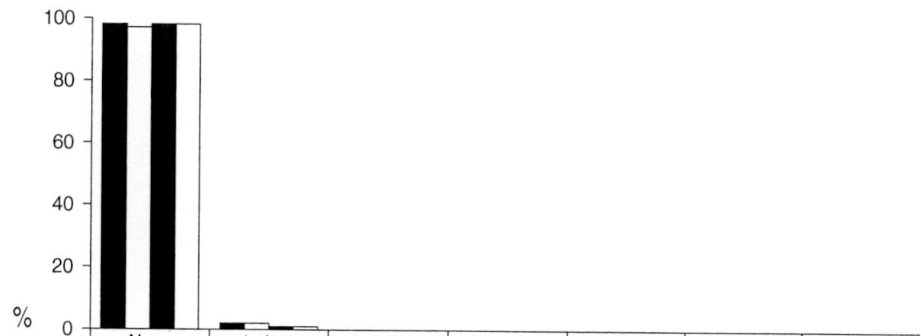

	None	1 glass	2 glasses	3 glasses	4 glasses	% or more	Valid responses
■ Yr 8 M	98	2	0	0	0	0	1930
□ Yr 8 F	97	2	0	0	0	0	1902
■ Yr 10 M	98	1	0	0	0	0	1547
□ Yr 10 F	98	1	0	0	0	0	1603

Comments

1. As with low-alcohol beer, this alternative drink does not seem to be popular with many young people. Is this because only normal-strength wine is available in many homes?

Fortified wine

Not much appeal for young people

During the last 7 days, how many glasses of fortified wine have you drunk? (30j)

One glass is taken as one unit of alcohol when assessing total alcohol intake.

1. Few Year 8 pupils had drunk any fortified wine; it is most popular with the Year 10 females.

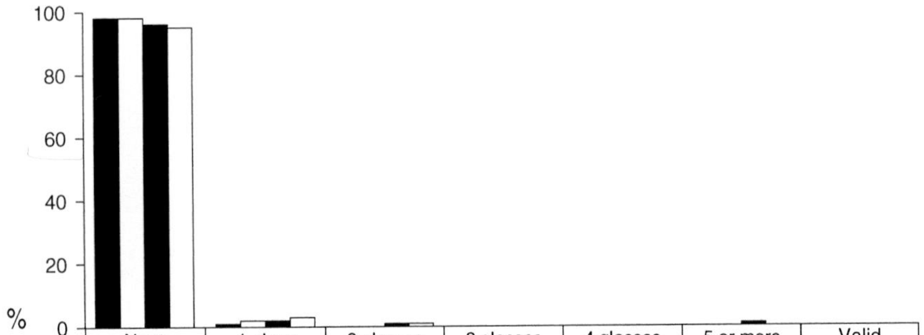

	None	1 glass	2 glasses	3 glasses	4 glasses	5 or more	Valid responses
■ Yr 8 M	98	1	0	0	0	0	2852
□ Yr 8 F	98	2	0	0	0	0	2737
■ Yr 10 M	96	2	1	0	0	1	2338
□ Yr 10 F	95	3	1	0	0	0	2330

Comments

1. The questionnaire gives *Martini, Cinzano, Sherry, etc.* as examples of fortified wine.
2. These drinks have generally declined in popularity with the exception of port.

Spirits

19% of Year 10 females
had drank one or more measures

During the last 7 days, how many measures of spirits have you drunk?
(30k)

One measure is taken as one unit of alcohol when assessing total alcohol intake.

1. Very little difference is noticeable between males and females with Year 10 females again consuming more than the males.

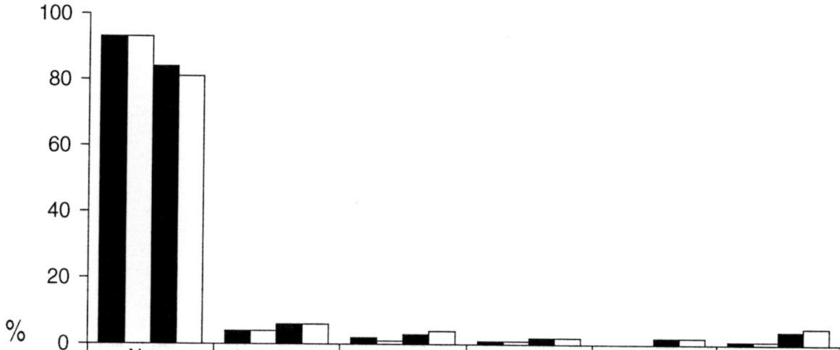

	None	1 measure	2 measures	3 measures	4 measures	5 or more	Valid responses
■ Yr 8 M	93	4	2	1	0	1	2832
□ Yr 8 F	93	4	1	1	0	1	2727
■ Yr 10 M	84	6	3	2	2	4	2308
□ Yr 10 F	81	6	4	2	2	5	2298

Comments

1. The Year 10 females 'overtook' the males as spirit-drinkers in 1996, although the females have always been behind the males in Year 8. Clearly they develop a taste for strong beverages around the age of 14.
2. We suspect that the amorphous nature of 'alcopops', which now include many spirit-based drinks, have enhanced the recent percentages (see page 59).
3. Data from 1983 (SHEU, 'Trends-Young People and Alcohol. 1983-2001'), show there is no overall downward trend in 12-15 year olds drinking spirits 'in the last 7 days'. However, the following table shows a comparison between 1991 and 2003 of those 14-15 year old females that drank at least 1 measure 'in the last 7 days':

During the last 7 days, how many measures of spirit have you drunk?	None	1	2	3	4	5+
Females 14-15yrs. (2003)	81%	6%	4%	2%	2%	5% (26%)
Females 14-15yrs. (1991)	87%	5%	3%	1%	1%	3% (23%)

In 2003, 19% drank at least 1 measure and, of those, 26% drank 5 or more measures 'in the last 7 days'.

Alcohol units consumed

15% of the Year 10 males drank more than 10 units

The total number of units of alcohol consumed in the last 7 days (30)

1. In both year groups, slightly more males recorded having drunk some alcohol.
2. 11% of Year 10 males drunk 15 or more units of alcohol in the previous 7 days compared with 9% of older females.

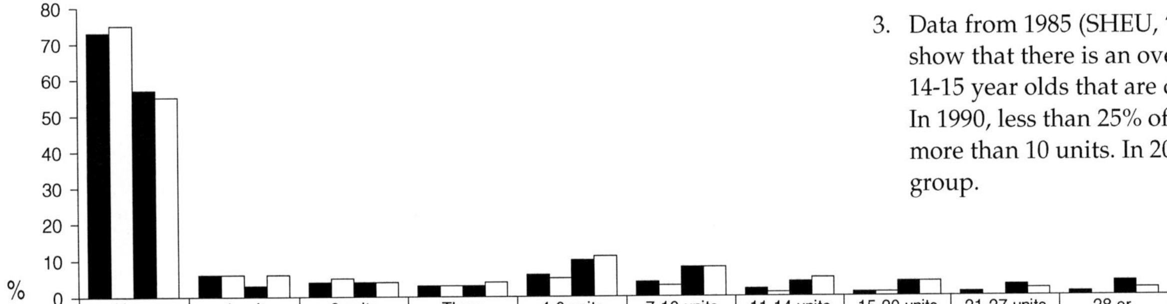

	None	1 unit	2 units	Three	4-6 units	7-10 units	11-14 units	15-20 units	21-27 units	28 or more units	Valid responses
■ Yr 8 M	73	6	4	3	6	4	2	1	1	1	2812
□ Yr 8 F	75	6	5	3	5	3	1	1	0	0	2706
■ Yr 10 M	57	3	4	3	10	8	4	4	3	4	2289
□ Yr 10 F	55	6	4	4	11	8	5	4	2	2	2281

Comments

1. On previous pages if the recorded amount of each individual type of drink includes a half measure, this is rounded up to the next whole amount. We feel this is justified in many cases, since glasses of drink poured between friends are likely to contain more liquid than official measures. However, when calculating the units for the table on this page, the original record is referred to.
2. The number of units of alcohol consumed by beer and cider drinkers is also certainly under-estimated, as the lowest alcohol levels (one unit per half-pint) are assumed for all beers and ciders drunk. The fact that young people's 'measures' of wines and spirits may in some cases be generous is another reason why the derived number of units may be on the low side.
3. Data from 1985 (SHEU, 'Trends-Young People and Alcohol. 1983-2001'), show that there is an overall decline in those reporting drinking. Those 14-15 year olds that are drinking are consuming more than they used to. In 1990, less than 25% of older males who drank alcohol 'last week' drank more than 10 units. In 2003, this figure is around 35% of the equivalent group.

Alcohol frequency

10% of the Year 10 males drank on 3 days or more

During the last 7 days, on how many days did you drink alcohol? (29) (Pri.38)

Canned shandy is not counted as an alcoholic drink.

1. In both year groups, the male drinkers outnumbered the females, and also tended to drink on more days.
2. However, on average more than half the 'drinkers' drank on only one day during the past week.
3. 10% of the Year 10 males and 8% of the Year 10 females drank on three days or more.

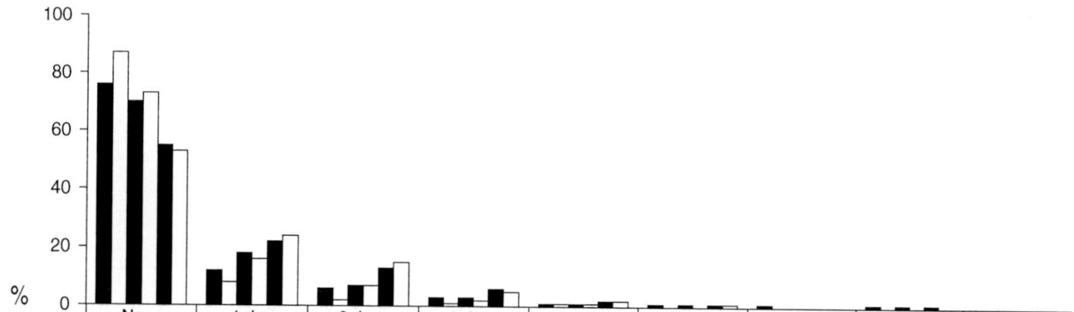

	None	1 day	2 days	3 days	4 days	5 days	6 days	7 days	Valid responses
■ Yr 6 M	76	12	6	3	1	1	1	1	2296
□ Yr 6 F	87	8	2	1	1	0	0	0	2228
■ Yr 8 M	70	18	7	3	1	1	0	1	2912
□ Yr 8 F	73	16	7	2	1	0	0	0	2771
■ Yr 10 M	55	22	13	6	2	1	0	1	2366
□ Yr 10 F	53	24	15	5	2	1	0	0	2354

Comments

1. We see that by Year 8 at least half the potential Year 10 'drinkers' have already acquired some taste for alcohol.
2. Drinking habits of adults in general are quite regular, while that of younger adults in the 18-25 age range is more likely to feature 'binge ' drinking. For young drinkers there is evidence to suggest that for some 13 – 16 year olds the figure of at least five alcoholic drinks in one session is not uncommon ('Education and Health', 2002, 20:3:46).

Sources of alcohol

Off-licences feature strongly

Have you bought alcoholic drink at any of these places during the last 7 days? (31)

1. The *off-licence* is clearly a most important source of purchased alcoholic drink, especially for the Year 10s, with the *pub or bar* as the next major source of alcohol purchased.
2. About 20% of the Year 10s bought some drink, but from the previous table we discover that around 47% of them drank some.

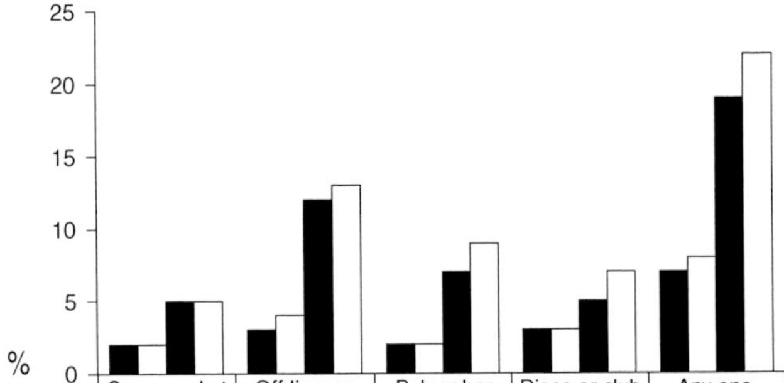

	Supermarket	Off-licence	Pub or bar	Disco or club	Any one of these	Available sample
■ Yr 8 M	2	3	2	3	7	3064
□ Yr 8 F	2	4	2	3	8	2865
■ Yr 10 M	5	12	7	5	19	2450
□ Yr 10 F	5	13	9	7	22	2425

Comments

1. The sites for drinking alcohol (whether purchased or not) are given overleaf.
2. It is suspected that alcohol purchased by young people is more likely to be connected to alcohol abuse and public nuisance than alcohol supplied in the home.
3. Purchases of alcoholic drink are age-restricted, and while at 16 you may buy cigarettes, (see page 70) you must be 18 before buying alcohol. Other age-restricted products in the questionnaire include National Lottery main draw tickets and 'Instants'. In any one week, probably many thousands of young people are making illegal purchases of these products.

Drinking venues

More young people consume alcohol at *home* than anywhere else

Have you had an alcoholic drink in any of these places during the last 7 days? (32)

1. Most 'drinkers' drank at *home*.
2. Substantial numbers of Year 10 'drinkers' used all the listed venues.

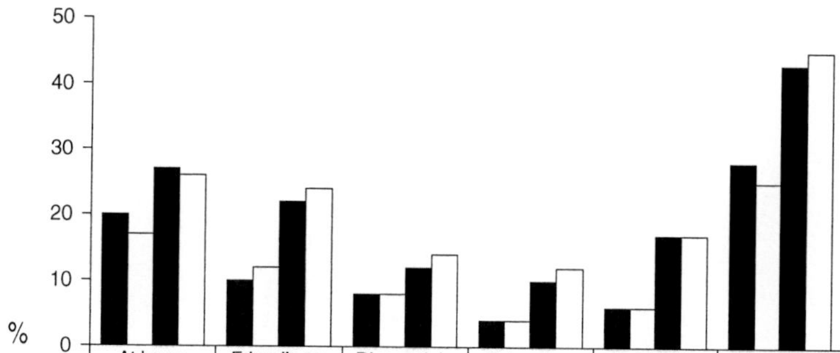

	At home	Friend's or relation's home	Disco, club or party	Pub or bar	Outside in a public place	Any one of these	Available sample
■ Yr 8 M	20	10	8	4	6	28	3064
□ Yr 8 F	17	12	8	4	6	25	2865
■ Yr 10 M	27	22	12	10	17	43	2450
□ Yr 10 F	26	24	14	12	17	45	2425

Comments

1. In 1990 we asked if they had been to a pub or bar, even if they didn't drink anything, and found that over 40% of the Year 10s had done so. If this single year was typical, then far more are visiting public houses (perhaps in a family outing) than are buying or being bought drink under-age.
2. Much media attention is paid to young people drinking in public venues, either outside or inside, but the most common places are the family home and relations' homes, where there could be greater control over drinking levels.
3. A review of research also found that the most popular location for drinking alcohol (among underage drinkers) was at home (Coleman & Cater, 2003). It is often observed that the home may be a safe and supportive environment in which to explore the use of alcohol, so that introducing children to alcohol in the home is a responsible thing for parents to do. Thus, we are effectively teaching young people to drink.
4. There is still a colossal burden of damage caused in society by alcohol, so that whatever is being done in the name of health education with children or adults, it has been inadequate to reach the roots of alcohol abuse.

Drinking at home

Parents of 14-15 year olds are less likely to know

If you ever drink alcohol at home, do your parents know? (33) (Pri. 40)

1. The Primary version of this question asks, 'Do your parents know if you drink alcohol?' and up to 51% of Year 6 pupils say their 'parents always know'.
2. Of those older pupils who do drink at home, about half do so with their parents always knowing about it.

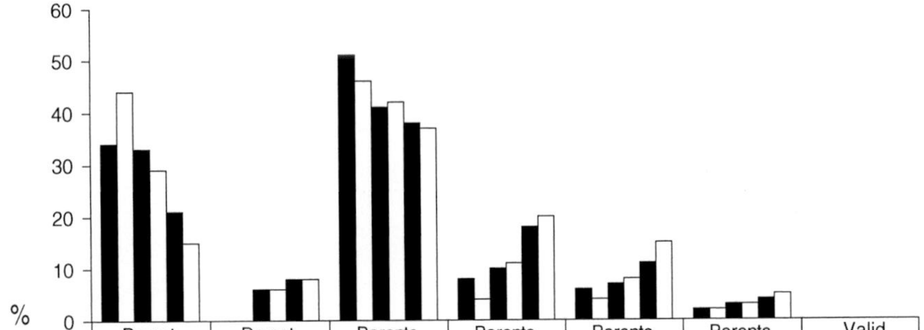

	Do not drink at all	Do not drink at home	Parents always know	Parents usually know	Parents sometimes know	Parents never know	Valid responses
■ Yr 6 M	34	*	51	8	6	2	2287
□ Yr 6 F	44	*	46	4	4	2	2213
■ Yr 8 M	33	6	41	10	7	3	2895
□ Yr 8 F	29	6	42	11	8	3	2779
■ Yr 10 M	21	8	38	18	11	4	2343
□ Yr 10 F	15	8	37	20	15	5	2370

* Option not available for Year 6

Comments

1. The question was added because of interest in the amount of alcohol being drunk during the previous week at home — always the most popular venue. The answer is that there is quite a lot of clandestine drinking going on among the older pupils.
2. The young people who say they do not drink at home may contain a substantial proportion who do not drink currently at all. These figures place an upper limit on the proportion of 'never drinkers', as we have no routinely collected information on drinking attitudes and experience to match that with respect to illegal drugs.

Cigarettes smoked

26% of the Year 10 females smoke

How many cigarettes have you smoked during the last 7 days? (23) (Pri.42)

1. More Year 8 & 10 females than males had smoked and there were more smokers in Year 10.
2. There is no significant gender difference in those Year 10 pupils reporting smoking more than 25 cigarettes. The majority of smokers smoke up to 25 cigarettes a week.

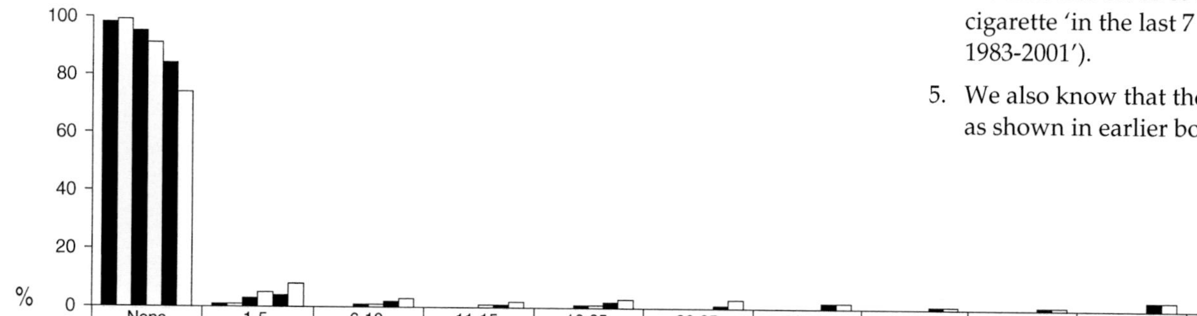

	None	1-5 cigarettes	6-10 cigarettes	11-15 cigarettes	16-25 cigarettes	26-35 cigarettes	36-45 cigarettes	46-55 cigarettes	56-65 cigarettes	66+ cigarettes	Valid responses
■ Yr 6 M	98	1	0	0	0	0	0	0	0	0	2325
□ Yr 6 F	99	1	0	0	0	0	0	0	0	0	2254
■ Yr 8 M	95	3	1	0	1	0	0	0	0	0	2978
□ Yr 8 F	91	5	1	1	1	0	0	0	0	0	2830
■ Yr 10 M	84	4	2	1	2	1	2	1	1	3	2394
□ Yr 10 F	74	8	3	2	3	3	2	1	1	3	2399

Comments

1. Assuming that many females may be going out with males older than themselves, it is possible that the Year 10s partners have smoking levels similar to the ones seen here.
2. Smoking levels of up to 25 a week are hardly addictive in adults; what is known about young people's addiction levels?
3. Smoking levels have increased rather than decreased since the publication of the 'Health of the Nation' targets in 1992 and 'Our Healthier Nation' in 1999.
4. Data from 1985 show an upward trend which may have peaked around the mid-late 1990s of those 12-15 years olds that report smoking at least 1 cigarette 'in the last 7 days' (SHEU, 'Trends-Young People and Smoking, 1983-2001').
5. We also know that the smoking levels vary widely from school to school, as shown in earlier books in this series.

Sources of cigarettes

Shops and *friends* were the main source

If you have smoked recently, where did you get your last cigarettes from?
(24)

1. For the Year 8 smokers, *friends* were the main source. In Year 10, *shops* were the most important source.

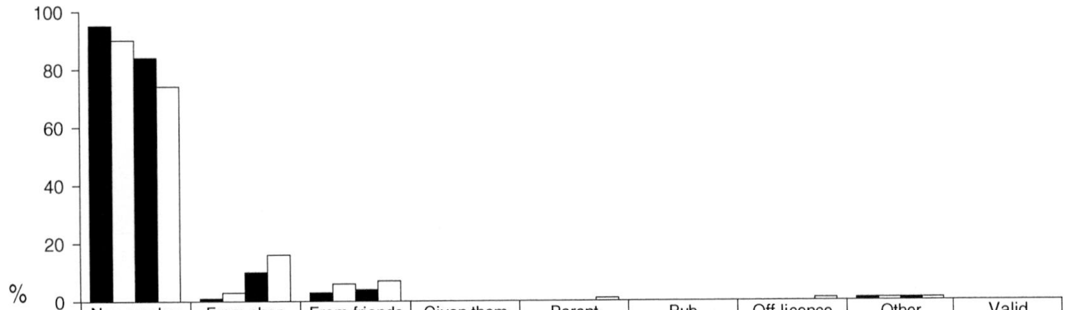

	Non-smoker	From shop	From friends	Given them	Parent	Pub	Off-licence	Other	Valid responses
■ Yr 8 M	95	1	3	0	0	0	0	1	2937
□ Yr 8 F	90	3	6	0	0	0	0	1	2794
■ Yr 10 M	84	10	4	0	0	0	0	1	2351
□ Yr 10 F	74	16	7	0	1	0	1	1	2353

Comments

1. Purchases by under-16s are illegal, but our sympathies are with any shop-keeper trying to judge the age of 14-15 year olds; fortunately there are age-verification cards available.
2. The friends that supplied cigarettes to the Year 8 smokers may be older than themselves.
3. The information about cigarette purchases can be related to the question on spending money (page 89). There is a very high degree of overlap — greater than 95%.

Type of smoker

Up to 63% will have smoked by Year 10

What kind of smoker are you? (25) (Pri.41)

1. Between Years 8 and 10 the number of regular smokers more than triples.
2. The majority of the current smokers say that they would *like to stop.*

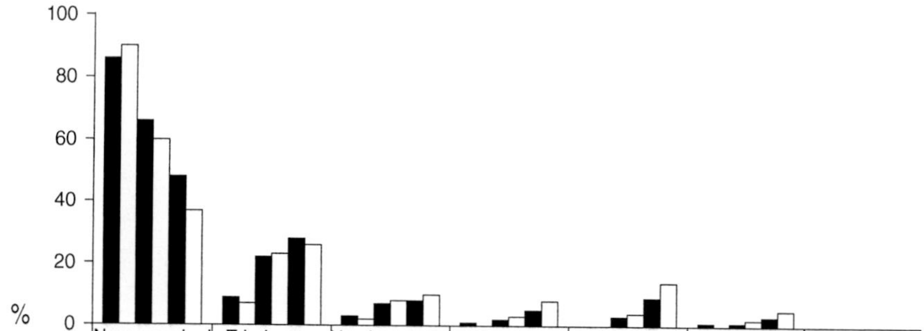

	Never smoked	Tried once or twice	Used to smoke	Smoke occasionally	Smoke, would like to stop	Smoke, don't want to stop	Valid responses
■ Yr 6 M	86	9	3	1	*	*	2319
□ Yr 6 F	90	7	2	0	*	*	2245
■ Yr 8 M	66	22	7	2	3	1	2991
□ Yr 8 F	60	23	8	3	4	2	2832
■ Yr 10 M	48	28	8	5	9	3	2402
□ Yr 10 F	37	26	10	8	14	5	2399

* Year 6 pupils were not asked about these activities

Comments

1. Two-thirds of smokers want to give up. If addiction is not their problem, can we help them? Raw et al's (1998) publication recommends interventions shown to be effective with adults should be considered for use with young people with the content modified as necessary - this includes stop-smoking groups and the possible use of nicotine replacement therapy.
2. We used to ask *Do we believe the ones who say that they want to give up?* It's an easy claim to make, but it might be offered that if they really wanted to quit they would. We believe them more since we related their level of anxiety about smoking to their desire to give up: those that want to give up are much more worried about smoking than other smokers ('No Worries?' Balding, 1998).
3. Data from 1986 (SHEU, 'Trends-Young People and Smoking, 1983-2001'), show no overall trend in those that report smoking regularly. This steady prevalence is seen very clearly from 1995 onward as around 22% of Year 10 females have reported smoking regularly.
4. By the time young people reach Year 10, it is unusual for them not to have tried cigarettes. Is it realistic to try to discourage experimentation? The table shows that fewer than half the number of those who have experimented are currently smoking.
5. It has been observed that the children of single or divorced parents are more likely to smoke (Brynin, 1999).

Smoker in the family

55% of the Year 10 females have a *close friend* who smokes

Do any of these people smoke on most days? (26)

1. A *close friend* has become the new chief smoking contact for all age groups.
2. Fewer than a third have no close family member or friend that smokes.

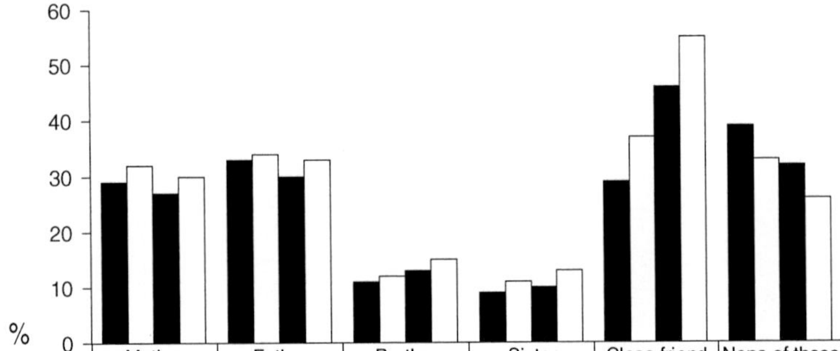

	Mother	Father	Brother	Sister	Close friend	None of these	Available sample
■ Yr 8 M	29	33	11	9	29	39	3064
□ Yr 8 F	32	34	12	11	37	33	2865
■ Yr 10 M	27	30	13	10	46	32	2450
□ Yr 10 F	30	33	15	13	55	26	2425

Comments

1. The greater the number of people smoking, the greater the incentive to follow suit and the chances of approval (at least from the smokers). We repeat below an analysis first published in 'Young People in 1996' showing powerful links between the smoking habit and smoking by family and friends — especially siblings and close friends.

   Percentages smoking among Year 10 females, by smoking among family and friends

Smoking by other?	Mother	Father	Brother	Sister	Friend
No	19%	19%	22%	23%	4%
Yes	40%	38%	46%	45%	43%

   The contrast in smoking between females with and without friends who smoke is dramatic, but the highest proportion of all is among females with a smoking sister.

2. On the other hand, since most young people will have both non-smokers and smokers in their immediate circle, it is clear that examples are not irresistible.

Smokers in the home

Around 50% live in a 'smoky' home

How many people smoke on most days in your home? (27)

The question asks the respondents to include themselves and regular visitors if they smoke at home.

1. Non-smoking/smoking households are evenly matched.
2. These figures seem to 'clump': smokers are more likely to be found where there is another smoker.

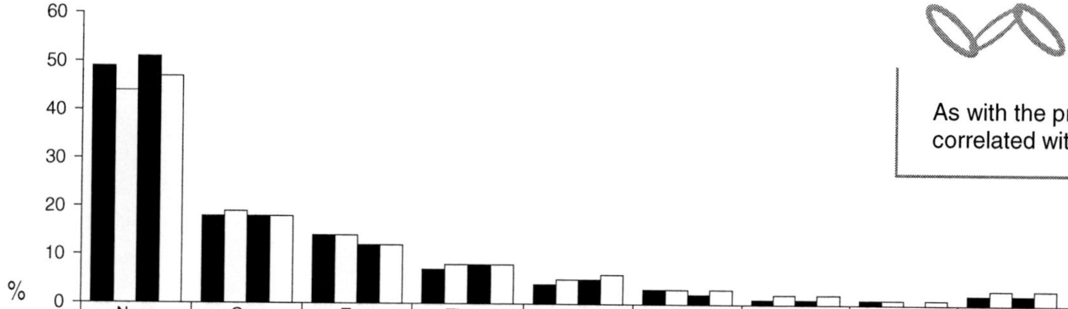

	None	One	Two	Three	Four	Five	Six	Seven	Eight or more	Valid responses
■ Yr 8 M	49	18	14	7	4	3	1	1	2	2913
□ Yr 8 F	44	19	14	8	5	3	2	1	3	2760
■ Yr 10 M	51	18	12	8	5	2	1	0	2	2365
□ Yr 10 F	47	18	12	8	6	3	2	1	3	2387

Comments

1. 'Smoking in the home' does not necessarily mean that the house is smoky. It could be banned from communal rooms, or smokers could even be sent outside.
2. Children in 'smoking' homes may experience approval, rather than just tolerance, of smoking, and are more likely to grow up thinking that it is a normal, even expected, behaviour with important pleasures and rewards.

As with the previous question, young people's own smoking habit is strongly correlated with the number of other people smoking at home.

Beliefs about drugs

As pupils get older fewer think that cannabis is *always unsafe*

What do you know about these drugs? (34) Response to 'Always unsafe'

1. There is little difference between the Year 8s and the Year 10s response to the dangers of cannabis, but uniquely it does decline with age.
2. In most cases, more females than males think that a drug will be *always unsafe.*
3. Generally, pupils think the most unsafe substances are ecstasy, cocaine, heroin and crack.

Comments

1. The format of this question has changed from that used in recent years to the following response options: *Never heard of them; Know nothing about them; Safe if used properly,* and *Always unsafe.* Thus it is not easy to say if young people have changed their perceptions of safety of these different drugs, but we are very confident that the response of year 10 pupils are now more complacent than in previous years.
2. We report responses to *Always unsafe* and can say that the relative safety of drugs has not changed with heroin, ecstasy and crack being thought most risky and cannabis the least.

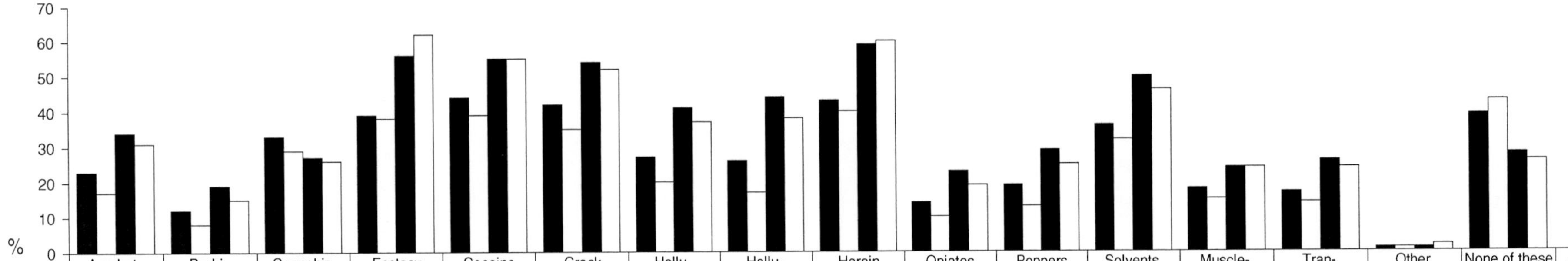

	Amphet-amines	Barbi-turates	Cannabis leaf/ resin	Ecstasy	Cocaine	Crack	Hallu-cinogens: natural	Hallu-cinogens: synthetic	Heroin	Opiates	Poppers	Solvents used as drugs	Muscle-building steroids	Tran-quillisers	Other illegal drugs	None of these	Available sample
■ Yr 8 M	23	12	33	39	44	42	27	26	43	14	19	36	18	17	1	39	3064
□ Yr 8 F	17	8	29	38	39	35	20	17	40	10	13	32	15	14	1	43	2865
■ Yr 10 M	34	19	27	56	55	54	41	44	59	23	29	50	24	26	1	28	2450
□ Yr 10 F	31	15	26	62	55	52	37	38	60	19	25	46	24	24	2	26	2425

Contact with drug users

Up to 58% of the 14-15 year olds are *fairly sure* or *certain* that they know a drug user

Do you know anyone personally who you think takes any of these drugs?

(35) (Pri.48)

1. Similar numbers of older males and females thought they knew someone.
2. 19%-27% of Year 6s, 28% of the Year 8s, and up to 58% of the Year 10s, claimed to be *fairly sure* or *certain.*

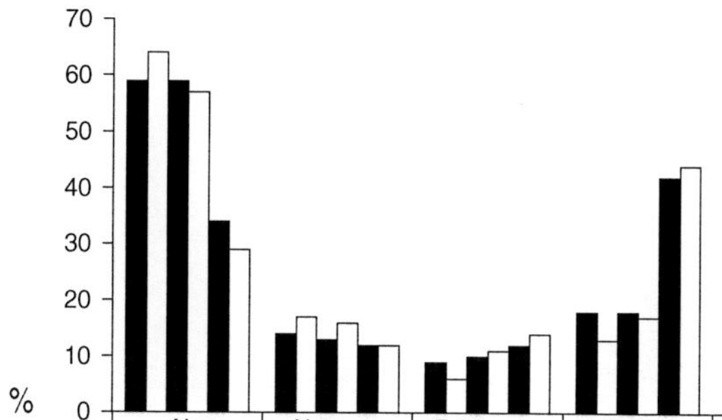

	No	Not sure	Fairly sure	Certain	Valid responses
■ Yr 6 M	59	14	9	18	1980
□ Yr 6 F	64	17	6	13	1877
■ Yr 8 M	59	13	10	18	2910
□ Yr 8 F	57	16	11	17	2787
■ Yr 10 M	34	12	12	42	2380
□ Yr 10 F	29	12	14	44	2379

Comments

1. Since knowledge of other drug users is a key to obtaining drugs, the proportion of Year 6s reporting that they think they know some one who uses at least one of the listed drugs presents concern for the potential future behaviour of these young people.
2. This does not mean that 20% of Year 6 pupils take drugs, since 99 pupils in a school could all be thinking of the same one person, who may not even be a school pupil. We emphasise personal knowledge to exclude depictions of drug use in the media, and give a prompt to exclude users of drugs as medicines.

Experience of drugs

Up to 24% of the Year 10 pupils have taken cannabis

Have you ever taken any of these drugs? (38)

1. About 1 in 5 pupils in Year 10 — four times as many as in Year 8 — have tried at least one of these drugs.
2. Cannabis is by far the most likely drug to have been tried, with 23% of males and 24% of females in Year 10 reporting having taken it. The percentage for other drugs taken are significantly lower, around 3%, for drugs such as amphetamines, ecstasy, and solvents up to 5%. The use of poppers is slightly higher being taken by 9% of Year 10 females.

Comments

1. We have reported elsewhere, 'Young People and Illegal Drugs' (Balding, 2000), that levels appear at least to have 'stabilised' and may have fallen, after a long period of increase. When we first saw a fall in our 1997 data, we were hesitant about its interpretation, but we now have further years of lower levels, and new reports from elsewhere are in line with our figures (Flood, 2000).
2. Clearly the drug careers of young people expand from Year 8 - an indicator of the need to review the timing of drug education within both primary and secondary schools.

	Amphet-amines	Barbi-turates	Cannabis leaf/ resin	Ecstasy	Cocaine	Crack	Hallu-cinogens: natural	Hallu-cinogens: synthetic	Heroin	Opiates	Poppers	Solvents used as drugs	Muscle-building steroids	Tran-quillisers	Other illegal drugs	None of these	Available sample
■ Yr 8 M	1	1	6	1	1	1	1	1	1	1	1	2	1	1	1	92	3064
□ Yr 8 F	1	0	4	1	1	1	0	0	1	0	1	1	0	0	0	94	2865
■ Yr 10 M	2	1	23	2	2	2	2	1	1	1	6	3	1	1	0	75	2450
□ Yr 10 F	3	1	24	3	2	2	2	1	1	1	9	5	0	1	0	72	2425

More than one drug

Up to 6% of the Year 10 pupils have combined more than one drug

Have you ever taken more than one type of drug on the same occasion? (40)

1. Over 5% of pupils in Year 10 say they have taken one or more type of drug on the same occasion.
2. The proportion in Year 8 is much smaller.
3. There is not a large gender difference.

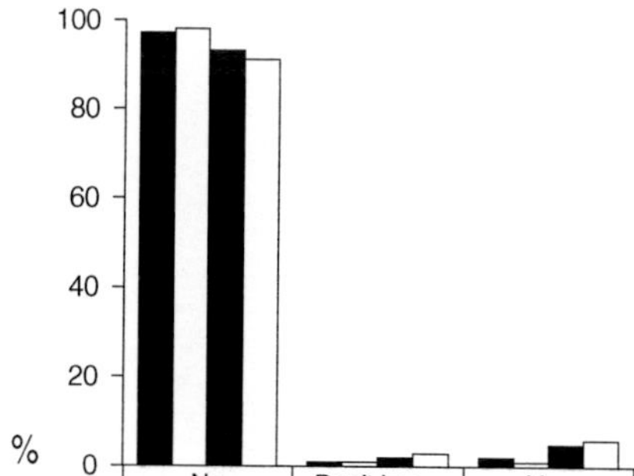

	No	Don't know	Yes	Valid responses
■ Yr 8 M	97	1	2	2889
□ Yr 8 F	98	1	1	2766
■ Yr 10 M	93	2	5	2348
□ Yr 10 F	91	3	6	2348

Comments

1. This was a new question in 2002 and pupils are referred to the list of drugs printed in the questionnaire. This list excludes alcohol which is the subject of the next question and reported on the following page.
2. This question tries to shift the emphasis from experimentation towards behaviour that is obviously risky.

Drugs and alcohol

Up to 18% of the Year 10 pupils have mixed drugs and alcohol

Have you ever taken drugs and alcohol on the same occasion? (41)

1. Nearly 20% of older pupils have taken drugs and alcohol on the same occasion.
2. The figures across genders are very similar.
3. The issue is age related as up to 3% of the 12-13 year olds report mixing drugs compared with up to 18% of 14-15 year olds.

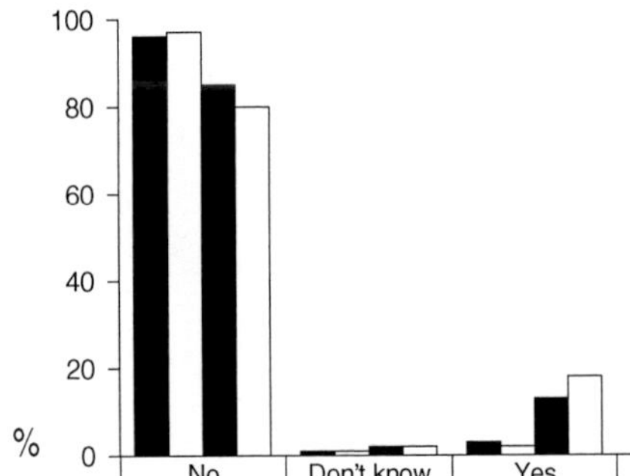

	No	Don't know	Yes	Valid responses
■ Yr 8 M	96	1	3	2886
□ Yr 8 F	97	1	2	2770
■ Yr 10 M	85	2	13	2348
□ Yr 10 F	80	2	18	2349

Comments

1. Drug use associated with alcohol use is not uncommon in the experience of young people who have ever taken drugs.
2. Again, we are looking at a behaviour that suggests a less cautious attitude to risk.

6 Money

The amount of money that young people have to spend is an important factor in determining their access to a host of behaviours. This section examines working for money, levels of income, and the sorts of things that they spend their money on, including National Lottery products.

Regular work

36% of the Year 10 pupils have regular paid work

Have you a regular paid job during term time? (77)

Respondents with more than one job were asked to record the one that paid the most money.

1. Up to 30% of 12-13 year olds have a regular paid job during term time.
2. By the time they are 14-15 years old, 36% of pupils report having a regular paid job.

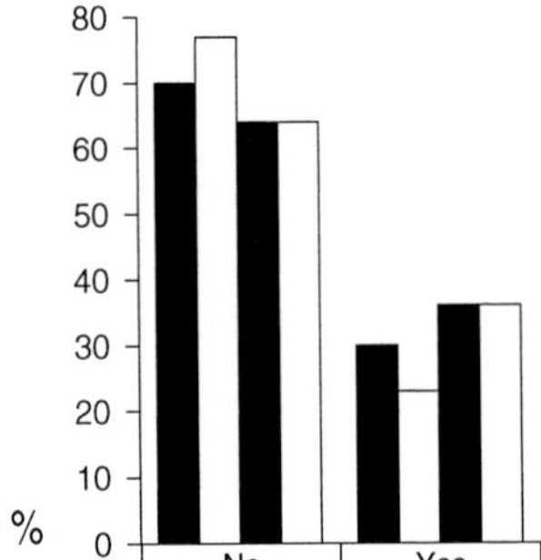

	No	Yes	Valid responses
■ Yr 8 M	70	30	2259
□ Yr 8 F	77	23	2257
■ Yr 10 M	64	36	1991
□ Yr 10 F	64	36	2075

Comments

1. The evenness of responses of the sexes to having a regular job by the Year 10 pupils is typical for this question and similar to previous years' results.
2. Since 1999 the numbers, of those reporting regular work, have followed a broadly similar pattern:

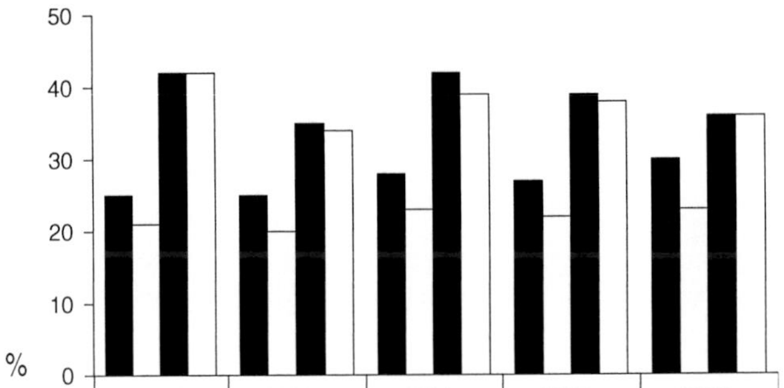

	1999	2000	2001	2002	2003
■ Yr 8 M	25	25	28	27	30
□ Yr 8 F	21	20	23	22	23
■ Yr 10 M	42	35	42	39	36
□ Yr 10 F	42	34	39	38	36

3. Unsurprisingly, the age differences have remained and data from the older pupils reflect the similarities between genders.

Type of paid work

Babysitting is the most popular for the females and *paper/milk round* for the males

What type of regular paid job do you do? (78)

Respondents with more than one job were asked to record the one that paid the most.

1. We note some gender contrasts; more females involved in *babysitting* and *paid housework* while more males report *manual work* and delivery rounds.
2. *Paid housework* diminishes in Year 10, but shop work, hotel and café work increases.

Comments

1. The distribution of jobs follows the pattern noted over recent years.
2. The involvement of some of these Year 8 pupils in regular paid work may be in violation of Section 18 of the Children and Young Persons Act, 1933. The Act places restrictions, including hours and conditions of work for children, especially for those under the age of 13.

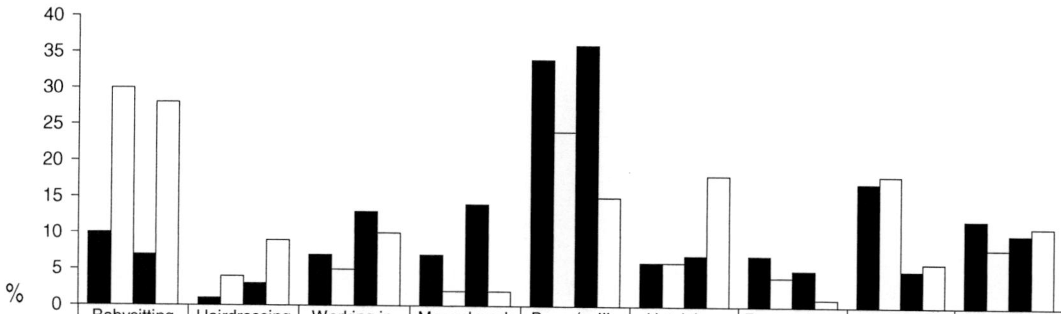

	Babysitting	Hairdressing	Working in a shop	Manual work	Paper/ milk round	Hotel, bar or cafe	Farmwork or gardening	Paid housework	Other work	Valid responses
■ Yr 8 M	10	1	7	7	34	6	7	17	12	671
□ Yr 8 F	30	4	5	2	24	6	4	18	8	510
■ Yr 10 M	7	3	13	14	36	7	5	5	10	708
□ Yr 10 F	28	9	10	2	15	18	1	6	11	720

Time spent working

13% of 14-15 year olds worked over 10 hours

How many hours did you work for money last week? (79)

1. The 14-15 year olds are working longer hours than the 12-13 year olds.
2. In Year 8 (12- 13 year olds), slightly more males than females are working the longer hours, but this is reversed for the Year 10 (14-15 year old) workers.
3. We observe a bimodal distribution, one maximum at 2 hours and the other at 6-7 hours (possibly a Saturday job?).

Comments

1. The figures for *None* represent those pupils who have a regular paid job but did not work in the last week.
2. The bimodal effect already noted could reflect the difference between morning or afternoon work and all-day working.
3. The average hours spent working by those who work in each group is:

Year 8 males	4.5
Year 8 females	4.3
Year 10 males	5.6
Year 10 females	6.0

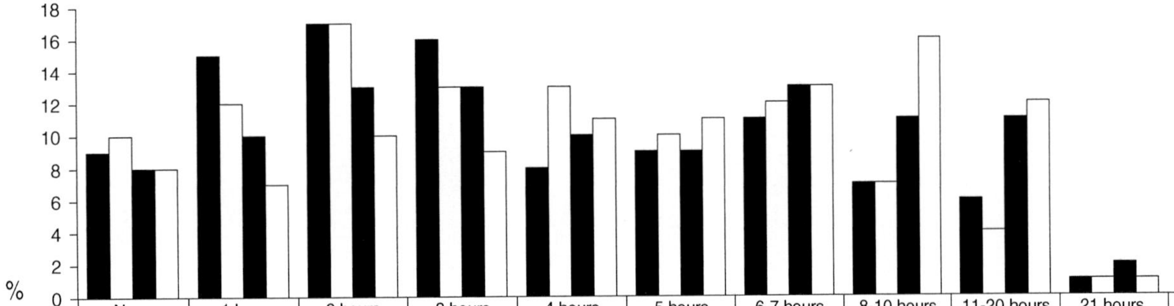

	None	1 hour	2 hours	3 hours	4 hours	5 hours	6-7 hours	8-10 hours	11-20 hours	21 hours or more	Valid responses
■ Yr 8 M	9	15	17	16	8	9	11	7	6	1	621
□ Yr 8 F	10	12	17	13	13	10	12	7	4	1	478
■ Yr 10 M	8	10	13	13	10	9	13	11	11	2	671
□ Yr 10 F	8	7	10	9	11	11	13	16	12	1	697

Money from paid work

Over 17% of 14-15 year olds earned more than £30 *last week*

How much money did you receive last week from your regular paid work? (80)

1. More money was earned by the Year 10 (14-15 year old) workers. There were more males among the high Year 8 earners.
2. Older females earn more than older males in £20-£40 range.
3. 13% of older males report earning over £40 'last week' and the older females are only 2% lower at 11%

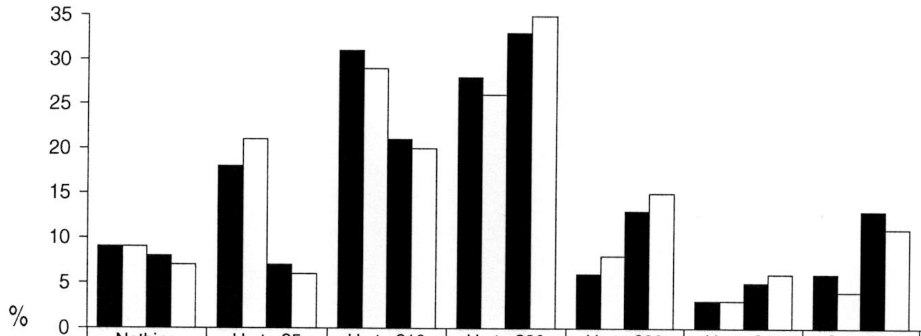

%	Nothing	Up to £5	Up to £10	Up to £20	Up to £30	Up to £40	Over £40	Valid responses
■ Yr 8 M	9	18	31	28	6	3	6	647
□ Yr 8 F	9	21	29	26	8	3	4	500
■ Yr 10 M	8	7	21	33	13	5	13	685
□ Yr 10 F	7	6	20	35	15	6	11	709

Comments

1. The figures for *Nothing* represent those pupils who have a regular paid job but did not work in the last week.
2. These amounts do not reflect the rates paid per hour, but it is possible to calculate these by using the data on the previous page.

Year	8	10
Males (£)	4.42	5.01
Females (£)	4.11	4.26

3. We note that the Year 10 females earn rather less than males of the same age, while on the previous page we find that, on average, they work slightly more hours.
4. The average earnings for workers can also be derived:

Year	8	10
Males (£)	14.54	22.02
Females (£)	13.78	20.81

Pocket money

The older they get
fewer receive weekly pocket money

Do you usually get pocket money?
(74) (Pri.9a)

1. Clearly, the majority receive pocket money each week although the regularity of this income declines as all get older.
2. More females than males receive money as they need it.
3. More males than females receive no pocket money.

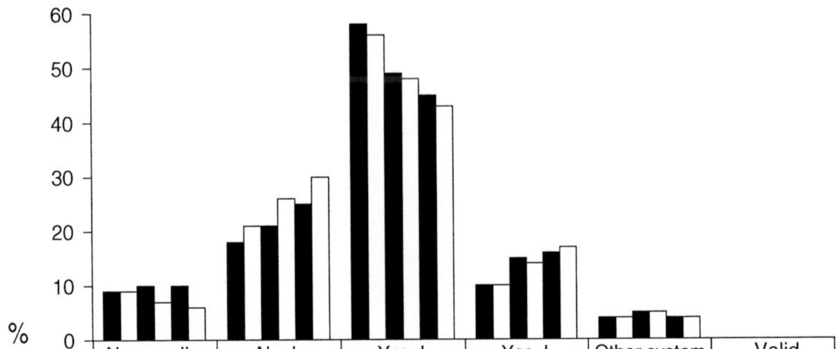

	No, usually none	No, I get money as I need it	Yes, I get money every week	Yes, I get money once a month	Other system	Valid responses
■ Yr 6 M	9	18	58	10	4	2110
□ Yr 6 F	9	21	56	10	4	2058
■ Yr 8 M	10	21	49	15	5	2197
□ Yr 8 F	7	26	48	14	5	2168
■ Yr 10 M	10	25	45	16	4	1908
□ Yr 10 F	6	30	43	17	4	1928

Comments

1. Up to 58% of Year 6 pupils (10-11 year olds) receive weekly pocket money. This falls to around 44% of Year 10 pupils (14-15 year olds) and is possibly replaced by money received from paid employment.
2. As pupils get older, the pattern of receiving pocket money shifts from weekly to 'once a month' and 'as I need it'. Again this may be influenced by the youngsters' ability to undertake paid work.
3. Around 92% of 10-15 year olds do receive pocket money.

Pocket money total

Up to 28% of 14-15 year olds receive more than £10

How much pocket money did you get last time? (75) (Pri.9b)

1. The males' percentages are slightly higher than the females' at the higher pocket money levels, and the Year 10 (14-15 year olds) amounts are greater than the Year 8.
2. Most of the younger pupils received *up to £5* and at least 27% of Year 10s received more than £10.

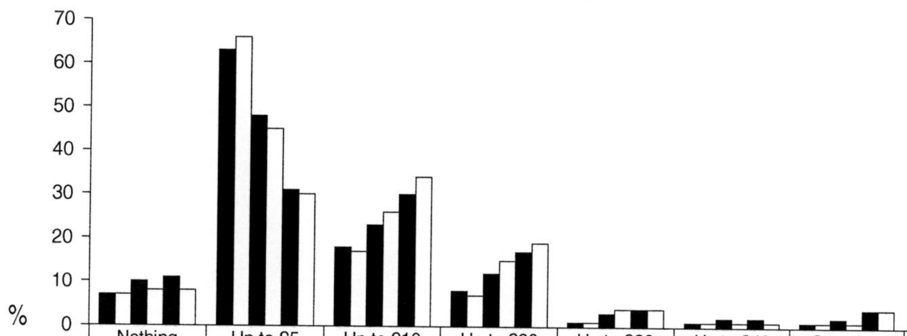

	Nothing	Up to £5	Up to £10	Up to £20	Up to £30	Up to £40	Over £40	Valid responses
■ Yr 6 M	7	63	18	8	1	1	1	1906
□ Yr 6 F	7	66	17	7	1	1	1	1935
■ Yr 8 M	10	48	23	12	3	2	2	2097
□ Yr 8 F	8	45	26	15	4	1	1	2052
■ Yr 10 M	11	31	30	17	4	2	4	1779
□ Yr 10 F	8	30	34	19	4	1	4	1795

Comments

1. We have occasionally had problems in deriving weekly amounts for those young people whose pocket money or allowance is paid monthly.

Total weekly income

14% of the 14-15 year olds received more than £30

Last week's combined income from paid work and pocket money (80a)

1. The majority are found within the £1.01-£10.00 range, around 25% of the Year 10 pupils (14-15 year olds) received more than £20, and 14% of this group received more than £30 'last week'.
2. The table reveals a similar level of higher income for the older pupils, even though we know from page 82 that more females than males are working more than 5 hours a week.

Comments

1. Disposable income is the key to doing many other things, some healthy, others less so. It is certainly a key to lifestyle.
2. The *Nothing* group may include some youngsters that receive money at longer than weekly intervals, or for particular purposes on a negotiated basis.

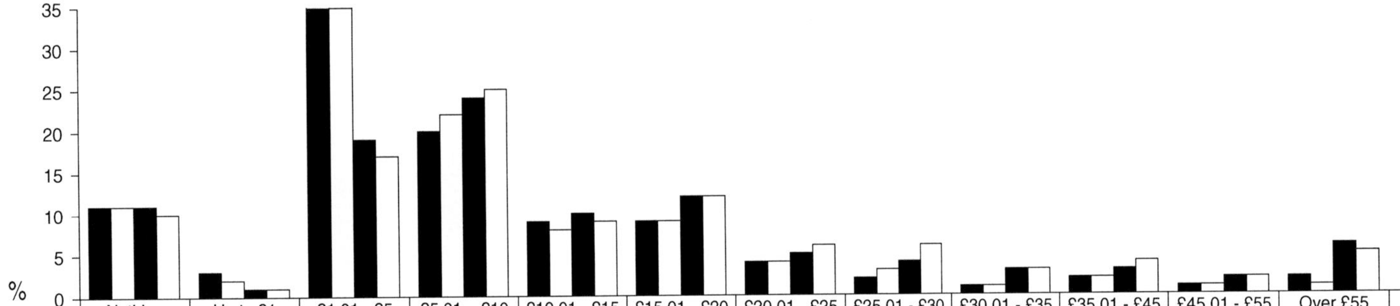

	Nothing	Up to £1	£1.01 - £5	£5.01 - £10	£10.01 - £15	£15.01 - £20	£20.01 - £25	£25.01 - £30	£30.01 - £35	£35.01 - £45	£45.01 - £55	Over £55	Valid responses
■ Yr 8 M	11	3	35	20	9	9	4	2	1	2	1	2	2208
□ Yr 8 F	11	2	35	22	8	9	4	3	1	2	1	1	2170
■ Yr 10 M	11	1	19	24	10	12	5	4	3	3	2	6	1877
□ Yr 10 F	10	1	17	25	9	12	6	6	3	4	2	5	1915

Saving money

Males save more than females

Have you put any of your own money into a savings scheme in the last 7 days? (76)

1. More males than females are savers, with little difference between the year groups for those who save anything.

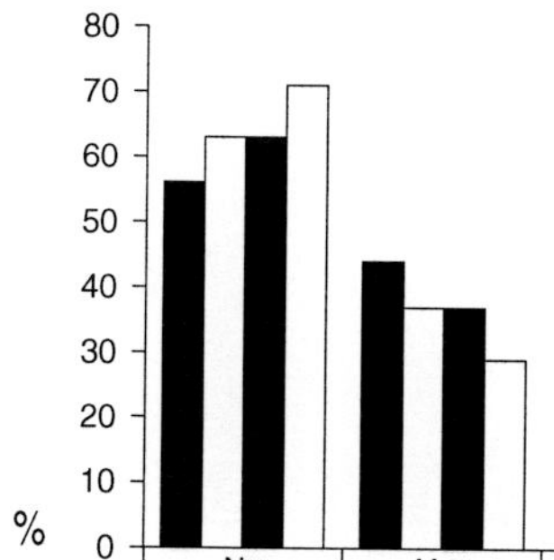

	No	Yes	Valid responses
■ Yr 8 M	56	44	2447
□ Yr 8 F	63	37	2405
■ Yr 10 M	63	37	2148
□ Yr 10 F	71	29	2195

Comments

1. Whether the greater proportion of males than females saving any money is a reflection of preference can only be speculation. Data from page 85 shows the older group to be generally receiving similar weekly amounts but 8% more older males than females are saving money.
2. These levels of saving may cause some surprise — the data certainly challenge the idea that young people are all living just for today.

Spending money

21% of older males spent more than £20

How much of your own money have you spent during the last 7 days? (81)

1. The distribution of percentages shows 'clumping' around certain values, the most obvious being *up to £5.00.*
2. Greater levels of spending over £5 are recorded by the Year 10 respondents. When compared with older males, older females report higher percentages when spending *up to £20*. 9% of older males report spending *over £40* 'during the last week'.

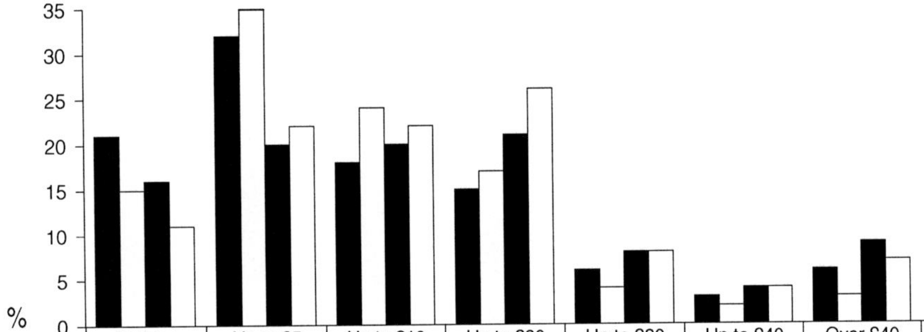

	Nothing	Up to £5	Up to £10	Up to £20	Up to £30	Up to £40	Over £40	Valid responses
■ Yr 8 M	21	32	18	15	6	3	6	1667
□ Yr 8 F	15	35	24	17	4	2	3	1742
■ Yr 10 M	16	20	20	21	8	4	9	1581
□ Yr 10 F	11	22	22	26	8	4	7	1623

Comments

1. This is one of our less 'precise' questions, in the sense that it is extremely difficult for most people to recall a week's spending. Rounding off to a likely figure could explain some of the 'clumping'.

Items bought last week (1)

Crisps remain popular for all groups

During the last 7 days, have you spent any of your own money on the following items? (81) (Pri. 10)

For convenience, this list has been divided into two parts and rearranged into alphabetical order within each part.

1. Within this section *crisps* were bought by at least 18% of all the groups. *Comics/magazines* are also popular items.
2. In Year 10, spending on *alcohol, cigarettes, fares* and *fast food* becomes important. 27% of older females spend on *cosmetics.* In Year 6, 27% of males spend on *arcade games* and 22% of females spend on *books.*
3. Overall, more females than males spend money on *cigarettes, clothes, comics/magazines, cosmetics,* and *discos.*

Comments

1. This list does not indicate the relative amounts spent on these different items, so it is not possible to reflect upon the amount of money spent on some of the less desirable activities.
2. Gender and age differences provide interesting comparisons particularly spending on *alcohol, books,* and *cigarettes.* The differences between groups is not restricted to this year's data. For example, over the years, we have seen a sharp reduction in book purchasing after the age of 11.

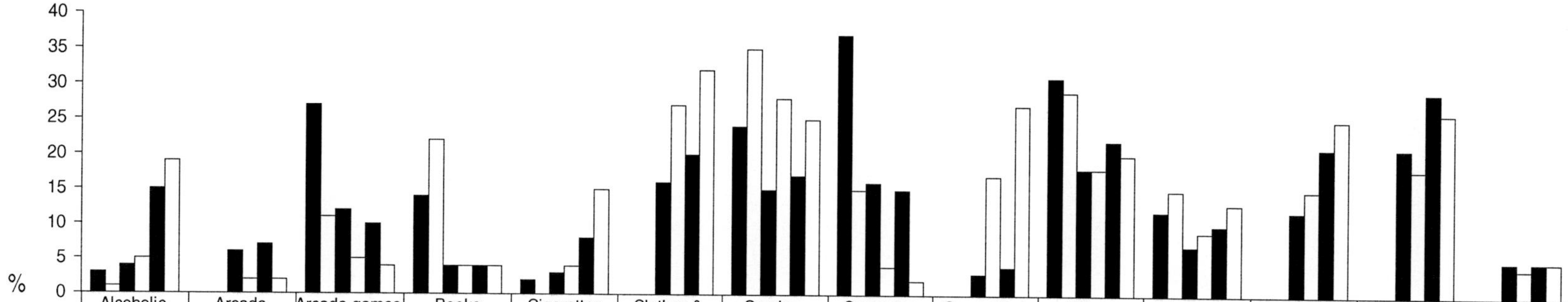

	Alcoholic drinks	Arcade gambling	Arcade games (for fun)	Books	Cigarettes	Clothes & footwear	Comics, Magazines	Computer games	Cosmetics/ Toiletries	Crisps	Discos or clubs	Fares	Fast food (hot)	Fresh fruit	Available sample
■ Yr 6 M	3	*	27	14	2	*	24	37	*	31	12	*	*	*	2422
□ Yr 6 F	1	*	11	22	0	*	35	15	*	29	15	*	*	*	2300
■ Yr 8 M	4	6	12	4	3	16	15	16	3	18	7	12	21	5	3064
□ Yr 8 F	5	2	5	4	4	27	28	4	17	18	9	15	18	4	2865
■ Yr 10 M	15	7	10	4	8	20	17	15	4	22	10	21	29	5	2450
□ Yr 10 F	19	2	4	4	15	32	25	2	27	20	13	25	26	5	2425

* Options not available for Year 6

Items bought last week (2)

Sweets remain the favourite item

During the last 7 days, have you spent any of your own money on the following items? (81) (Pri. 10)

For convenience, this list has been divided into two parts and rearranged into alphabetical order within each part.

1. Within this section *records/CD/tapes*, *soft drinks* and *sweets* are clearly the items on which money was most frequently spent.
2. Gender differences in which higher percentages of males report are apparent for items such as *leisure/sports centres* and *sports equipment*. Female biased responses are observed for items such as *pets, school equipment* and *sweets*.

Comments

1. This list does not indicate the relative amounts spent on these different items, so it is not possible to reflect upon the amount of money spent on some of the less desirable activities.
2. Spending on *sweets* has remained the favourite item for many years and older females consistently report spending most of their money on this item – 58% of 14-15 year old females selected *sweets* in 1999.

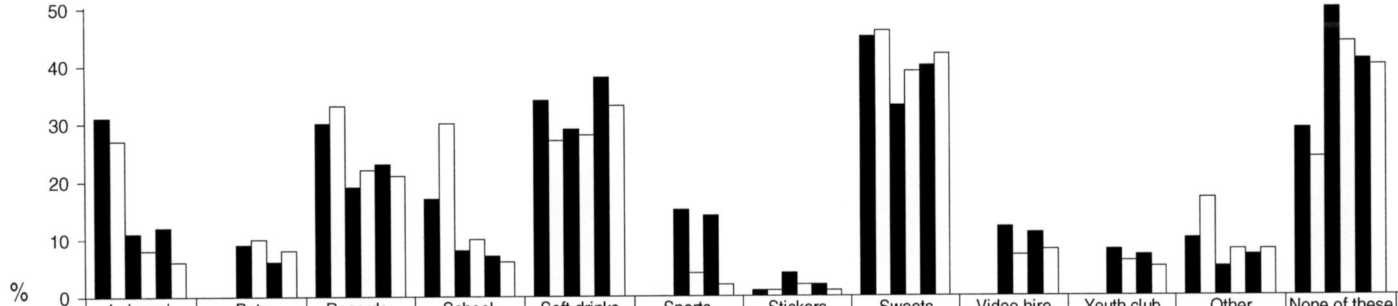

	Leisure/ sports centre	Pets	Records, CDs, tapes	School equipment	Soft drinks	Sports equipment	Stickers	Sweets	Video hire	Youth club	Other	None of these	Available sample
■ Yr 6 M	31	*	30	17	34	*	1	45	*	*	10	29	2422
□ Yr 6 F	27	*	33	30	27	*	1	46	*	*	17	24	2300
■ Yr 8 M	11	9	19	8	29	15	4	33	12	8	5	50	3064
□ Yr 8 F	8	10	22	10	28	4	2	39	7	6	8	44	2865
■ Yr 10 M	12	6	23	7	38	14	2	40	11	7	7	41	2450
□ Yr 10 F	6	8	21	6	33	2	1	42	8	5	8	40	2425

* Options not available for Year 6

Draw tickets and 'Instants'

More 14-15 year-old males own National Lottery draw tickets

Who paid over your money for National Lottery products in the last 7 days? (82 & 83)

1. Between 2%-8% owned a lottery ticket or scratch card.
2. Most of the tickets and cards owned by the Year 10 (14-15 years old) males were purchased themselves.

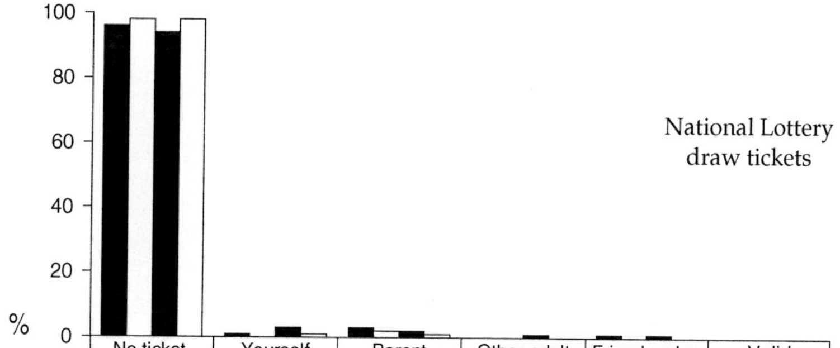

	No ticket bought	Yourself	Parent	Other adult	Friend under 16 years	Valid responses
■ Yr 8 M	96	1	3	0	1	2065
□ Yr 8 F	98	0	2	0	0	2087
■ Yr 10 M	94	3	2	1	1	1878
□ Yr 10 F	98	1	1	0	0	1913

Comments

1. This question was introduced in 1996 and in recent years we have seen slightly fewer older males owning tickets.
2. Purchase of these tickets by under-16s is illegal, and so is the collection of any prize. However, a winning ticket could be claimed on their behalf by an adult, if they have not written their own name on the ticket.
3. We have heard it suggested that just the successful purchase of a ticket can itself count as a successful 'gamble' for some of these young people.

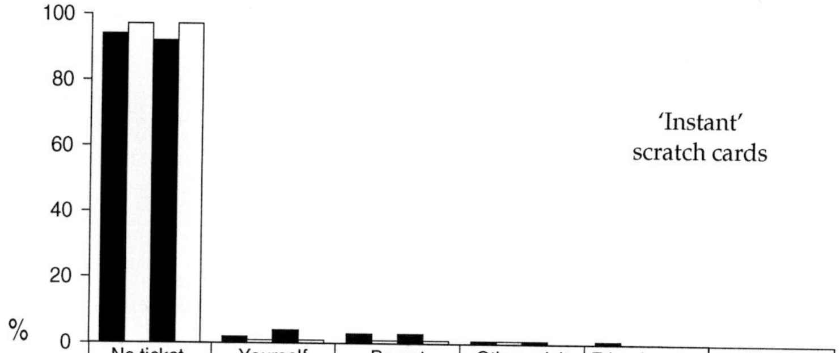

	No ticket bought	Yourself	Parent	Other adult	Friend under 16 years	Valid responses
■ Yr 8 M	94	2	3	1	1	1372
□ Yr 8 F	97	1	1	1	0	1466
■ Yr 10 M	92	4	3	1	0	1259
□ Yr 10 F	97	1	1	0	0	1319

7 Exercise and Sport

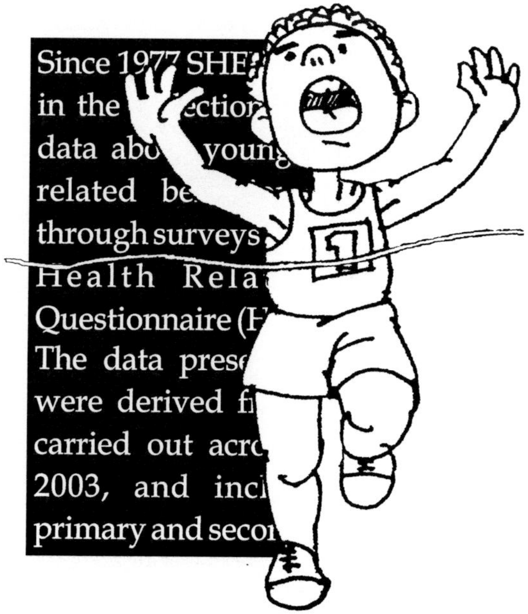

There is widespread concern at what appear to be generally low levels of physical activity in the daily life of young people. If, as has been suggested, the four-year-olds starting in our primary schools will have a life expectancy in excess of a hundred years, then we need to ensure that they have a healthy respect for the role that physical fitness plays in their quality and enjoyment of life. The questions in this section cover physical activity, perceived fitness, and which sporting activities (if any) young people took part in out of school time.

Question

Enjoying sport

47% of the 10-11 year old females enjoy physical activities *a lot*

How much do you enjoy physical activities? (84) (Pri.22)

1. There is a large gender difference: far fewer females in each year group report liking sport *a lot*. The gender difference is already distinct in Year 6 (10-11 year olds) but the gap becomes wider as the age of the pupils increase.
2. The difference is especially marked in Year 10, nearly half as many females as males say they enjoy physical activities *a lot*.
3. It is noticeable, that as males get older fewer respond that they enjoy physical activities *a lot*.
4. Nevertheless, around 80% of primary school pupils and up to 87% of the older groups enjoy sport *quite a lot* or *a lot*.

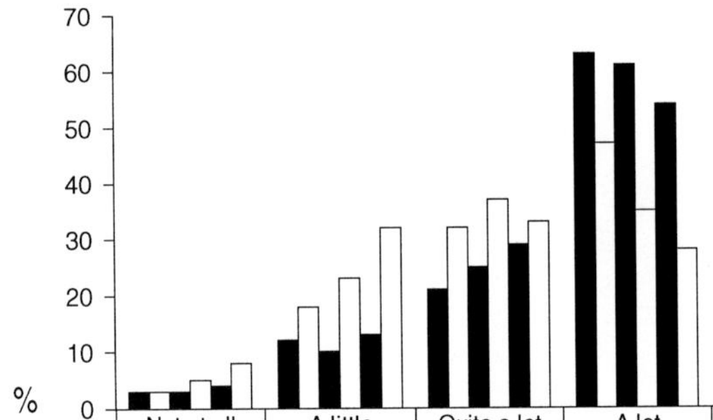

	Not at all	A little	Quite a lot	A lot	Valid responses
■ Yr 6 M	3	12	21	63	2369
□ Yr 6 F	3	18	32	47	2272
■ Yr 8 M	3	10	25	61	2337
□ Yr 8 F	5	23	37	35	2317
■ Yr 10 M	4	13	29	54	2120
□ Yr 10 F	8	32	33	28	2133

Comments

1. 54% of 14-15 year old males report enjoying physical activities *a lot*. Since 1999, this percentage has ranged between 54%-59% and, generally, shown a similar decline in relation to age. Is it realistic to attempt to reverse this decline and try to achieve a level of 60% for all age groups?
2. Is it uncool for females in secondary schools to show an interest in sport?
3. Does the changing room experience for females play a role in the rapid decline in an interest in physical activity? Many schools have found that by installing shower curtains in their changing rooms they have seen a positive effect on the interest their female students show for PE.
4. There is also a call for PE specialists to look into the provision of the types of activity that will appeal to the groups involved. Basketball is seen to have some success with female students; what other activities might be similarly attractive to them?

Participation in active sports (1)

Riding a bicycle still remains the most popular activity for all pupils

Sports and activities participated in, at least weekly, during the past 12 months outside school (87a) (Pri.25)

The responses to this question have been divided into three pages.

1. These figures should be seen in the context of the figures on the following pages.
2. *Riding a bicycle* still remains a popular activity for all groups.
3. *Jogging/Running for exercise* involves all groups but the levels are not maintained.

Comments

1. These sports and activities are carried out in the pupils' own time or in school clubs and not in school lessons.
2. For the females, interest in *soccer, hockey, tennis* and *basketball*, increases from primary to secondary school and then declines as they reach 14-15 years old. Interest in *netball, riding a bike* and *running for exercise/jogging*, generally decreases as the females get older.
3. Interest in soccer, for the females, is slightly higher than last year. In America and Canada, female soccer leagues have proved a great success, and soccer is one of the fastest growing women's sports in the UK.

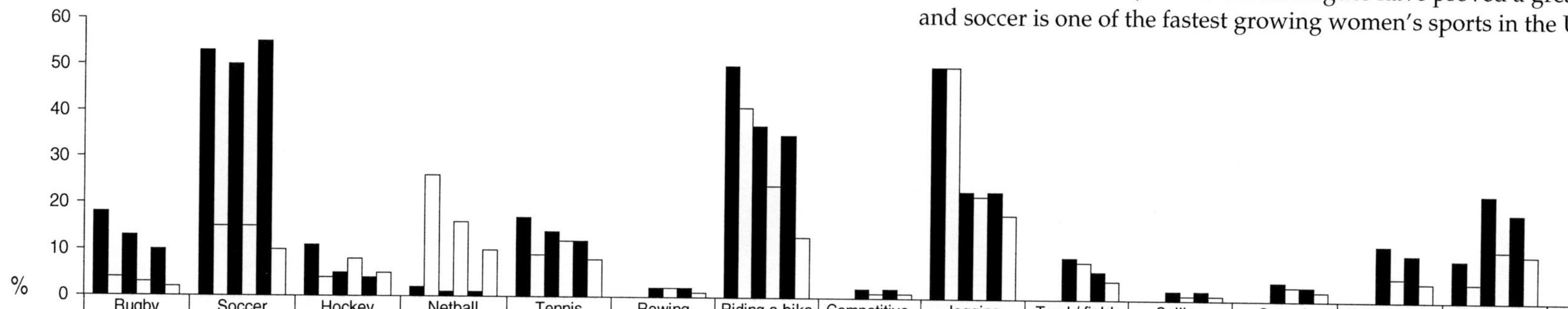

	Rugby	Soccer	Hockey	Netball	Tennis	Rowing	Riding a bike	Competitive cycling	** Jogging	Track/ field events	Sailing	Squash	Table tennis	Basketball	Available sample
■ Yr 6 M	18	53	11	2	17	*	50	*	50	*	*	*	*	9	2422
□ Yr 6 F	4	15	4	26	9	*	41	*	50	*	*	*	*	4	2300
■ Yr 8 M	13	50	5	1	14	2	37	2	23	9	2	4	12	23	3064
□ Yr 8 F	3	15	8	16	12	2	24	1	22	8	1	3	5	11	2865
■ Yr 10 M	10	55	4	1	12	2	35	2	23	6	2	3	10	19	2450
□ Yr 10 F	2	10	5	10	8	1	13	1	18	4	1	2	4	10	2425

* Options not available for Year 6

** *Jogging* appears as *Running for exercise* for Year 6

Participation in active sports (2)

Swimming remains a popular activity particularly with younger people

Sports and activities participated in, at least weekly, during the past 12 months outside school (87b) (Pri.25)

The responses to this question have been divided into three pages.

1. *Swimming* is the most popular activity with most age groups and genders in this section.
2. *Dancing/gymnastics* are undertaken, outside school, each week by 47% of Year 6 females.
3. *Fitness exercises* is the only activity that shows an upward trend for all pupils in the secondary age group in this section.

Comments

1. American football may be becoming more popular in this country with new clubs forming but is not reflected in figures in recent years. Martial arts continue to receive interest from the younger males.
2. Dancing remains popular with females across the age range. Although it declines as age increases, perhaps this is an activity that could be further encouraged in secondary schools.

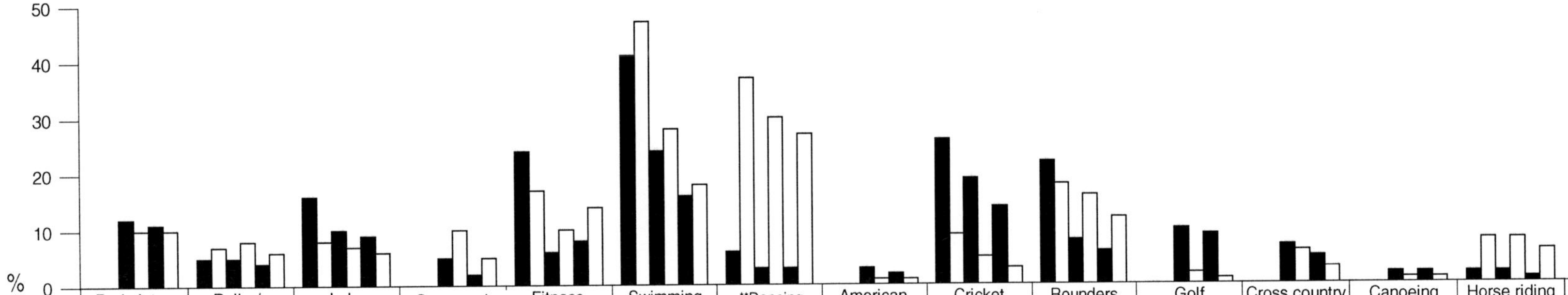

	Badminton	Roller/ Ice skating	Judo, Karate, Boxing	**Gymnastics	Fitness exercises	Swimming	**Dancing	American football	Cricket	Rounders	Golf	Cross country	Canoeing	Horse riding	Available sample
■ Yr 6 M	*	5	16	*	24	41	6	*	26	22	*	*	*	2	2422
□ Yr 6 F	*	7	8	*	17	47	37	*	9	18	*	*	*	8	2300
■ Yr 8 M	12	5	10	5	6	24	3	3	19	8	10	7	2	2	3064
□ Yr 8 F	10	8	7	10	10	28	30	1	5	16	2	6	1	8	2865
■ Yr 10 M	11	4	9	2	8	16	3	2	14	6	9	5	2	1	2450
□ Yr 10 F	10	6	6	5	14	18	27	1	3	12	1	3	1	6	2425

* Options not available for Year 6

** *Gymnastics/Dancing* appears as one item for Year 6

Participation in active sports (3)

Up to 38% of females choose *going for a walk*

Sports and activities participated in, at least weekly, during the past 12 months outside school (80c) (Pri.25)

The responses to this question have been divided into three pages.

1. 16% of the Year 10 females and 10% of the Year 8 females do not participate in any active sport on a weekly basis.
2. The considerable increase in popularity of weight training for the older males is against the general trend of decreasing involvement.
3. *Going for walks* was a new category in 2002 and is a popular activity with up to 38% of females.

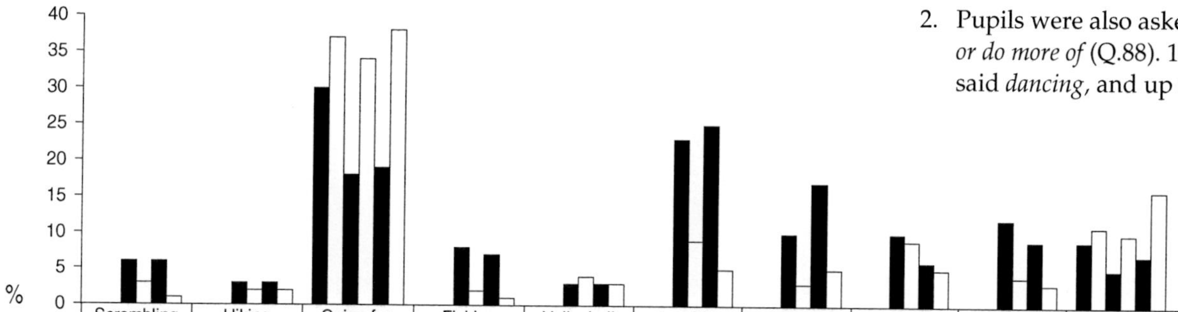

	Scrambling	Hiking	Going for walks	Fishing	Volleyball	5-a-side football	Weight training	** Roller blading	Skateboarding	No active sports at all	Available sample
■ Yr 6 M	*	*	30	*	*	*	*	*	*	9	2422
□ Yr 6 F	*	*	37	*	*	*	*	*	*	11	2300
■ Yr 8 M	6	3	18	8	3	23	10	10	12	5	3064
□ Yr 8 F	3	2	34	2	4	9	3	9	4	10	2865
■ Yr 10 M	6	3	19	7	3	25	17	6	9	7	2450
□ Yr 10 F	1	2	38	1	3	5	5	5	3	16	2425

* Options not available for Year 6

** *Rollerblading* appears as *Roller skating* for Year 6

Comments

1. Comparing the Year 10 female *no active sports at all* data since 1992 shows a range from 14%-23%. In the past five years the average has been around 20%.

1992	*19%*	1998	*14%*
1993	*18%*	1999	*20%*
1994	*18%*	2000	*21%*
1995	*23%*	2001	*22%*
1996	*20%*	2002	*14%*
1997	*19%*	2003	*16%*

2. Pupils were also asked about which activites they *would like to start doing or do more of* (Q.88). 10% of females said *roller/ice skating*, 13% of females said *dancing*, and up to 17% of older females said *swimming*.

Participation in 'pub/club' sports

Up to 25% of males play snooker or pool each week

Sports and activities participated in, at least weekly, during the past 12 months outside school (87d)

1. There is a distinct gender difference seen in the data for these options.
2. 11% of the males play darts on a weekly basis and over 20% of them regularly play snooker and pool.

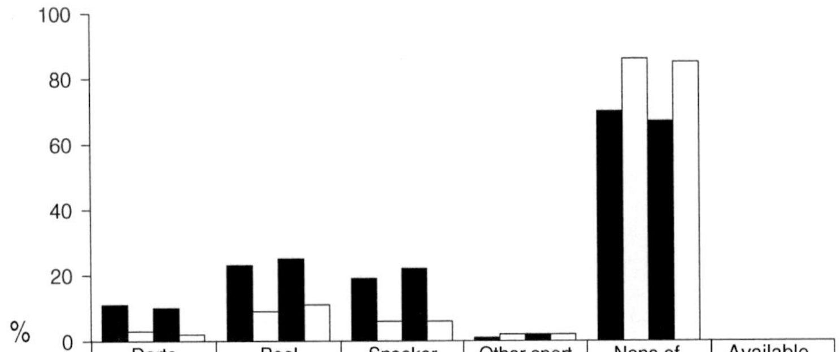

	Darts	Pool	Snooker	Other sport	None of the above	Available sample
■ Yr 8 M	11	23	19	1	70	3064
□ Yr 8 F	3	9	6	2	86	2865
■ Yr 10 M	10	25	22	2	67	2450
□ Yr 10 F	2	11	6	2	85	2425

Comments

1. Are these activities being pursued within a pub setting, or at a youth club, or do these youngsters have access to pool tables etc at home? We can see that among Year 10 males that the more often they take part in these games, the more often they have drunk alcohol in the previous week:

   Mean number of days drinking alcohol last week for different frequencies of 'pub and club' sports.

	Pool	Snooker	Darts
Never or hardly ever	0.7	0.8	0.8
Once or twice in a month	0.8	0.8	1.1
Weekly	1.0	0.9	1.0
Twice a week or more	1.0	1.0	1.0

2. These highly social games, like many computer games, also require hand and eye co-ordination skills, as well as some strategic thought.

Personal fitness

26% of 14-15 year old females think they are *unfit* or *very unfit*

How fit do you think you are? (85) (Pri.20)

1. More Year 6 males continue to assess themselves as *very fit* than any of the other groups.
2. 26% of the Year 10 (14-15 year old) females describe themselves as *unfit* or *very unfit*.
3. Perceived fitness declines with age in males and females.

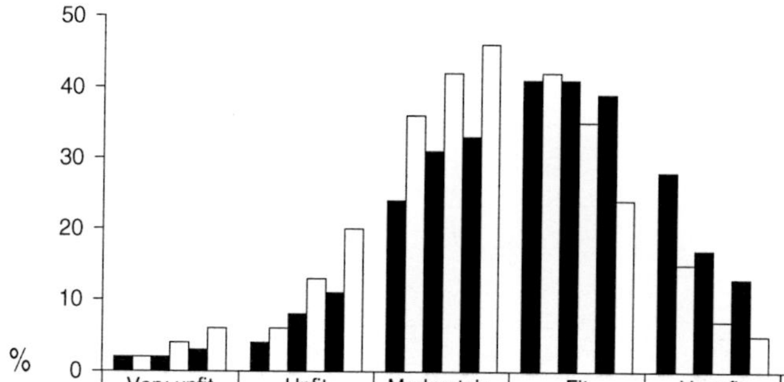

	Very unfit	Unfit	Moderately fit	Fit	Very fit	Valid responses
■ Yr 6 M	2	4	24	41	28	2378
□ Yr 6 F	2	6	36	42	15	2278
■ Yr 8 M	2	8	31	41	17	2325
□ Yr 8 F	4	13	42	35	7	2313
■ Yr 10 M	3	11	33	39	13	2112
□ Yr 10 F	6	20	46	24	5	2129

Comments

1. The higher self-assessment of the males is consistent with their higher participation in sporting activities.
2. Do the females see themselves as less fit than the males because they participate in less physical activity or indeed are they less fit than the males?
3. This subjective method of assessing fitness may not seem very rigorous, but individual physiological measurements, in conjunction with similar questions, have shown good agreement.

Aerobic exercise

Over 86% of 10-15 year olds report exercising at least once *last week*

How many times last week did you exercise and have to breathe harder and faster? (86) (Pri.21)

1. Over 86% of all groups report exercising at least once last week, but again the gap is seen to widen between males and females among the frequent exercisers as they increase in age.
2. Between 9%-14% of over 13,000 10-15 year olds, report taking no exercise *last week.*
3. Up to 25% of all males and between 30%-41% of all females report doing no exercise or exercising only once *last week.*

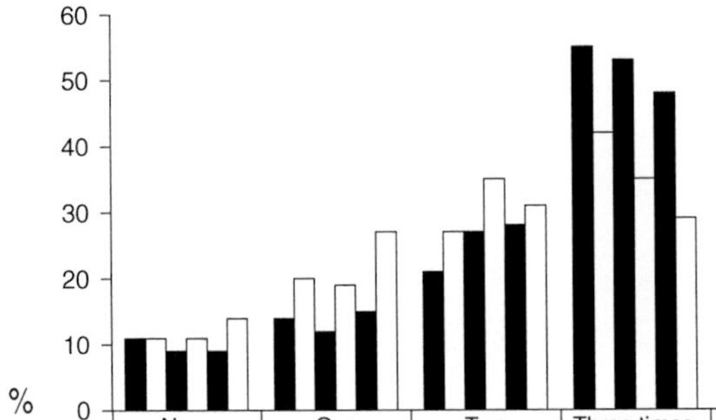

	None	One	Two	Three times or more	Valid responses
■ Yr 6 M	11	14	21	55	2370
□ Yr 6 F	11	20	27	42	2272
■ Yr 8 M	9	12	27	53	2329
□ Yr 8 F	11	19	35	35	2296
■ Yr 10 M	9	15	28	48	2113
□ Yr 10 F	14	27	31	29	2116

Comments

1. The data suggest that around 50% of males, and between 29%-42% of females, report exercising vigorously three times or more.
2. We have increasing opportunities for youngsters to adopt sedentary lifestyles: many youngsters today have seemingly endless choices for the time they spend watching television with the increased viewing options available on satellite TV, they even have televisions in their rooms; or they spend time playing computer games; and indeed the popularity of surfing the Internet is increasing on a daily basis. But how much do young people depend on parents/carers for permission and support to be active?
3. Are we observing the collection of mini time-bombs where youngsters are choosing leisure options that are likely to have a detrimental effect to their general health and fitness in the years to come?
4. The question has in mind the old recommendation of exercising vigorously for at least 20 minutes a time, three times a week. Current recommendations are more likely to suggest *daily* exercise.

8 Social and Personal

The questions included in this group refer to social relationships, sources of information about sex, school lessons and problem-sharing. Questions to discover the pupils' awareness about contraceptive methods and services are also included.

Question

8 Social and Personal

Meeting others

Around 28%
are *quite* or *very uneasy*

How do you usually feel when meeting people of your own age for the first time? (56)

1. Males are more likely to say that they are *at ease*. The Year 10 pupils express slightly more confidence than the Year 8 pupils. However, the differences are not very large.
2. Around 28% are *quite* or *very uneasy*.

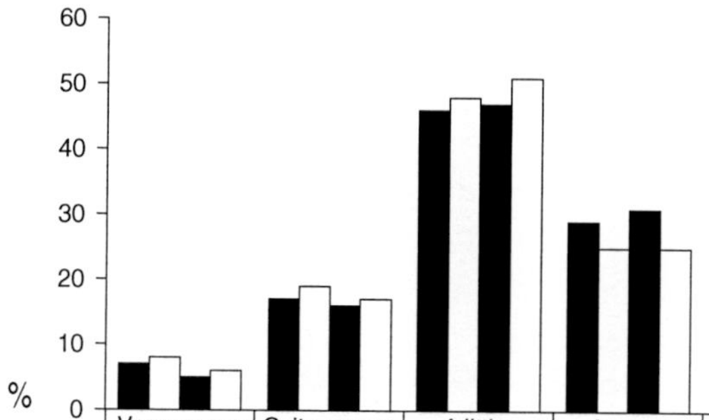

	Very uneasy	Quite uneasy	A little uneasy	At ease	Valid responses
■ Yr 8 M	7	17	46	29	2656
□ Yr 8 F	8	19	48	25	2577
■ Yr 10 M	5	16	47	31	2241
□ Yr 10 F	6	17	51	25	2237

Comments

1. This question is specific to age and does not refer to the 'opposite sex' as in previous years, and is closely related to our measurement of self-esteem (page 118), which includes questions about self-confidence.
2. Should we be surprised that around a quarter of young people in this ample, aged from 12-15 years, say they are *quite* or *very* uneasy when meeting people of their own age for the first time?

Information about sex (1)

School lessons are an important source of information

Which of these is your main source of information about sex? (61)

1. Between Years 8 and 10 we see a trend away from *parents* and *school lessons*, and a trend towards friends.
2. There are quite striking gender differences with respect to *TV or films* and *magazines.*
3. The main source of information for males are *school lessons.* Younger females prefer *parents* and older females choose *friends* as their main source of information about sex.

Comments

1. Respondents are asked to choose their main source, but this may not necessarily be their most accurate source.
2. 'Information about sex' could mean different things to different people, and the range of preferred sources presented here may reflect these differences.
3. *School lessons* are an important source of information and schools are conscientious in their teaching about sex and relationships, but teaching about parenthood, relationships and the prevention of infection is often poor (OFSTED, *Education and Health* 2002:20(2), 38-39).

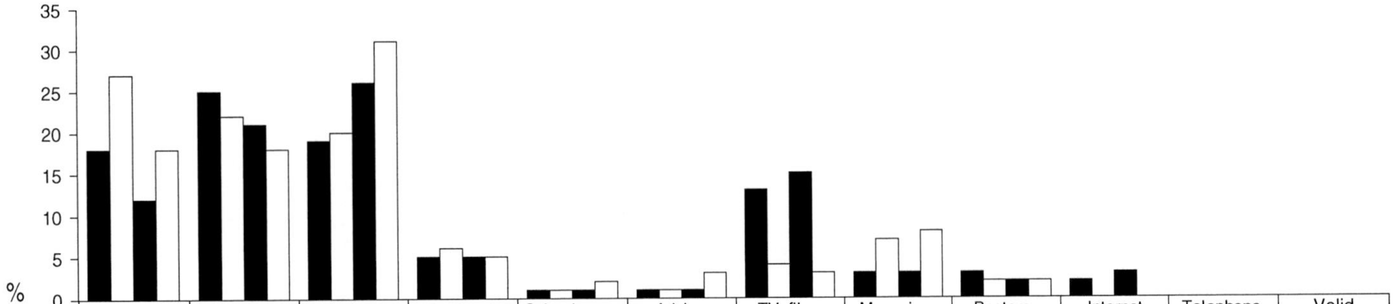

	My parents	School lessons	Friends	Brothers, sisters, other relations	School nurse	Advice Centre e.g. Family Planning	TV, films	Magazines	Posters, leaflets, reference books	Internet	Telephone helpline	Valid responses
■ Yr 8 M	18	25	19	5	1	1	13	3	3	2	0	2530
□ Yr 8 F	27	22	20	6	1	1	4	7	2	0	0	2469
■ Yr 10 M	12	21	26	5	1	1	15	3	2	3	0	2101
□ Yr 10 F	18	18	31	5	2	3	3	8	2	0	0	2133

Information about sex (2)

My parents topped the list

Which of these do you think should be your main source of information about sex? (62)

1. *Parents* are the preferred group particularly for Year 8 females, with school lessons second.

Comments

1. These higher percentages for parents compared with the previous table do not necessarily mean that pupils feel their parents are failing them. The 'should' condition seems to refer to an ideal world where information can be exchanged without constraint on either side. Many parents find it difficult to talk openly and frankly about sex with their children and often they are thankful to know that the school is doing something.

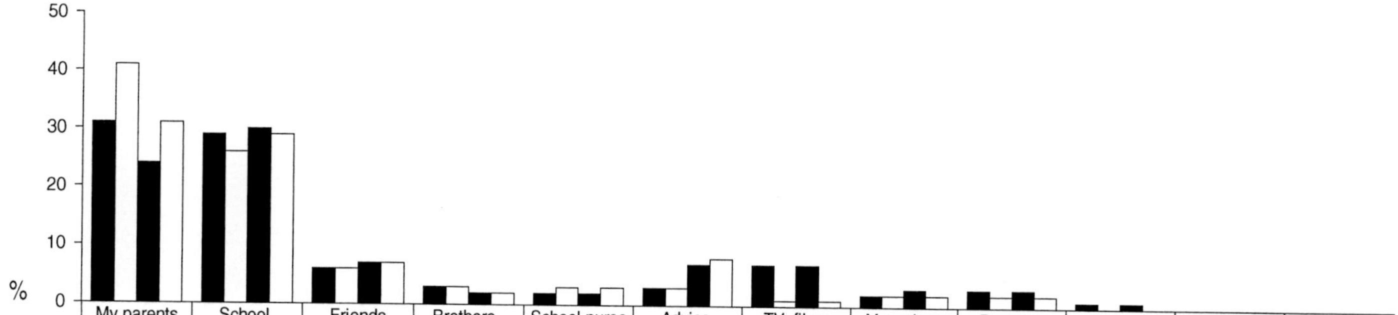

	My parents	School lessons	Friends	Brothers, sisters, other relations	School nurse	Advice Centre e.g. Family Planning	TV, films	Magazines	Posters, leaflets, reference books	Internet	Telephone helpline	Valid responses
■ Yr 8 M	31	29	6	3	2	3	7	2	3	1	0	2602
□ Yr 8 F	41	26	6	3	3	3	1	2	2	0	0	2541
■ Yr 10 M	24	30	7	2	2	7	7	3	3	1	0	2168
□ Yr 10 F	31	29	7	2	3	8	1	2	2	0	0	2172

Useful school lessons

Most lessons in the list are reported to be less 'useful' as pupils get older

How useful have you found lessons about the following subjects? (63)

Responses to 'quite useful / very useful'

1. Lessons about *Drug education, Safety, Physical Activity* and *Sex and Relationships education* are the most useful for both age groups and genders.
2. Least useful are *PSHE* and *Citizenship* lessons.
3. It is noticeable how 'usefulness' declines with age for all subjects except *Sex and Relationships education.*
4. The *Healthy eating* lessons appear to be less 'useful' as reported by older pupils e.g. 43% of 12-13 year old females find these lessons 'quite useful/very useful', compared with 29% of the 14-15 year old females.

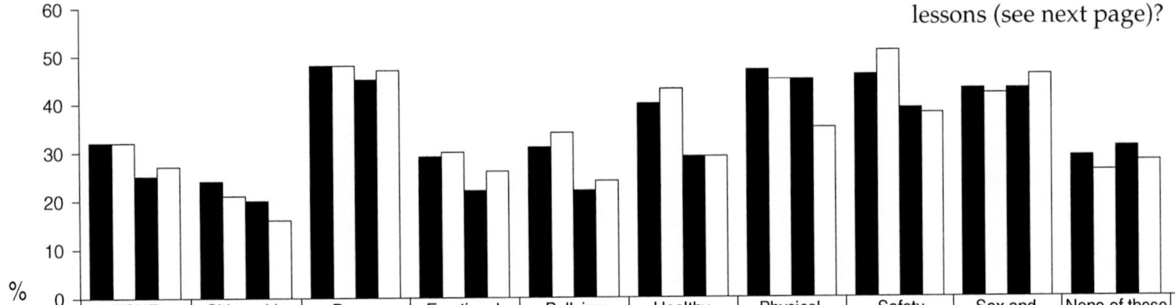

	PSHE	Citizenship	Drugs (legal/ illegal)	Emotional health and well-being	Bullying	Healthy eating	Physical activity	Safety	Sex and relationship education	None of these	Available sample
■ Yr 8 M	32	24	48	29	31	40	47	46	43	29	3064
□ Yr 8 F	32	21	48	30	34	43	45	51	42	26	2865
■ Yr 10 M	25	20	45	22	22	29	45	39	43	31	2450
□ Yr 10 F	27	16	47	26	24	29	35	38	46	28	2425

Comments

1. We first asked this question in 1999. The range of lesson options has changed but the 'usefulness' scale has remained. Pupils are asked to 'circle one number for each answer' and each number refers to a scale of 'usefulness'. This scale ranges from *can't remember any, not at all useful, some use, quite useful,* to *very useful.*
2. The drugs subject is written as 'Drug education (including alcohol and tobacco)' in the current version of the questionnaire.
3. What factors influence the degrees of 'usefulness' reported for each subject?
4. Is it surprising that the reported levels of 'usefulness' decline with age? How do these data relate to the general question about enjoying school lessons (see next page)?

Enjoyable school lessons

Up to 34% report enjoying 'all' or 'most' school lessons

How many school lessons do you enjoy at school? (9)

1. The majority of 12-15 year olds report enjoying 'most' or 'about half' of their school lessons.
2. Up to 34% report enjoying 'all' or 'most' school lessons.
3. For the majority, the percentages remain similar across gender and age groups. Slightly more females (32%) compared with males, report enjoying 'most' of their lessons.
4. More younger males (38%), compared with females and older males report enjoying 'less than half ' or 'hardly any' lessons.

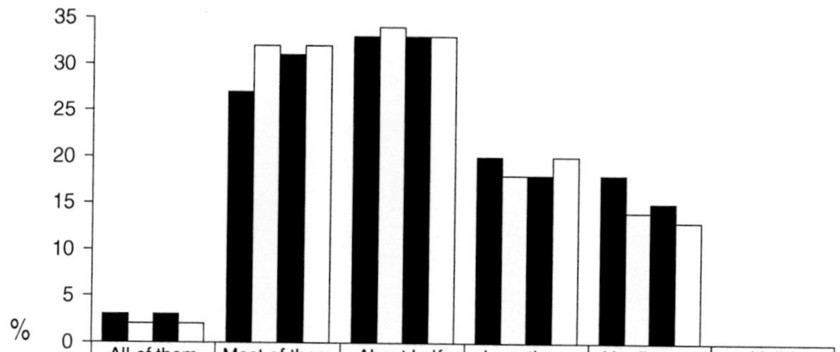

	All of them	Most of them	About half of them	Less than half of them	Hardly any of them	Valid responses
■ Yr 8 M	3	27	33	20	18	2864
□ Yr 8 F	2	32	34	18	14	2725
■ Yr 10 M	3	31	33	18	15	2369
□ Yr 10 F	2	32	33	20	13	2346

Comments

1. This is the second time we have included this question and it appears early on in the questionnaire (question number 9).
2. The question is about school lessons in general and not subject specific.
3. There appears to be slight difference, as pupils get older, in those reporting 'enjoying' lessons.

We found a positive relationship between pupils enjoying lessons and finding PSHE lessons useful. Those pupils that report enjoying 'all' or 'most' lessons were also more likely to rate the subjects on the list (see previous page) as 'quite useful' or 'very useful'.

GCSEs

53% of 14-15 year olds expect good grades at GCSEs

Which of these statements about GCSEs best describes you? (10)

1. The majority of 12-15 year olds *expect to take several GCSEs and get mostly good grades (A-C).*
2. As pupils get older their expectations, about taking more GCSEs and getting good grades, increase.
3. Females report higher expectations than males and younger males report the lowest levels of expectation with 22% expecting to take less than 5 GCSEs.

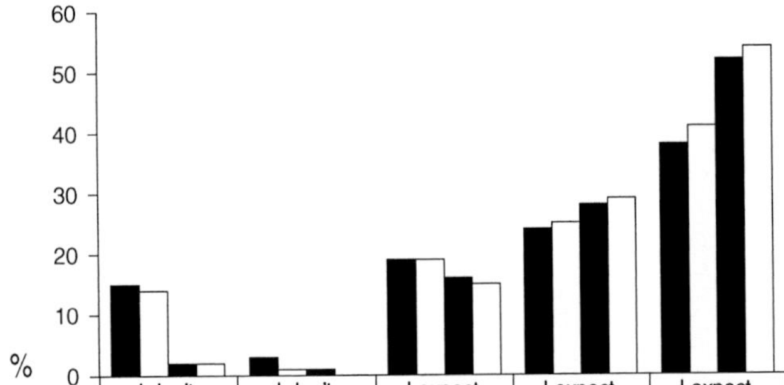

	I don't know what GCSEs I'm going to	I don't expect to take any GCSEs	I expect to take a few GCSEs (1-4)	I expect to take several GCSEs (5+)	I expect to take several GCSEs (A-C)	Valid responses
■ Yr 8 M	15	3	19	24	38	2865
□ Yr 8 F	14	1	19	25	41	2702
■ Yr 10 M	2	1	16	28	52	2359
□ Yr 10 F	2	0	15	29	54	2337

Comments

1. This is the second time we have asked this question.
2. By the time they are 13 years old, around 40% of pupils expect good grades at GCSEs. This figure rises to 53% by the time they reach 15 years of age.
3. Do the responses confirm our understanding of young people's expectations of involvement with GCSEs? Do we think more young people would expect to get good grades?
4. In England in 2003, 53% of pupils achieved GCSEs at grades A-C (http:// www.dfes.gov.uk/rsgateway).

After Year 11

60% of 14-15 year old females want to continue with full-time education

After the end of Year 11 what would you like to do? (11)

Responses to 'Yes'

1. From this sample, 60% of 14-15 year old females want to to continue in full-time education after Year 11 and 31% want to stay in the neighbourhood where they live.
2. For the older males, 49% want to continue in full-time education and 42% want to get training for a skilled job.
3. The aspirations of the younger pupils lie in the direction of skills training and not full-time education or finding a job.
4. Around 28% responded to the option *Finding a job as soon as you can.*

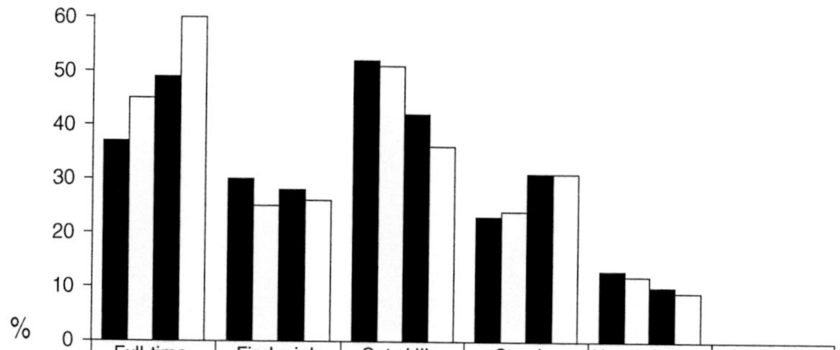

	Full-time education	Find a job	Get skills training	Stay in the neighbourhood	None of these	Available sample
■ Yr 8 M	37	30	52	23	13	3064
□ Yr 8 F	45	25	51	24	12	2865
■ Yr 10 M	49	28	42	31	10	2450
□ Yr 10 F	60	26	36	31	9	2425

Comments

1. This is the second time this question has been asked. Pupils are asked to circle a three point scale ranging from *0=No, 1=Don't know* and *2=Yes* in response to four options.
2. It is noticeable that the gender and age differences show that, as the females get older, more are interested in continuing full-time education and staying in their neighbourhood. As they get older the females are less interested in *finding a job as soon as you can* and getting training for a skilled job.
3. Both males and females show more of an interest in staying in the neighbourhood as they get older.
4. Figures from the Department for Education and Skills show that at the end of 2003, 72% of 16 year olds and 60% of 17 year olds in England were in full-time education. (http://www.dfes.gov.uk/rsgateway).

Worries

Around 28% of 10-11 year olds worry about *family problems*

How much do you worry about these problems? (59) (Pri.49)

Responses to 'quite a lot / a lot'

1. *Family problems* cause concern for around 28% of 10-11 year olds.
2. *The way you look* worries the 12-15 year old females more than anything else on the list.
3. For 14-15 year old males, problems with *school-work* and *career* appears to worry them the most.
4. The *none of these* category shows that more females than males worry about things in the list.

Comments

1. These problems do not necessarily concern the respondents themselves, they could indicate worry about family or friends or even 'society'.
2. As girls grow older, higher percentages worry about all the categories listed here apart from *puberty and growing up* and *bullying*.
3. The percentage of 10-11 year olds, that worry about *family problems*, is simlar when compared with figures from recent years.
4. Since 1991, fewer young people worry 'about the way they look' although it has always been the main worry for 14-15 year old females (SHEU, 2004, 'Trends-Young People and Emotional Health and Well-Being 1983-2003').

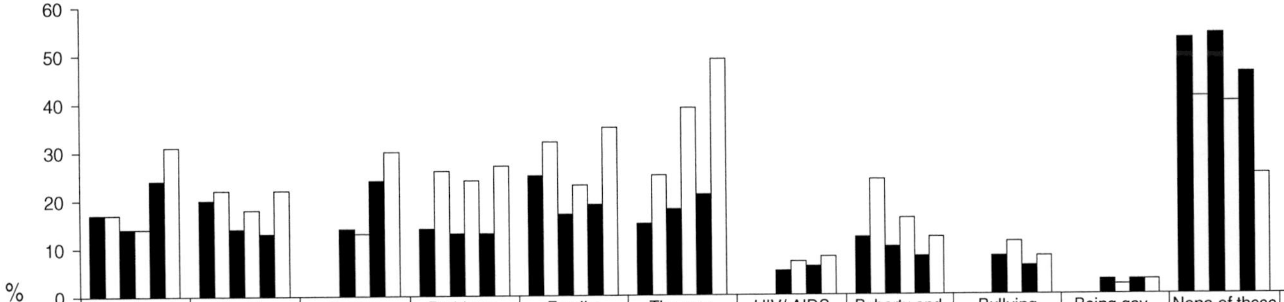

	School-work problems	Health problems	Career problems	Problems with friends	Family problems	The way you look	HIV/ AIDS	Puberty and growing up	Bullying	Being gay, lesbian or bisexual	None of these	Available sample
■ Yr 6 M	17	20	*	14	25	15	*	12	*	*	53	2422
□ Yr 6 F	17	22	*	26	32	25	*	24	*	*	41	2300
■ Yr 8 M	14	14	14	13	17	18	5	10	8	3	54	3064
□ Yr 8 F	14	18	13	24	23	39	7	16	11	2	40	2865
■ Yr 10 M	24	13	24	13	19	21	6	8	6	3	46	2450
□ Yr 10 F	31	22	30	27	35	49	8	12	8	3	25	2425

* Options not available

School-work problems

Up to 23% of pupils
look to *Teachers* for support

If you wanted to share school-work problems, to whom would you probably turn? (60a)(Pri.50)

1. *Mother and father* are the most common source of support which declines as pupils get older.
2. Up to 23% would turn to *Teacher*.
3. The proportion, of older pupils, who would keep such a problem to themselves is small, smaller at least than for most other problems.
4. The various sources of support rise (*Teacher, Friend*) or fall (*Mother and Father*) with age, and there are some marked gender differences.

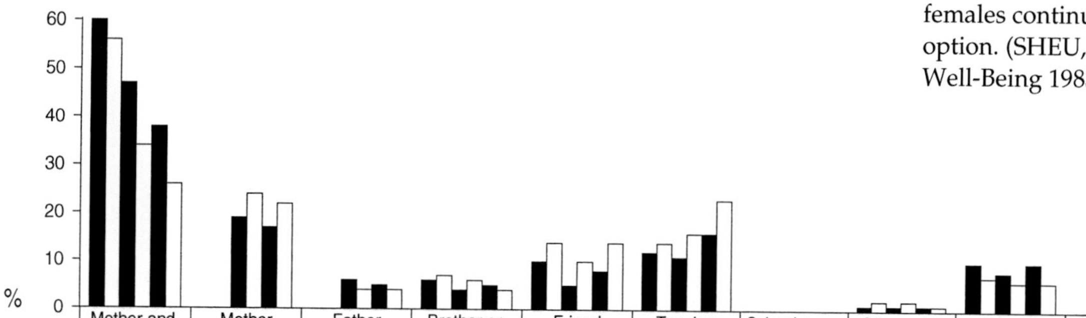

	Mother and father	Mother	Father	Brother or sister	Friend	Teacher	School nurse	Other adult	Keep it to myself	Valid responses
■ Yr 6 M	60	*	*	6	10	12	*	1	10	2203
□ Yr 6 F	56	*	*	7	14	14	*	2	7	2143
■ Yr 8 M	47	19	6	4	5	11	0	1	8	2649
□ Yr 8 F	34	24	4	6	10	16	0	2	6	2589
■ Yr 10 M	38	17	5	5	8	16	0	1	10	2215
□ Yr 10 F	26	22	4	4	14	23	0	1	6	2219

* Options not available

Comments

1. Since 1999, between 35%-39%, of 14-15 year old females, have reported worrying 'quite a lot' or 'a lot' about school-work problems. The figure for 14-15 year old males is around 25%
2. Figures, from older pupils seeking support from a *Teacher*, have risen from 12% in 1999 to up to 23% in 2003.
3. Around 8% of 10-11 year olds report that they would not share a school-work problem but *keep it to myself.*
4. Since 1990, there has been an overall increase in the numbers of pupils reporting sharing school problems with a *Teacher*. Data from older females continue to show an increase in those choosing the *Teacher* option. (SHEU, 2004, 'Trends-Young People and Emotional Health and Well-Being 1983-2003').

Money problems

Around 50% would talk to *Mother and Father*

If you wanted to share money problems, to whom would you probably turn? (60b)

1. *Mother and father* are the most common source of support.
2. The percentage giving *father* is higher than for any of the other listed problems.

Comments

1. Young people seem to keep money problems more firmly within the family compared with the other problems listed.
2. Are *fathers* more likely to have money than *mothers?*

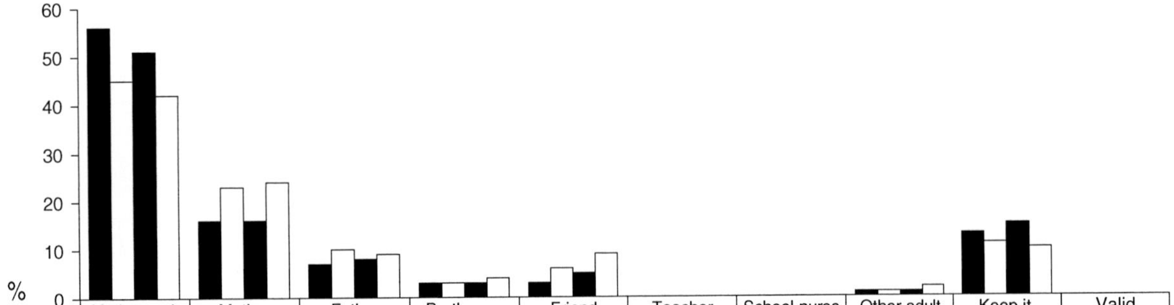

	Mother and father	Mother	Father	Brother or sister	Friend	Teacher	School nurse	Other adult	Keep it to myself	Valid responses
■ Yr 8 M	56	16	7	3	3	0	0	1	13	2612
□ Yr 8 F	45	23	10	3	6	0	0	1	11	2563
■ Yr 10 M	51	16	8	3	5	0	0	1	15	2182
□ Yr 10 F	42	24	9	4	9	0	0	2	10	2208

Health problems

Mother features strongly for the females

If you wanted to share health problems, to whom would you probably turn? (60c) (Pri.50)

1. Again, *Mother and Father*, are the popular choice but are less popular as pupils get older.
2. *Keep it to myself* is the third choice for males — 1 in 7 of the Year 10s would not share a health problem with anybody.
3. The *School nurse*, the only health professional on the list, secures up to 5% of votes for this topic.

Comments

1. The expression 'health problems' is open to wide interpretation.
2. Although Mum and Dad might be the first port of call, it may be only through them that a young person will seek access to Health Care Professionals. We wonder if the small proportion responding *School nurse* reflects a lack of opportunity rather than a reluctance to see them. We know that School Nursing services have been cut from earlier levels.

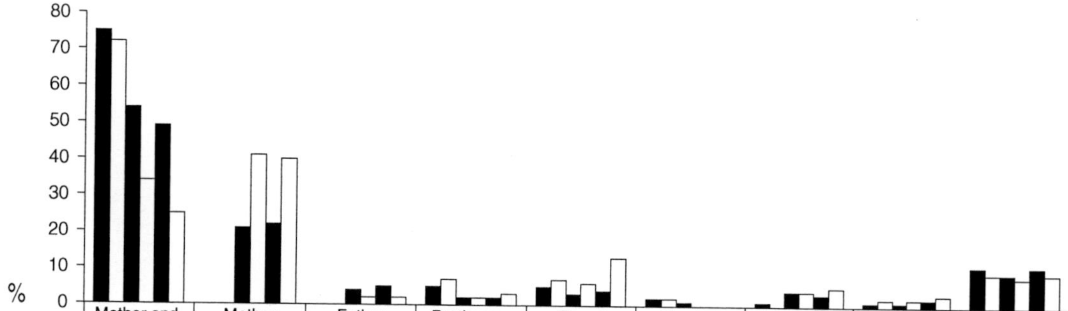

	Mother and father	Mother	Father	Brother or sister	Friend	Teacher	School nurse	Other adult	Keep it to myself	Valid responses
■ Yr 6 M	75	*	*	5	5	2	1	1	11	2184
□ Yr 6 F	72	*	*	7	7	2	0	2	9	2128
■ Yr 8 M	54	21	4	2	3	1	4	1	9	2638
□ Yr 8 F	34	41	2	2	6	0	4	2	8	2580
■ Yr 10 M	49	22	5	2	4	0	3	2	11	2212
□ Yr 10 F	25	40	2	3	13	0	5	3	9	2222

* Options not available

Career problems

Up to 14% of older pupils would turn to *Teacher*

If you wanted to share career problems, to whom would you probably turn? (60d)

1. For males and females the most likely source of support is *Mother and father* with *Mother* being the second most likely choice.
2. *Teacher* figures feature more strongly for the older pupils.

Comments

1. The large difference between *Mother and father*, for what would appear to be a problem they could both help with, may reflect their accessibility.
2. This problem is perhaps still fairly remote for many of these youngsters, particularly the younger pupils.
3. The low standing of *brother or sister* and *friend* suggests that these young people expect to have to look to older people for advice.

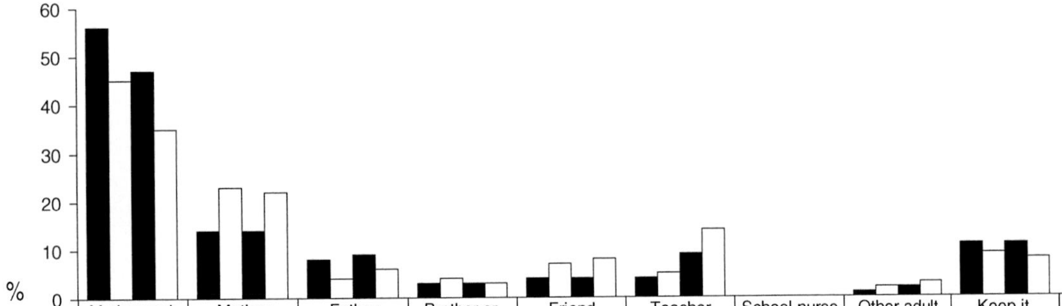

	Mother and father	Mother	Father	Brother or sister	Friend	Teacher	School nurse	Other adult	Keep it to myself	Valid responses
■ Yr 8 M	56	14	8	3	4	4	0	1	11	2599
□ Yr 8 F	45	23	4	4	7	5	0	2	9	2541
■ Yr 10 M	47	14	9	3	4	9	0	2	11	2191
□ Yr 10 F	35	22	6	3	8	14	0	3	8	2209

Friend problems

Gender differences are pronounced

If you wanted to share problems about friends, to whom would you probably turn? (60e) (Pri.50)

1. Gender differences are pronounced. More males say *mother and father*, or would *keep it to myself*; more females say *mother* and also more females would share the problem with another *friend.*
2. Older pupils tend to seek less support from their parents and teachers but rely more on *friends* or simply keep things to themselves.
3. 24% of 14-15 year old males would keep the problem with friends to themselves.

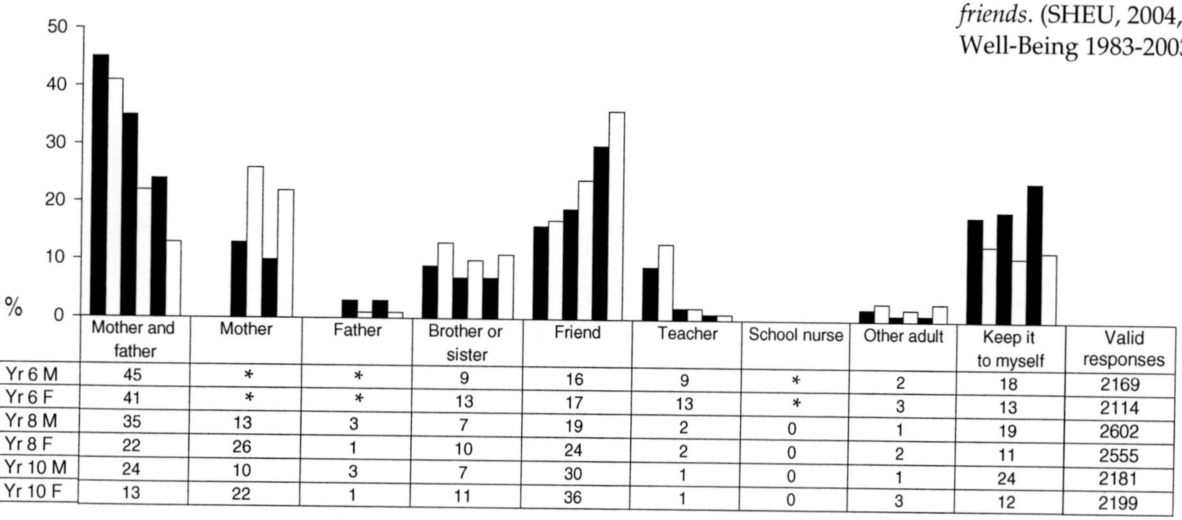

	Mother and father	Mother	Father	Brother or sister	Friend	Teacher	School nurse	Other adult	Keep it to myself	Valid responses
■ Yr 6 M	45	*	*	9	16	9	*	2	18	2169
□ Yr 6 F	41	*	*	13	17	13	*	3	13	2114
■ Yr 8 M	35	13	3	7	19	2	0	1	19	2602
□ Yr 8 F	22	26	1	10	24	2	0	2	11	2555
■ Yr 10 M	24	10	3	7	30	1	0	1	24	2181
□ Yr 10 F	13	22	1	11	36	1	0	3	12	2199

* Options not available

Comments

1. Year 6 pupils were more likely to turn to their teacher than the older pupils within secondary schools. Perhaps this is due to the closer bonds they have with their primary school teachers, developed through the higher level of contact.
2. The importance of seeking support from other friends is clearly seen as pupils get older.
3. Since 1985, there has been an underlying increasing trend to share problems with friends with *mother and father* and other *friends.* Older males and females have, since the late 1990s, consistently chosen other *friends.* (SHEU, 2004, 'Trends-Young People and Emotional Health and Well-Being 1983-2003').

Family problems

Females are twice as likely than males to turn to a *friend*

If you wanted to share family problems, to whom would you probably turn? (60f) (Pri.50)

1. For the females, a *friend* is the likeliest resource and *Mother* is a more popular choice compared with the males. The males are much more likely to go to *Mother and father*, or to *keep it to myself.*

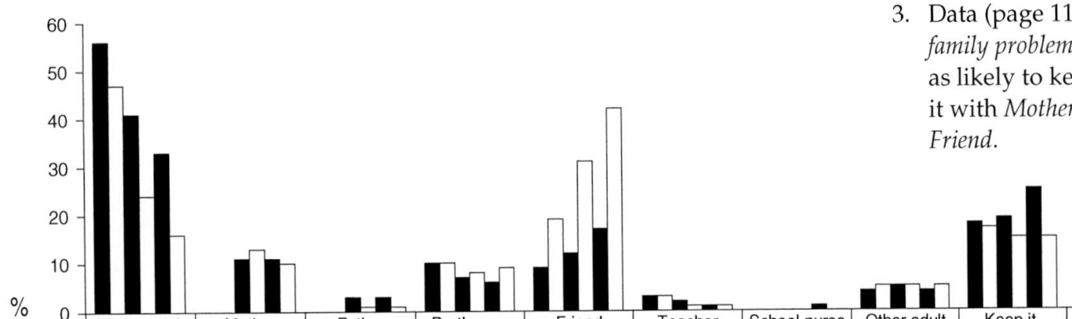

	Mother and father	Mother	Father	Brother or sister	Friend	Teacher	School nurse	Other adult	Keep it to myself	Valid responses
■ Yr 6 M	56	0	0	10	9	3	0	4	18	2203
□ Yr 6 F	47	0	0	10	19	3	0	5	17	2132
■ Yr 8 M	41	11	3	7	12	2	0	5	19	2596
□ Yr 8 F	24	13	1	8	31	1	0	5	15	2552
■ Yr 10 M	33	11	3	6	17	1	1	4	25	2176
□ Yr 10 F	16	10	1	9	42	1	0	5	15	2196

Comments

1. It is interesting that many more males than females would seek help with family problems from *Mother and father*. It is possible that the interpretation of 'family problems' is not the same for the two genders.
2. This observation is further supported by looking at the source of support and comparing the large differences in percentages reported by the 14-15 year olds. 16% of older females, compared with 33% of the older males, share family problems with *Mother and father.* 42% of older females, compared with 17% of the older males, share family problems with a *Friend.*
3. Data (page 110) showed that around 28% of 10-11 year olds, worry about *family problems.* When compared with other pupils, the Year 6 pupils are as likely to keep family problems to themselves and more likely to share it with *Mother and father,* but least likely to share the problem with a *Friend.*

Bullying problems

Up to 23% would *keep it to themselves*

If you wanted to share bullying problems, to whom would you probably turn? (60g)

1. *Mother and father* would be the most common resource, but another large group say that they would *keep it to myself.*
2. The percentage seeking support from their friends is higher for the older females.

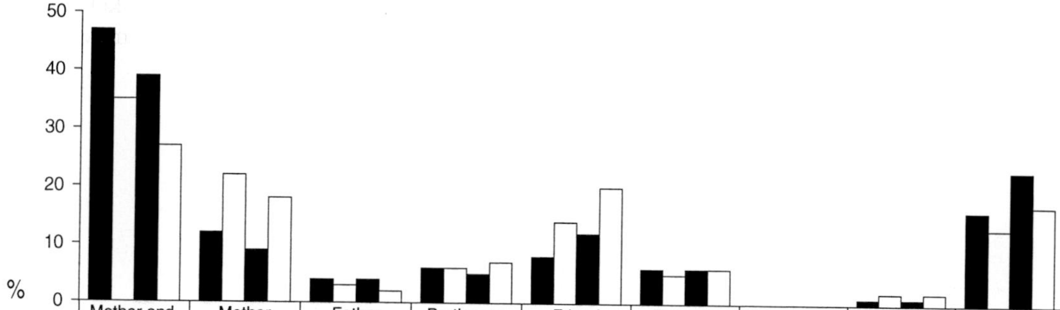

	Mother and father	Mother	Father	Brother or sister	Friend	Teacher	School nurse	Other adult	Keep it to myself	Valid responses
■ Yr 8 M	47	12	4	6	8	6	0	1	16	2445
□ Yr 8 F	35	22	3	6	14	5	0	2	13	2393
■ Yr 10 M	39	9	4	5	12	6	0	1	23	2085
□ Yr 10 F	27	18	2	7	20	6	0	2	17	2070

Comments

1. Bullying (page 28 and pages 134-136) is an issue for females more than males and pupils in Year 6 and Year 8 are more concerned than pupils in Year 10. Since 1999 we have seen that in the Year 6 group, up to 13% more females than males report feeling afraid of going to school because of bullying.
2. The high percentage, saying that they would not talk to anyone about this problem, is cause for concern. For example, 23% of 14-15 year old males would not share their bullying problem with anyone and hardly any pupils would choose to talk to a school nurse.

Index of self-esteem

The level of self-esteem tends to increase with age

Self-esteem measurement (0–18) (12)
Self-esteem measurement (0–14) (12) (Pri.32)

1. The scales used in the primary and secondary versions of the survey are not directly comparable; we give two sets of figures below, the overall secondary figures, and figures from the primary dataset which are comparable.
2. The *high* group included more males than females.
3. The first measure (0-18) shows that the great majority scored more than 10/14, and more than a third of the whole sample were in the *high* group.
4. The second measure (0-14), includes Year 6 pupils.
5. The level of self-esteem tends to increase with age.

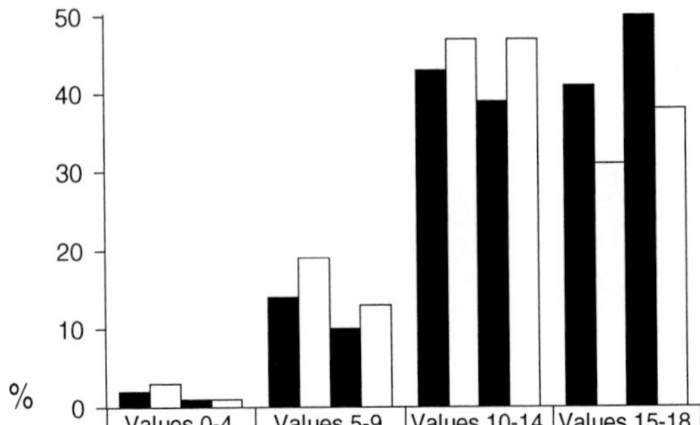

	Values 0-4 (low)	Values 5-9 (med-low)	Values 10-14 (med-high)	Values 15-18 (high)	Valid responses
■ Yr 8 M	2	14	43	41	2929
□ Yr 8 F	3	19	47	31	2796
■ Yr 10 M	1	10	39	50	2386
□ Yr 10 F	1	13	47	38	2388

Self-esteem measurement (0-18) (12)

Comments

1. This measurement is derived from the responses to a set of nine statements, taken from a standard self-esteem enquiry method developed by Denis Lawrence (Lawrence 1981).
2. Many health educators believe high self-esteem may motivate positive behaviour, as well as being a general contributor to emotional well-being
3. The gender differences are a challenge: we do not see them in every school, which means that they are more marked in some other schools.

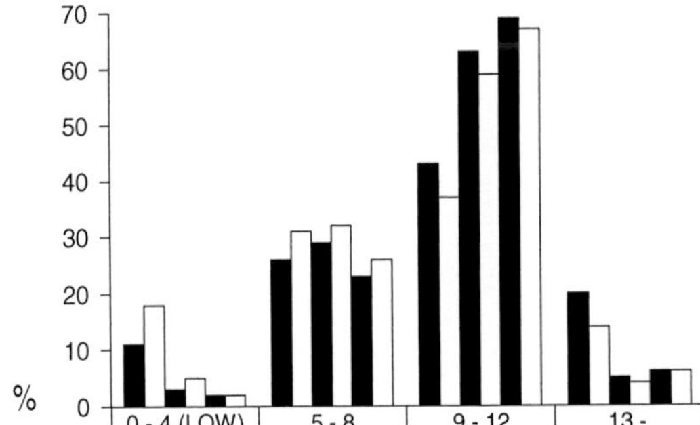

	0 - 4 (LOW)	5 - 8	9 - 12	13 - 14 (HIGH)	Valid responses
■ Yr 6 M	11	26	43	20	2330
□ Yr 6 F	18	31	37	14	2236
■ Yr 8 M	3	29	63	5	2933
□ Yr 8 F	5	32	59	4	2798
■ Yr 10 M	2	23	69	6	2388
□ Yr 10 F	2	26	67	6	2390

Self-esteem measurement (0-14) (12) (Pri 32)

Control over health (1)

The majority feel they are in control of their health

"I am in charge of my health." (13a) "If I keep healthy, I've just been lucky." (13b)

1. The four groups in the sample were fairly close in their responses, although more males than females agreed with (*"I am in charge of my health"*) and disagreed with (*"If I keep healthy,I've just been lucky"*).

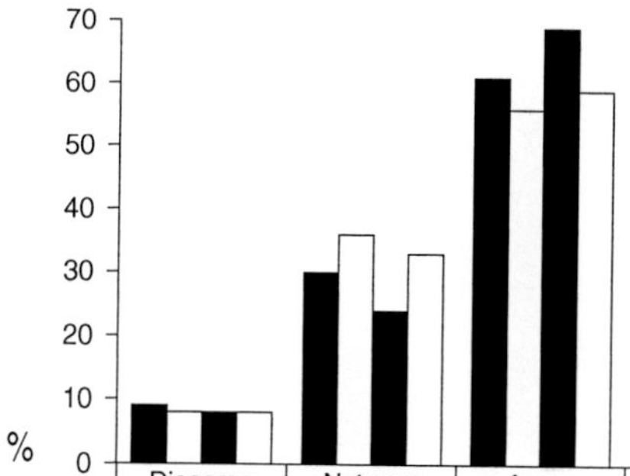

	Disagree	Not sure	Agree	Valid responses
■ Yr 8 M	9	30	61	2988
□ Yr 8 F	8	36	56	2816
■ Yr 10 M	8	24	69	2407
□ Yr 10 F	8	33	59	2403

"I am in charge of my health" (13a)

Comments

1. These two sets of statements are used, together with the two on the following page to generate a 'health locus of control' score (page 121).
2. We have discovered some interesting correlations with these responses. For example, a feeling of low health control links with fear of bullying (page 28).

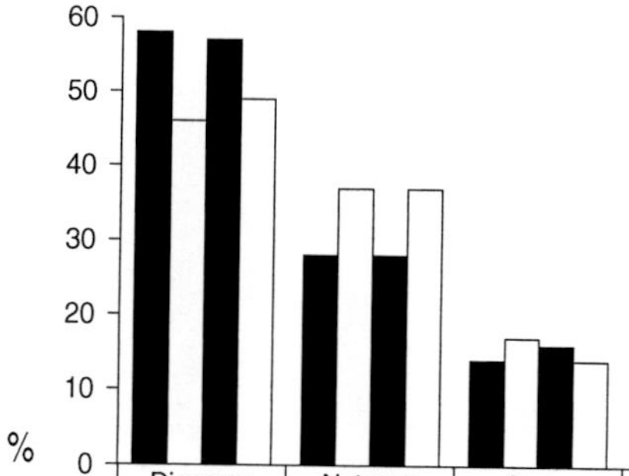

	Disagree	Not sure	Agree	Valid responses
■ Yr 8 M	58	28	14	2945
□ Yr 8 F	46	37	17	2800
■ Yr 10 M	57	28	16	2379
□ Yr 10 F	49	37	14	2391

"If I keep healthy, I've just been lucky." (13b)

Control over health (2)

Most feel they can do something about their health

"If I take care of myself I'll stay healthy."(13c) "Even if I look after myself, I can still easily fall ill." (13d)

1. The four groups in the sample were fairly close in their responses, although more males than females agreed with (*"If I take care of myself I'll stay healthy"*) and disagreed with (*"Even if I look after myself, I can still easily fall ill"*).

Comments

1. We find that about 79% think they will stay healthy if they take care, and around 45% think that they can still fall ill even if they do take care. The apparent contradictions between the items seem to be more in the mind of the logician than the young person.

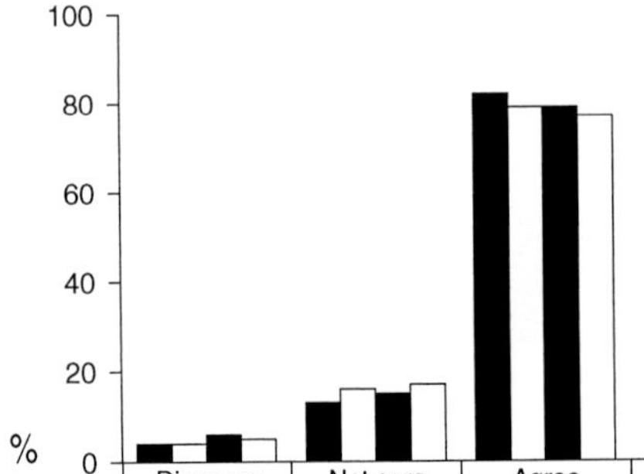

	Disagree	Not sure	Agree	Valid responses
■ Yr 8 M	4	13	82	2963
□ Yr 8 F	4	16	79	2814
■ Yr 10 M	6	15	79	2392
□ Yr 10 F	5	17	77	2401

"If I take care of myself I'll stay healthy." (13c)

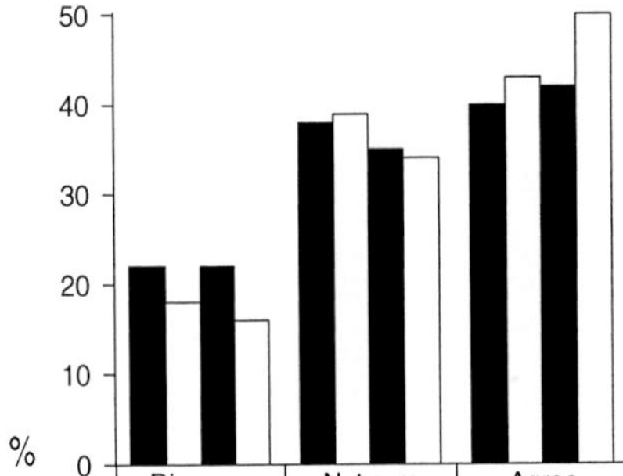

	Disagree	Not sure	Agree	Valid responses
■ Yr 8 M	22	38	40	2943
□ Yr 8 F	18	39	43	2810
■ Yr 10 M	22	35	42	2382
□ Yr 10 F	16	34	50	2399

"Even if I look after myself, I can still easily fall ill." (13d)

Control over health (3)

The majority recorded positive control

Health locus of control score (-4 to +4) (13e)

1. Half of all the groups recorded positive control at the +1 to +2 level.
2. Slightly more males than females felt that they were in positive control of their health.

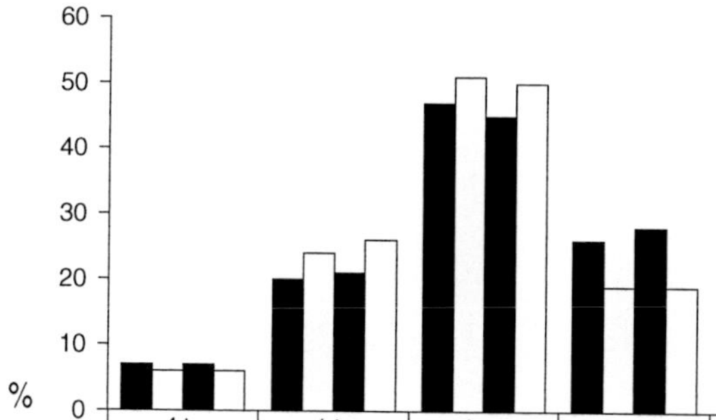

	-4 to -2 (external)	-1 to 0 (neutral)	1 to 2 (internal)	3 to 4 (internal)	Valid responses
■ Yr 8 M	7	20	47	26	3064
□ Yr 8 F	6	24	51	19	2865
■ Yr 10 M	7	21	45	28	2450
□ Yr 10 F	6	26	50	19	2425

Comments

1. 'Health locus of control' is an attempt to establish whether young people feel in control of their health (positive score) or unable to influence it (negative score).
2. The HLOC score reflects the person's overall perception of whether they are personally in control of their health ('internal locus of control') or not and are thereby at the mercy of outside influences ('external locus').
3. We learn from these results that at least a quarter of all the groups do not think that they can influence their health by their own efforts.
4. We know from the work of ourselves and others that the answers to these questions can be strongly correlated with behaviours. For example:

40% of Year 10 females with scores of 3 or 4 on this scale have never smoked at all, whereas of the females whose replies yield neutral or negative scores 29% have never smoked.

In *Bully Off* (Balding, 1996), we described a strong link between scores of these questions and fear of going to school because of bullying.

Favourite adult

Up to 60%
get on best with both parents

With which of these adults do you get on best? (54)

1. One or both parents are the favourite adult for the great majority.
2. The Year 10s show a move away from *Mother and father*. The percentages saying *Mother* or *Father* alone are higher for this age group but we also see increases in the percentages selecting *Adult brother or sister* and *Adult friend*.
3. Up to 3% 'get on best' with no one (compare next page).

Comments

1. It is reassuring to see that the great majority within this age group find their favourite adult within their immediate family.
2. It must be remembered that not all pupils live with both *Mother and father*.

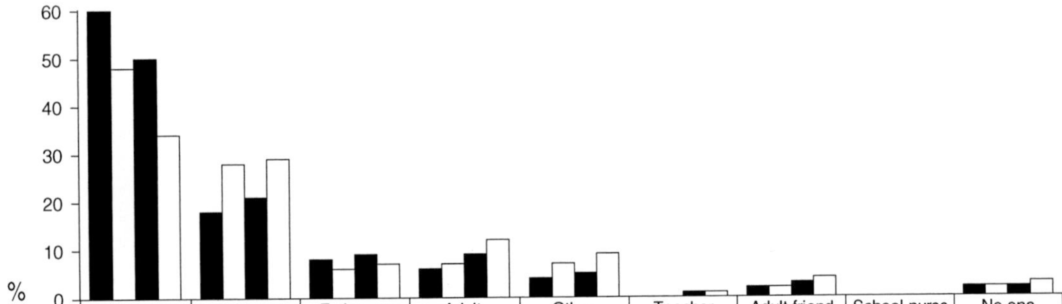

	Mother and father	Mother or step-mother	Father or step-father	Adult brother or sister	Other relation	Teacher	Adult friend	School nurse	No one	Valid responses
■ Yr 8 M	60	18	8	6	4	0	2	0	2	2718
□ Yr 8 F	48	28	6	7	7	0	2	0	2	2607
■ Yr 10 M	50	21	9	9	5	1	3	0	2	2236
□ Yr 10 F	34	29	7	12	9	1	4	0	3	2251

Trustworthy adults

Around 5% of pupils trust no one

How many adults can you really trust? (55)

1. More than 78% trust at least two adults.
2. We notice that trustworthiness levels drop slightly in Year 10, and that more males than females are inclined to trust a lot of adults.

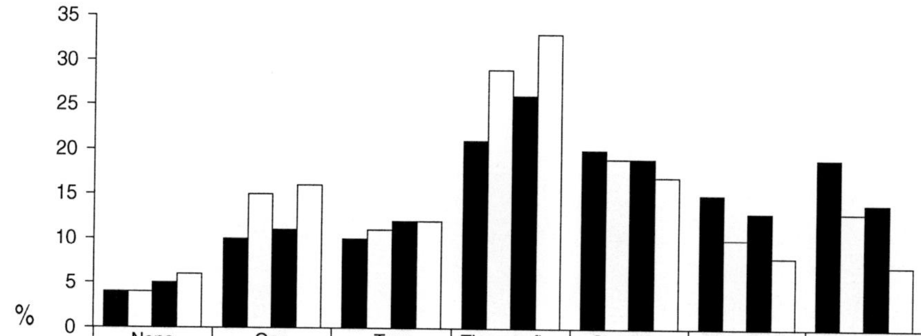

	None	One	Two	Three to five	Six to ten	Eleven to twenty	More than twenty	Valid responses
■ Yr 8 M	4	10	10	21	20	15	19	2783
□ Yr 8 F	4	15	11	29	19	10	13	2690
■ Yr 10 M	5	11	12	26	19	13	14	2304
□ Yr 10 F	6	16	12	33	17	8	7	2304

Comments

1. The group that demand particular attention are those responding none — 4% in Year 8 and up to 6% in Year 10. This is slightly larger than the proportion saying that they 'get on best' with no one (previous page); but getting on with someone does not necessarily mean really trusting them.

Satisfaction with life

Males are more satisfied than females

In general, how satisfied do you feel with your life at the moment? (8)

1. Slightly more males record *a lot*; and slightly more females record *not much*.
2. Overall, more than 60% report *quite a lot* or *a lot*, and around 12% are dissatisfied to some extent (reporting *not much* or *not at al).*
3. The females' level of dissatisfaction increases a little with age.

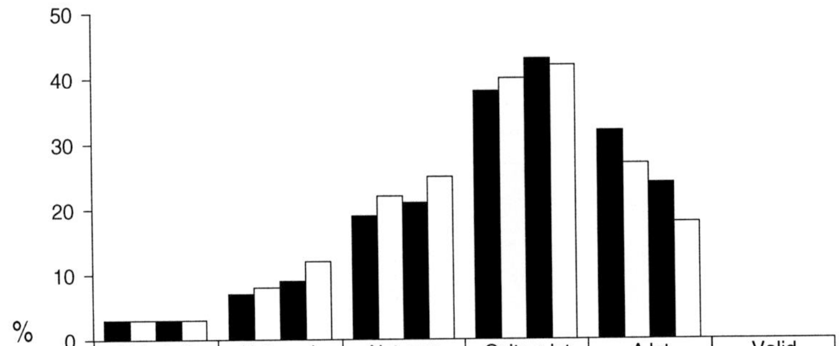

	Not at all	Not much	Not sure	Quite a lot	A lot	Valid responses
■ Yr 8 M	3	7	19	38	32	2967
□ Yr 8 F	3	8	22	40	27	2818
■ Yr 10 M	3	9	21	43	24	2402
□ Yr 10 F	3	12	25	42	18	2405

Comments

1. The difference in the percentage of satisfied males and females is in line with the evidence on page 110 that females worry about more things than males do.
2. Since 1995, there has been an upward trend for all groups choosing the satisfied *a lot* option. Males more than females have consistently reported higher levels of satisfaction with life. Younger males have always been the most satisfied group. Older females have consistently been the group most likely to report *not much* satisfaction with life *at the moment*. (SHEU, 2004, 'Trends-Young People and Emotional Health and Well-Being 1983-2003').

Sexually transmitted diseases

6-11% think HIV/AIDS can be treated or cured

What you know about sexually transmitted diseases and infections? (64)

Responses to 'Can be treated and cured'.

1. Most commonly identified treatable infections are warts and pubic lice.
2. Between 6-11% of pupils think that HIV/AIDS can be treated and cured.
3. Older females, compared with males, responded most frequently across categories.

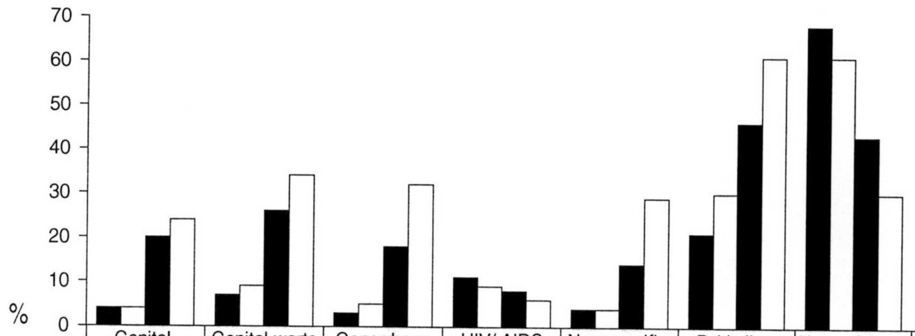

	Genital herpes	Genital warts	Gonorrhoea	HIV/ AIDS	Non-specific urethritis, e.g. Chlamydia	Pubic lice (crabs)	None of these	Available sample
■ Yr 8 M	4	7	3	11	4	21	68	3064
□ Yr 8 F	4	9	5	9	4	30	61	2865
■ Yr 10 M	20	26	18	8	14	46	43	2450
□ Yr 10 F	24	34	32	6	29	61	30	2425

Comments

1. This was a new question in 2002 that provides four possible options: *Never heard of it. Know nothing about it. Can be treated but not cured. Can be treated and cured.* Responses *Can be treated and cured* are shown in the chart opposite. This need not mean that young people think sexually transmitted diseases/infections (STDs and STIs) cannot be treated and cured, they may have opted for one of the other options.
2. The current figures about HIV/AIDS needs to be compared with our reporting (May 2004) on the apparent decline in 12-15 year olds' knowledge about the dangers of HIV/AIDS (www.sheu.org.uk/pubs/trends/hivmay.htm).
3. Should the apparent knowledge of the 12-15 year olds, and in particular the older females, in this sample cause us concern? For information about STDs and STIs contact the Health Protection Agency (www.hpa.org.uk).

Methods of contraception

76% of males selected *Condoms*
70% of females selected *The Pill*

What do you know about methods of contraception? (67a)

Responses to 'Reliable to stop pregnancy'

1. The most popular method chosen by the males, that is 'reliable to stop pregnancy', was *Condoms.* For older females, the most popular methods chosen were *The Pill, Condoms* and *The Morning After Pill* (emergency contraception used up to 3 mornings after).
2. Between 62%-76% of all pupils selected *Condoms.*

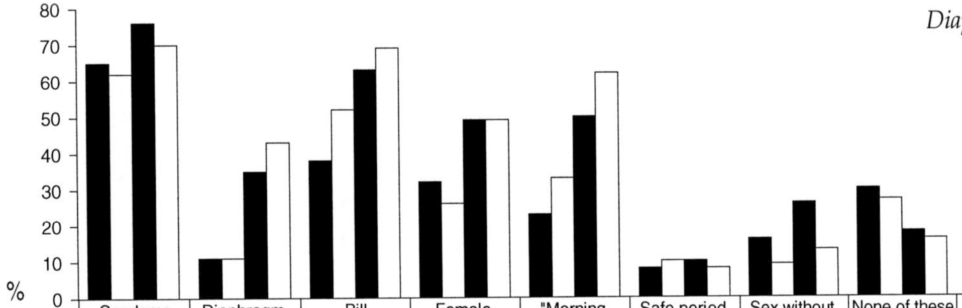

	Condoms	Diaphragm (cap)	Pill	Female condom (Femidom)	"Morning after" pill	Safe period (Rhythm method)	Sex without penetration	None of these	Available sample
■ Yr 8 M	65	11	38	32	23	8	16	30	3064
□ Yr 8 F	62	11	52	26	33	10	9	27	2865
■ Yr 10 M	76	35	63	49	50	10	26	18	2450
□ Yr 10 F	70	43	69	49	62	8	13	16	2425

Comments

1. This is the second time we have asked this specific question. Pupils have a choice of four answers to describe best what they know about the list of contraceptive methods. The answers are 'Never heard of it', 'Know nothing about it', 'Not reliable to stop pregnancy', and 'Reliable to stop pregnancy'. Responses shown in the chart are from the last answer.
2. The data show clear gender and age differences. For many of the contraceptive methods there is a marked shift in response rates particularly between the females from 12-13 years old to 14-15 years old. The most noticeable – *Diaphragm* and *Female condom* methods show a difference of around 28%. The most popular choice for the females, *Condoms,* shows only a 8% difference between the age groups.
3. For differences, from the reponses between younger and older males, the *Diaphragm, The Pill* and *Morning After Pill* methods show a difference of around 24%. The most popular choice for the males, *Condoms,* shows an 11% difference between the age groups.
4. This chart presents combined responses to several sub-questions and thus there is no single value for 'valid responses', the percentages of 'missing data' are included in the *None of the these* column. With this in mind we see that up to 30% of young people did not respond to the answer option 'Reliable to stop pregnancy'.

Contraception and HIV/AIDS

Up to 13% selected *sex without penetration*

Which contraceptive methods are reliable to stop infections like HIV/AIDS? (67b)

1. The item *Condoms* was selected by up to 69% of all pupils and between up to 42% selected *Female condoms*.
2. There are differences in percentages between some choices made by Year 8 and Year 10 pupils. For example, as they get older 19% more females choose *Condoms* and 16% choose *Female condoms*.
3. More males than females think *sex without penetration* is a reliable method to stop infections like HIV/AIDS. However, the maximum number choosing this option is 13% of older males.

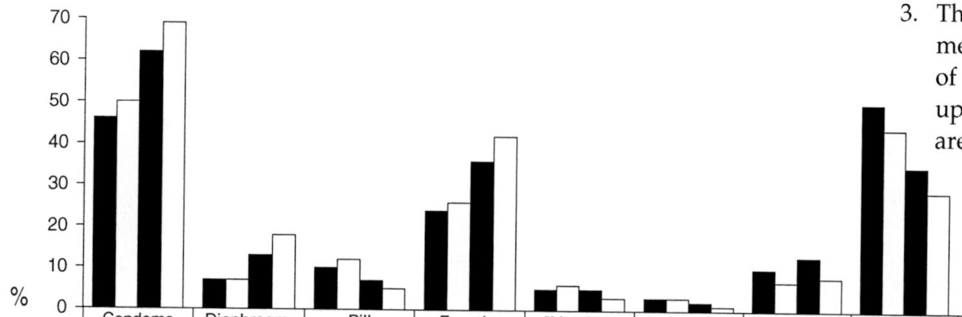

	Condoms	Diaphragm (cap)	Pill	Female condom (Femidom)	"Morning after" pill (emergency contraceptio-	Safe period (Rhythm method)	Sex without penetration	None of these	Available sample
■ Yr 8 M	46	7	10	24	5	3	10	50	3064
□ Yr 8 F	50	7	12	26	6	3	7	44	2865
■ Yr 10 M	62	13	7	36	5	2	13	35	2450
□ Yr 10 F	69	18	5	42	3	1	8	29	2425

Comments

1. This is the second year we have asked this specific question. In the questionnaire it follows the question on the previous page. Pupils are asked to circle each letter, corresponding with a list of contraceptive methods, that they think is reliable to stop infection like HIV/AIDS.
2. If we accept that the barrier contraceptive methods (male and female condoms) and 'sex without penetration' offer protection against infections (see www.fpa.org.uk and www.avert.org.uk) then should the apparent level of knowledge of the 12-15 year olds in this sample cause us concern?
3. The *None of these* data refer to those pupils who did not choose any of methods. For example, 29% of 14-15 year old females did not choose any of the options on the list. We do not know the reasons for this choice but up to 35% of older pupils could not decide which contraceptive methods are reliable to stop infections.
4. Often in a question we can distinguish between missing data and a definite *No* response. Because of the design of this particular question no such distinctions can be made.

Free condoms

43% of the Year 10 males
do not know where to get free condoms

Do you know where you can get condoms free of charge? (65)

1. The increased knowledge, or belief, of the Year 10 respondents is clear.
2. In Year 10, two-thirds of the females say they know of a source, whereas fewer than half the males do.

Comments

1. 'Knowing of a source' does not mean that it will or could be used, and we in Exeter have no means of knowing if the information is accurate. The schools and health authorities examining the data from their own surveys should be in a position to judge.
2. Respondents were asked to write down the name of the source, rather than refer to a checklist. It is possible that some knew of more than one source, and wrote down the one they could most easily spell rather than the one they were most likely to use.
3. This question needs to be considered together with question on page 125.
4. We quote, with respect to teenage pregnancy, 'boys are half the problem'.
5. Females are often considered to be 'more mature', dating older boys, and the gender difference observed here need not represent a reluctance on the part of the males to accept responsibility for contraception.

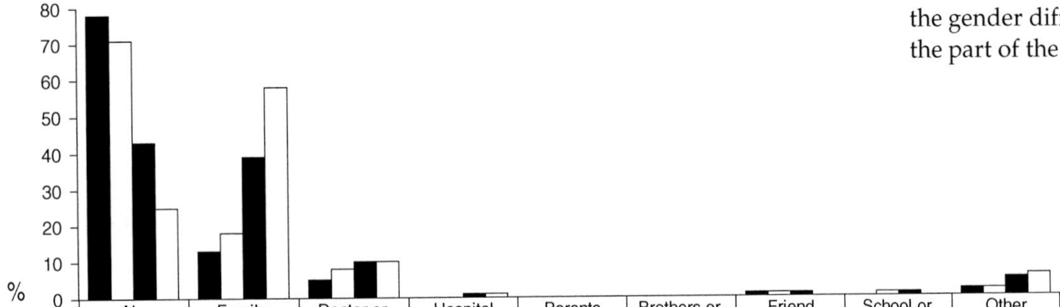

	No	Family planning or other clinic	Doctor or Health Centre	Hospital	Parents	Brothers or Sisters	Friend	School or College nurse	Other	Valid responses
■ Yr 8 M	78	13	5	0	0	0	1	0	2	1943
□ Yr 8 F	71	18	8	0	0	0	1	1	2	2052
■ Yr 10 M	43	39	10	1	0	0	1	1	5	1425
□ Yr 10 F	25	58	10	1	0	0	0	0	6	1532

Birth control service

52% of the Year 10 females knew about a local service

Is there a special birth control service for young people available locally? (66)

1. The females were more likely to know if there was one, and knowledge was much greater in Year 10.
2. Up to 64% *don't know* about a local service and up to 51% are aged 14-15 years old.

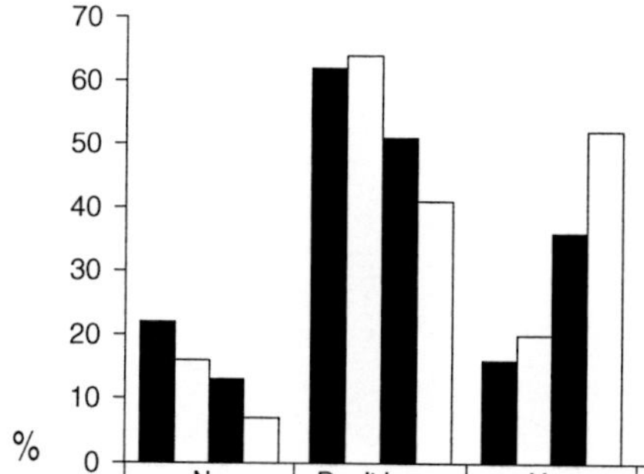

	No	Don't know	Yes	Valid responses
■ Yr 8 M	22	62	16	2529
□ Yr 8 F	16	64	20	2506
■ Yr 10 M	13	51	36	2173
□ Yr 10 F	7	41	52	2205

Comments

1. With the continuing concern over teenage pregnancies, as well as the spread of AIDS, a lot of money and effort is being directed towards this area of health education. The charts on this and the preceding page are two measures of its success.
2. As with the previous question, local knowledge will be required to assess the responses. Districts vary in the amount of publicity given to contraceptive services for young people, as well as in the nature and scale of provision.
3. Is it a satisfactory state of affairs when up to 51% of 14-15 year olds don't know about local services — even the fact that there aren't any?

9 The Primary Questionnaire Responses

The primary Health Related Behaviour Questionnaire contains 50 questions, compared with more than a hundred in the secondary version. Overall, therefore, many more secondary questions lack a primary equivalent than the other way round. However, some questions in the primary version do not match up with any of the 'secondary' questions. There are also questions that cover similar aspects whose data are difficult to merge, so that some information is lost. We present the major omissions here, as they cover important aspects of the lives of these very young people.

Question

Schoolday breakfast

6% had nothing to eat or drink before 'coming to school today'.

What did you eat or drink for breakfast this morning? (Pri.6)

1. *Cereal* is by far the most popular breakfast choice.
2. Up to 56% of primary school pupils have *something to drink* and up to 48% have *cereal* before school.

Comments

1. Primary school pupils generally are more likely than secondary school pupils to have a substantial breakfast before school. This is probably due to parental influence. (See page 2 'Schoolday breakfast' to see the secondary school comparison for some of the items listed.)
2. The category *something to drink* replaced categories in previous surveys which were: *drink of milk, tea or coffee, fruit juice.* Around 50% report having *something to drink* suggesting that around 50% of the sample did not have a drink before 'coming to school today'. This is not to suggest they had no liquid, as some ate *cereal* which would include milk.

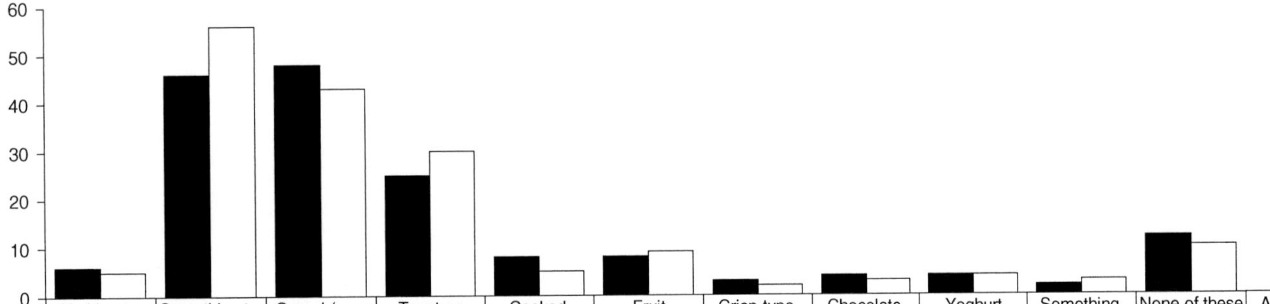

	Nothing to eat or drink	Something to drink	Cereal (e.g. Porridge/ Readybrek)	Toast or bread	Cooked breakfast	Fruit	Crisp-type packet snack	Chocolate bar, sweets	Yoghurt	Something else	None of these	Available sample
■ Yr 6 M	6	46	48	25	8	8	3	4	4	2	12	2422
□ Yr 6 F	5	56	43	30	5	9	2	3	4	3	10	2300

Vegetarian diet

Up to 7% of 10-11 year old pupils are vegetarian

Are you a vegetarian? (Pri.7)

1. Up to 7% of Year 6 primary school pupils describe themselves as vegetarian.
2. There is little difference between male and female pupils.

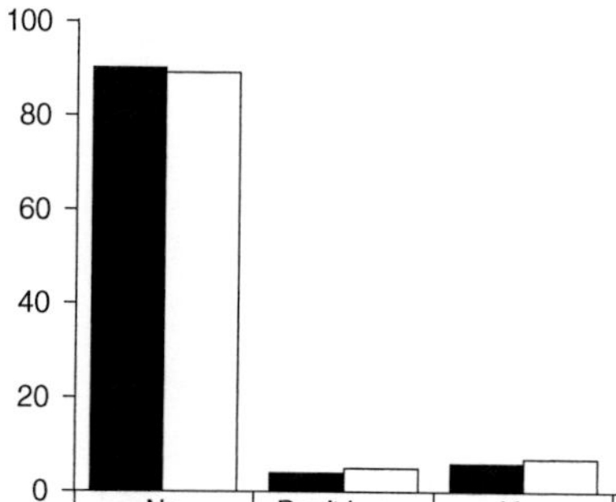

	No	Don't know	Yes	Available sample
■ Yr 6 M	90	4	6	1404
□ Yr 6 F	89	5	7	1330

Comments

1. We do not define 'vegetarian', neither do we ask what these young people mean by the term.

   From our work in the 1990s, we know that young people have a variety of dietary styles with respect to meat and fish which are too complex to be shoehorned into the one term. Nonetheless, it does indicate a proportion of children who are consciously not eating meat. Since 1999 we have reported that between 4%-7% primary pupils are vegetarian.

Being bullied (1)

Around 26% experience some form of bullying

Have any of the following happened to you in the last month? (Pri.13)

Responses to 'often' or 'every day'.

1. Around 26% of primary pupils report that they have been bullied *often* or *every day* in one or more of the listed ways.
2. *Being teased/made fun of* or *called nasty names* are the main causes of unhappiness for many primary school pupils.

Comments

1. Slightly more males than females report incidences of physical rather than verbal forms of bullying. It is the females, however, who report more fear of going to school because of bullying (See page 28).
2. The *none of these* data reveal that around 26% of pupils report at least one of these things happening to them *often* or *every day*. It is evident that some of these pupils are experiencing more than just one of these forms of bullying.

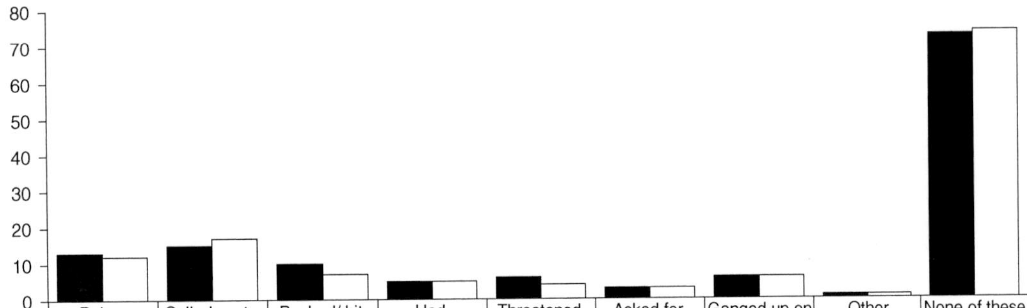

	Being teased/ made fun of	Called nasty names	Pushed/ hit for no reason	Had belongings taken/ broken	Threatened for no reason	Asked for money	Ganged up on	Other	None of these	Available sample
■ Yr 6 M	13	15	10	5	6	3	6	1	73	2422
□ Yr 6 F	12	17	7	5	4	3	6	1	74	2300

Being bullied (2)

Playtime and *lunchtime* can cause anxiety for up to 17%

Where did these unpleasant experiences happen? (Pri. 14)

Responses to 'often' or 'every day'.

1. Outside and inside during *playtime* and *lunchtime* causes problems for up to 17% of primary children
2. Up to 9% of pupils report being bullied *at or near home.*
3. Up to 10% report being bullied *during lesson time.*

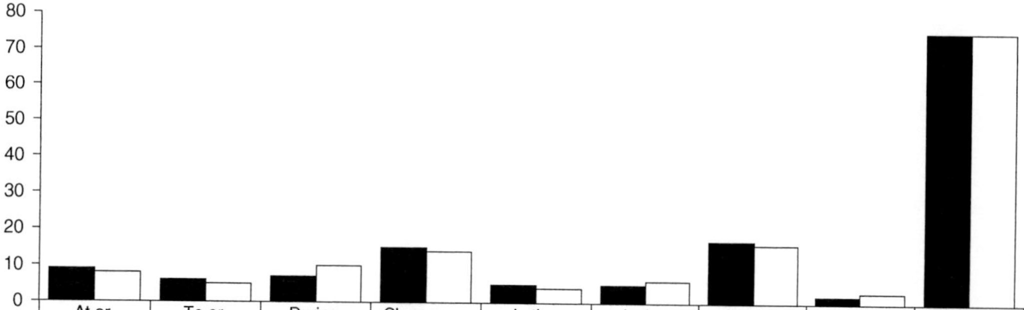

	At or near home	To or from school	During lesson time	Classroom (playtime/ lunchtime)	In the toilets	In the corridors	Outside (playtime/ lunchtime)	Somewhere else	None of these	Available sample
■ Yr 6 M	9	6	7	15	5	5	17	2	75	2422
□ Yr 6 F	8	5	10	14	4	6	16	3	75	2300

Comments

1. The top two categories unsurprisingly relate to free time during school hours – outside and inside during *playtime* and *lunchtime.* It can often be difficult for staff to monitor how much bullying behaviour occurs in this free time because of the nature of the playground.
2. Teachers may well be concerned to learn that up to 10% of pupils report being bullied *during lesson time.*
3. Since 1997, more primary pupils have consistently reported being bullied during free times, ie. outside and inside during *playtime* and *lunchtime.* (SHEU, 2004, 'Trends-Young People and Emotional Health and Well-Being 1983-2003').

Being bullied (3)

25% of the females picked on for 'the way they look'

Do you think you are being 'picked on' or bullied for any of the following reasons? (Pri. 15)

1. Around 45% responded to being 'picked on' or bullied, most felt it was due to their 'size or weight' or to the 'way they looked'.
2. Generally there are little differences between genders, but more of the 10-11 year old females, compared with the males, thought they were being 'picked on' because of the their size and weight or the 'way they looked'.

Comments

1. This was a new question in 2002 and since than has provided information from over 12,700 primary pupils about possible reasons for being bullied.
2. We note that among secondary pupils 'the way you look' is a significant worry and clearly 'size and weight' are related to this.

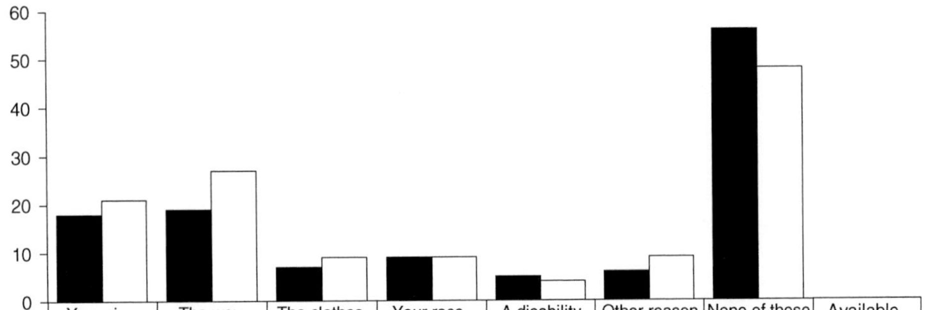

	Your size or weight	The way you look	The clothes you wear	Your race, colour or religion	A disability	Other reason	None of these	Available sample
■ Yr 6 M	18	19	7	9	5	6	56	2247
□ Yr 6 F	21	27	9	9	4	9	48	2133

'Stranger danger' (1)

Up to 27% have had some sort of upsetting experience

Have you ever been approached by an adult stranger who scared you or made you upset? (Pri. 16)

1. Up to 27% report that they have been 'scared or upset' by an adult stranger.
2. Since 1999 between 28%-32% of primary pupils have reported being 'scared or upset'.
3. Another 11% of pupils also report some element of disquiet about an incident or incidents that may have happened to them.

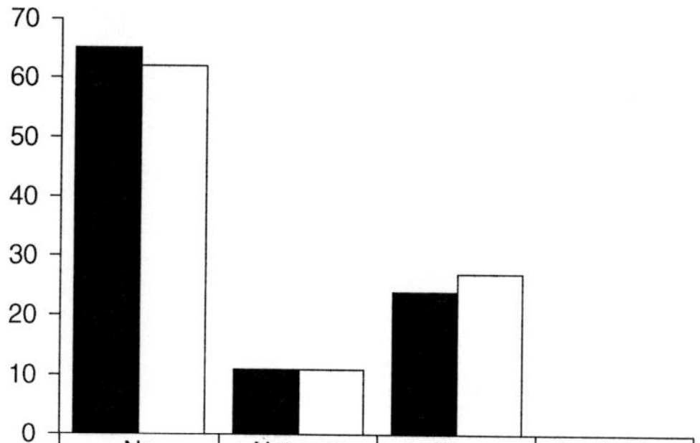

	No	Not sure	Yes	Available sample
■ Yr 6 M	65	11	24	2311
□ Yr 6 F	62	11	27	2222

Comments

1. The figures for both genders are worryingly high. It is important to note here, that these figures denote the percentage who felt anxious at the approach of a stranger, not necessarily an incident.
2. These data indicate that 'Stranger Danger' education in primary schools is important for both males and females.
3. The question doesn't ask for any details about the behaviour they were worried about, but it does ask a follow-up question 'what did you do?'
4. We recognise that adults known to a child are more likely to threaten or abuse that child than strangers. However, we do not wish to be responsible for introducing this idea to children in the context of a questionnaire when there might not be an opportunity to discuss all issues arising.

'Stranger danger' (2)

Ran or walked away
was the most frequent course of action

What did you do when an adult stranger scared or upset you? (Pri. 17)

1. About 20% of primary school pupils *ran or walked away* when approached by a stranger who upset them.
2. Up to 9% told an adult straightaway.
3. 5% reported the incident to the police but 6% never told anyone.
4. The 'none of these' column also includes the children who have never been so approached.

Comments

1. The percentage of children recording that they *ran or walked away* is consistent with figures from 1999 onwards and range between 14%-23%.

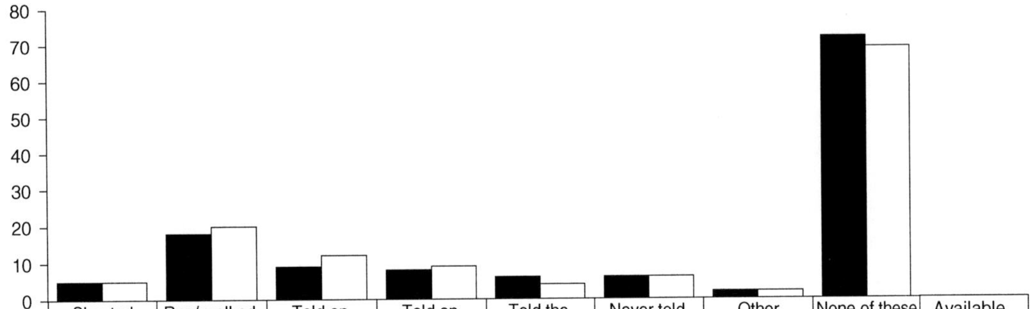

	Shouted	Ran/ walked away	Told an adult straightaway	Told an adult afterwards	Told the police	Never told anyone	Other	None of these	Available sample
■ Yr 6 M	5	18	9	8	6	6	2	72	2422
□ Yr 6 F	5	20	12	9	4	6	2	69	2300

Bicycle ownership

Up to 91% have a bike

Have you got a bicycle? (Pri. 23)

1. Up to 91% children report owning their own bicycle.

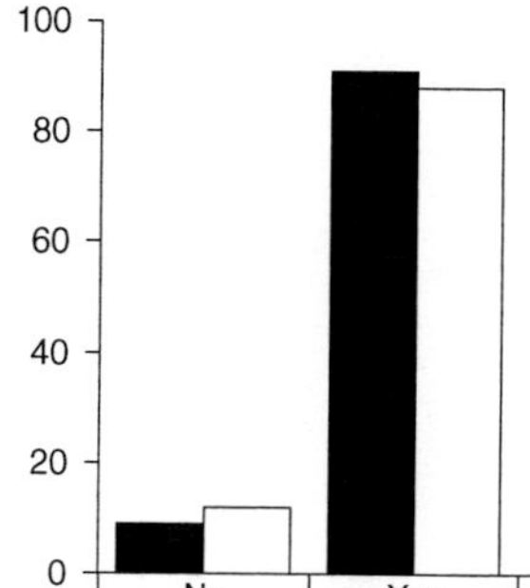

	No	Yes	Available sample
■ Yr 6 M	9	91	2422
□ Yr 6 F	12	88	2300

Comments

1. Refer also to page 10, 'safety helmets,' to see the age-related differences in answers to 'When you cycle, do you wear a safety helmet?' These data suggest that although young people have access to bicycles they don't necessarily cycle, and this is particularly true for females.
2. These figures show that the majority of primary school pupils could cycle as a means of travel to school, although very few currently do so. The reasons for this, no doubt, include the lack of safe (off-road) cycle routes and the lack of facilities for parking bicycles securely at schools. It seems, however, that these current difficulties are gradually being reduced with the development of the country's cycle network infrastructure.

Alcoholic drinks

59% of 10–11 year old females have tasted wine

Which of these alcoholic drinks have you tasted? (Pri. 36)

1. Wine has been tasted by up to 59% of 10-11 year olds.
2. Males top the list in all categories of alcoholic drink except wine.

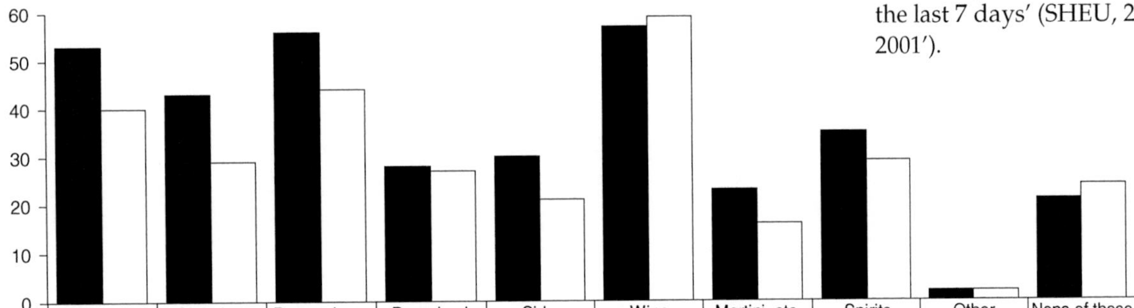

	Shandy - canned	Shandy - mixed	Beer or lager	Pre-mixed spirits and Alcopops	Cider	Wine	Martini, etc.	Spirits	Other	None of these	Available sample
■ Yr 6 M	53	43	56	28	30	57	23	35	2	21	2422
□ Yr 6 F	40	29	44	27	21	59	16	29	2	24	2300

Comments

1. The relative frequencies of the drinks are not surprising, and may reflect their availability in the home.
2. There may be some kudos in being able to say that you have tasted a variety of drinks, even if these are just sips of parents' drinks.
3. Figures from 1999 show that more 10-11 year old females have consistently reported tasting wine compared with males. Over this period, percentages for the females range from 59%-69%.
4. It is also worth considering the *wine* figures from 10-11 year old females with trends data for older females. From 1983–2001, wine has been the preferred drink for females aged 14-15 years old. In relation to the amount of wine drunk by older females in 2001, 20% reported drinking at least 1 glass of wine and, of this 20%, 15% drank 5 or more glasses 'in the last 7 days' (SHEU, 2003, 'Trends-Young People and Alcohol 1983-2001').

Alcohol in last week

25% of males and 14% of females drank alcohol last week

Have you had an alcoholic drink (more than just a sip) in the last 7 days? (Pri. 37)

1. Up to 25% of the 10-11 year olds report having had an alcoholic drink, which was more than just a sip, in the last 7 days. There is a noticeable 11% difference in the responses from males and females.

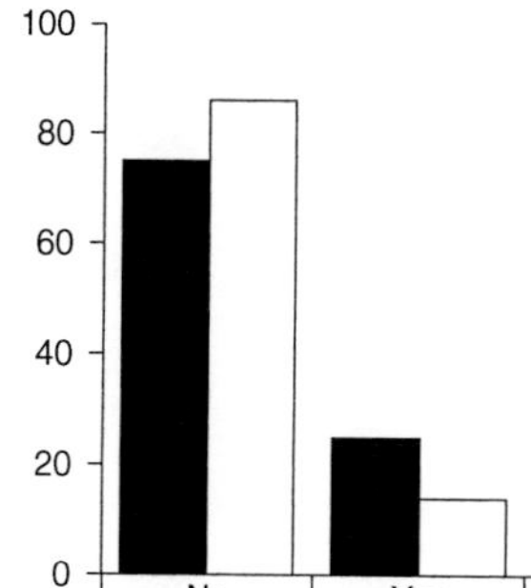

	No	Yes	Available sample
■ Yr 6 M	75	25	2317
□ Yr 6 F	86	14	2235

Comments

1. Does this reflect an increase in the availability of alcohol to youngsters in the home, or do they have access to alcohol when they are out with parents in social settings?
2. The difference in response rates from males and females has been consistent over the years. Since 1999 between 20-25% of males and 14%-15% of females report having more than a sip of alcohol 'in the last 7 days'.

Smoking

At least 18% said *maybe* or *yes*

Do you think you will smoke when you are older? (Pri. 42)

1. Over 79% of these youngsters said that they don't think they will smoke when they are older. Up to 83% of females said 'no'.
2. 5% of the males are sure that they will smoke when they are older.
3. At least 18% say that they might well smoke.

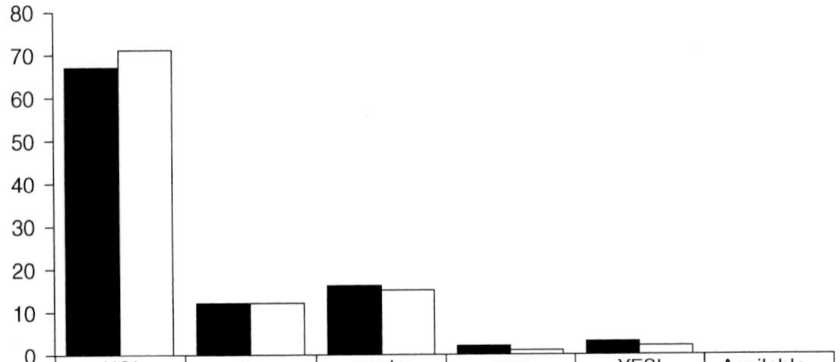

	NO!	no	maybe	yes	YES!	Available sample
■ Yr 6 M	67	12	16	2	3	2305
□ Yr 6 F	71	12	15	1	2	2218

Comments

1. As at least 18% of primary school pupils say that they might well smoke, then their perception of the dangers may be outweighed by their perceptions of smoking by role models.
2. On page 71 we see that at age 10-11 years old, 90% of the females report having never smoked at all. By the time they are 14-15 years old, 37% of the females report having never smoked at all and, around 32% smoke occasionally/regularly. 14% of the regular smokers group say that they would like to give it up, so why do they want to start in the first place?
3. If the messages about the dangers of smoking could be reinforced earlier, would fewer young people take up smoking? Most primary pupils are adamantly anti-smoking.

Awareness of AIDS or HIV

A declining trend in knowledge is suggested with this year's data

Do you know about an illness called AIDS (or HIV)? (Pri. 45)

1. 57% of males and 56% of females in the top year of the primary school age range say that they do know about an illness called AIDS.

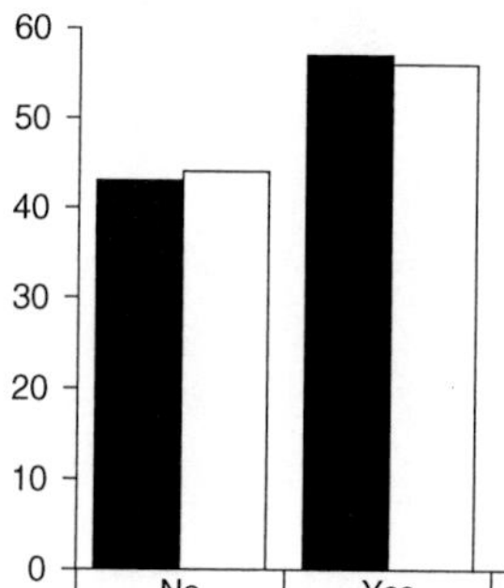

	No	Yes	Available sample
■ Yr 6 M	43	57	2234
□ Yr 6 F	44	56	2192

Comments

1. This years figures are lower than in previous years and suggest a declining trend in primary pupils' knowledge of HIV/AIDS:

Responding 'Yes'	1999	2000	2001	2002	2003
Year 6 Males	66%	60%	61%	58%	57%
Year 6 Females	69%	63%	66%	62%	56%

2. These results seem to underline the findings from research (see for example Balding, Regis & Wise, 1998, p21), that concern about AIDS/HIV has reduced significantly since the mid 1990s. A more up to date picture of 12-15 year olds can be seen on our website: (www.sheu.org.uk/pubs/trends/hivmay.htm).
3. The follow-up question 'Have any of the following talked to you about AIDS (or HIV)?' gives more detail about their sources of information.

Talking about AIDS or HIV

Parents are the most likely source of information

Have any of the following talked with you about AIDS (or HIV)? (Pri. 46)

1. Pupils report that only about 12% of Year 6 teachers have talked to them about AIDS (or HIV).
2. The highest group recorded is 'parents'. 30% of males and 32% of females have talked to their parents about this condition.

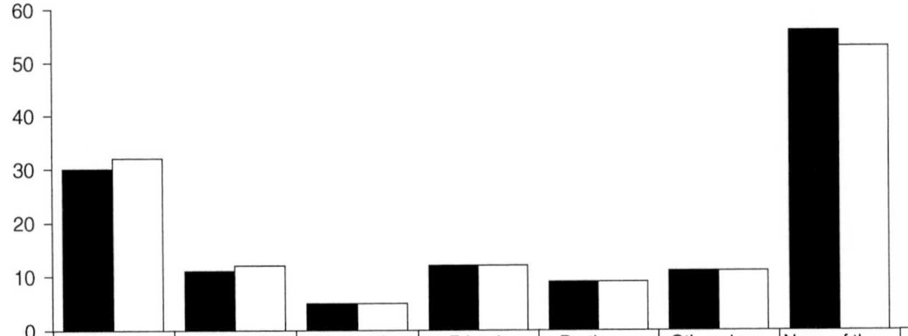

	Parents	Teachers	Visitors in school lessons e.g. nurse	Friends	Brothers, sisters	Other close relations	None of these	Available sample
■ Yr 6 M	30	11	5	12	9	11	56	2422
□ Yr 6 F	32	12	5	12	9	11	53	2300

Comments

1. The proportions of youngsters who have talked with their parents about AIDS (or HIV) may well result from coverage given to the issue via media sources.
2. It is interesting to note the proportions of pupils discussing these issues with siblings, other close relations and friends.
3. Over 53% (*none of these*) of the sample have not talked to anyone about AIDS (or HIV). This high proportion indicates that discussions about AIDS are not common within this age group. Since 1999, figures for *none of these* have ranged from 47%-54% for females and 52%-58% for males

Talking about drugs

Up to 67% say *parents* talked with them about drugs

Have any of the following talked with you about drugs? (Pri.47)

1. Up to 67% of primary school youngsters said that their parents talked to them about drugs.
2. Up to 56% said that their teachers talked to them about drugs.

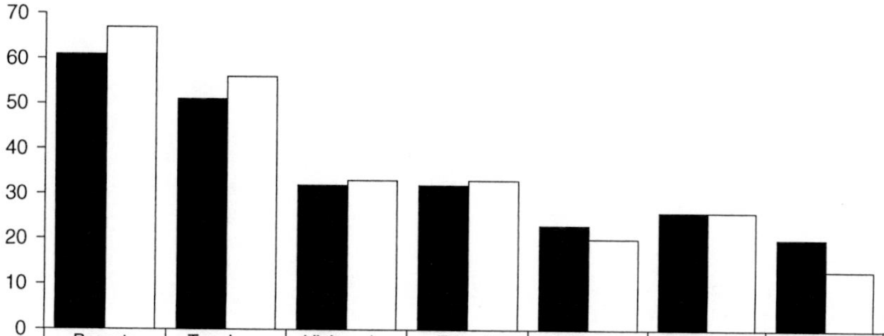

	Parents	Teachers	Visitors in school lessons e.g. police	Friends	Brothers, sisters	Other close relations	None of these	Available sample
■ Yr 6 M	61	51	32	32	23	26	20	2422
□ Yr 6 F	67	56	33	33	20	26	13	2300

Comments

1. Parents remain by far the most popular choice. Is this a signal for literature to be made more widely available for parents in order to help them in discussion with their children?
2. Teachers can also take positive messages from these data. Pupils are keen to have accurate information and they are aware that friends or siblings are perhaps less likely to provide them with this.
3. This question was new in 2002; previously we asked 'who would you like to talk with about drugs', when *parents* got the top vote.

Playtime and dinner time

15% of males favour *reading quietly* compared with 29% in 1997

During playtimes (including dinner times), do you spend time...? (Pri.19)

Responses to 'sometimes' or 'often'.

1. More females than males spend time chatting at playtime.
2. More males than females report playing ball games.
3. 15% of males and 20% of females favour *reading quietly*.

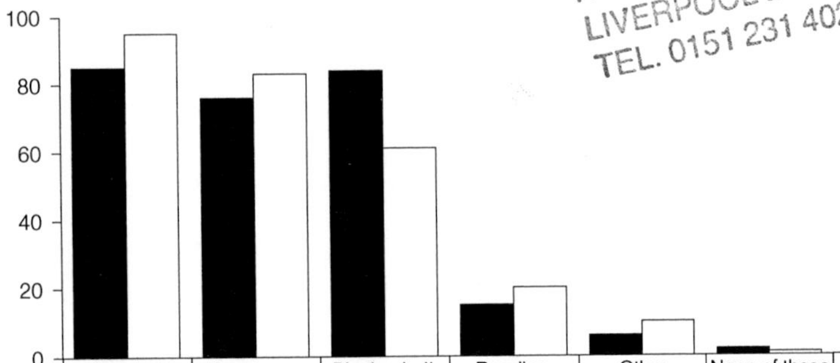

	Chatting/ talking	Running or skipping games	Playing ball games	Reading quietly	Other	None of these	Available sample
■ Yr 6 M	85	76	84	15	6	2	2422
□ Yr 6 F	95	83	61	20	10	1	2300

Comments

1. Significantly more males than females take part in ball games during playtime, while more females than males report playing running or skipping games. We know that games such as football can occupy a large proportion of the available space in the playground.
2. The figures for *reading quietly* continue to decline with 15% of males and 20% of females favour *reading quietly*. These figures compare with 19% of males and 25% of females in 1999.

Reading quietly during playtimes	1999	2000	2001	2002	2003
Year 6 Males	19%	20%	19%	17%	15%
Year 6 Females	25%	26%	22%	22%	20%

However, if one looks at figures from 1999-2003 (see below) it would appear that there is not a decline in those 10-11 year olds buying books with their own money (see page 89 for a breakdown of items 'bought last week'). Perhaps school play/dinner times are less conducive to *reading quietly* than they were in the past. (See www.sheu.org.uk/pubs/read.htm)

Buying books with own money	1999	2000	2001	2002	2003
Year 6 Males	11%	13%	15%	15%	14%
Year 6 Females	17%	20%	21%	22%	22%